WAKE ISLAND WILDCAT

A Marine Fighter Pilot's Epic Battle at the Beginning of
World War II

WILLIAM L. RAMSEY

STACKPOLE BOOKS

Essex, Connecticut
Blue Ridge Summit, Pennsylvania

STACKPOLE BOOKS

An imprint of Globe Pequot, the trade division of The Rowman & Littlefield Publishing Group, Inc.
4501 Forbes Blvd., Ste. 200
Lanham, MD 20706
www.rowman.com

Distributed by NATIONAL BOOK NETWORK

British Library Cataloguing in Publication Information available

Library of Congress Cataloging-in-Publication Data
Names: Ramsey, William L., 1961– author.
Title: Wake Island Wildcat : A Marine fighter pilot's epic battle at the beginning of World War II / William L. Ramsey.
Other titles: A Marine fighter pilot's epic battle at the beginning of World War II
Description: Essex, Connecticut : Stackpole Books, [2024] | Includes bibliographical references.
Identifiers: LCCN 2023055674 (print) | LCCN 2023055675 (ebook) | ISBN 9780811776677 (cloth) | ISBN 9780811776684 (ebook)
Subjects: LCSH: Elrod, Henry Talmage, 1905–1941. | Wake Island, Battle of, Wake Island, 1941. | Fighter pilots—United States—Biography. | United States. Marine Fighter Squadron, 211th—Biography. | World War, 1939–1945—Aerial operations, American. | Wildcat (Fighter plane) | United States. Marine Corps—Aviation—Biography.
Classification: LCC D767.99.W3 R36 2024 (print) | LCC D767.99.W3 (ebook) | DDC 940.54/4973092 [B]—dc23/eng/20240207
LC record available at https://lccn.loc.gov/2023055674
LC ebook record available at https://lccn.loc.gov/2023055675

♾️™ The paper used in this publication meets the minimum requirements of American National Standard for Information Sciences—Permanence of Paper for Printed Library Materials, ANSI/NISO Z39.48-1992.

To Farrar Elrod Ramsey and Mei-Yee Kung

Contents

ACKNOWLEDGMENTS

Any effort to express gratitude to those who have assisted with this project must begin with my grandmother, Farrar Elrod Ramsey. She flooded our dinner table with stories about her famous brother, Henry Talmage Elrod, from my earliest days to her last. When she and I inevitably ended up the last ones at the table, the stories became more vivid, and my questions evoked even more vividness. In one of those discussions, when I was in my middle teens, she asked what I wanted to be. I had begun writing poems, but I dared not say "a poet." So I told her instead "a writer." She pointed a finger at me and said, "Write a book about Talmage." From that point onward, this was the typical conclusion to all our conversations. I always said I would, never meaning it. Even when life surprised me and led me to pursue a PhD in history, I chose to write about colonial affairs, not Talmage. Yet here, in my seventh decade, I have done what I promised. The book exists solely because of her.

I owe thanks to so many archives and archival staff members around the country that it's hard to name them all. Ephraim Rotter of the Thomasville Historical Society went above and beyond the call of duty to help me find new sources of information on the Elrod family's early days in Thomasville, Georgia. He even helped me locate my great-grandfather's grave, where I subsequently spent a solemn hour contemplating the fateful actions of that troubled soul. Alyson Mazzone of the Marine Corps Archives at Quantico was kind enough to send me a digitized file of correspondence from the Henry T. Elrod Papers in 2020, when personal visits to the archives had been discontinued due to COVID-19. It allowed me to keep working until I was able to visit in person two years later. Once there, the friendly staff of the Marine Corps Archives spent many days cheerfully bringing me box after box. They carried the lion's share of the illustrations in this book to my desk. Meagan May and Sara Wilson of the University of North Texas Special Collections and Oral History Program also made Herculean efforts to send me digitized records during the COVID-19 shutdown. And lastly, Bonnie Towne, a marine herself, and Bob Thomas at the National Naval Aviation Museum in Pensacola, Florida, continued searching their collections long after I had left town, to find materials that could be helpful.

In the end, it was my wife, Mei-Yee Kung, who persuaded me to honor my long-standing promise to write about Talmage, and I could not have done it without her support and unwavering faith. My daughter, Jing Mei Ramsey, already one of the world's great readers and writers at age ten, read many passages while the manuscript was still in progress and offered helpful feedback and encouragement. By the same token, my son Zhen listened to my endless anecdotes with his usual patience and kind demeanor. His only lapse came at age four at the National Air and Space Museum in Washington, DC, where he wandered away from the Grumman F4F-3 display while I had my back turned, pointing out features of the airplane. The museum announced the presence of a lost child at the reception desk while I was describing the drawbacks of the landing gear. So this book is his chance to hear the rest of my presentation.

Introduction

In the fall of 1925, a twenty-year-old Henry Talmage Elrod sat at his dorm room desk at Yale University, attempting to write a letter to a young woman he had dated in high school. He felt lost, he told her, both on the Yale campus itself and in the larger world of modern science and technology that he was studying in its classrooms. Connecticut seemed like a foreign country to him, in comparison to rural south Georgia. He imagined himself as a "piece of flotsam" swirling randomly on ocean currents and despaired of his ability to navigate the challenges ahead. It was an incongruous metaphor, given the winter landscape and falling snow outside his window, but he felt it. He wrote it. As his troubles deepened that fall, Elrod came to relish the idea of escaping it all like driftwood carried to a remote tropical island, washing up on a sunny beach somewhere far beyond the eyes of the civilized world. In one letter that same semester, written to the same young woman, he even envisioned himself dying in such a place.[1]

He had probably forgotten those undergraduate ramblings by December 4, 1941, when he touched down on Wake Island as a pilot in the legendary marine fighter squadron, VMF-211. Yet just as he fantasized in college so long ago, he had indeed found his way to a remote Pacific island. There were, in fact, few islands as remote. Japan lay over two thousand miles westward, and Hawaii about the same distance to his east. And just as he had envisioned in 1925, he died there. He lived only nineteen days on the atoll, just long enough to see the full moon whittled down to a slender crescent, less time than he once spent writing term papers at Yale. In that blink of an eye, however, he accomplished military feats for which he is still celebrated today. He was awarded a Medal of

Honor, and countless books and articles have told the story of those nineteen days again and again. The Marine Corps named a street by the airfield at Quantico "Elrod Avenue," and the US Navy named a frigate after him, the USS *Elrod*. As we speak, his portrait hangs in the Hall of Honor at the National Naval Aviation Museum in Pensacola, Florida.

Despite the attention paid to his final days, however, there is no scholarship to date about his early life or the path that led him to those fateful shores. This book tells that story. It is not a long one, for his life was cut short at the age of thirty-six. Yet his journey to Wake Island was unique and tortured in ways that few lives are, and which fewer still survive. Indeed, Elrod's undergraduate musings apply here, too. He said he felt like "a piece of flotsam," and I can think of no better image. He never graduated from Yale University, due to his father's suicide, and running away from his troubles by climbing into a westbound boxcar only carried him to fresh hardships. It is the story of a young man drifting aimlessly for long periods, moved by a myriad of conflicting currents, turning, circling, tossed by waves, returning to his original position, moving sideways. Flotsam.

Some of it was his own fault. He possessed a keen, mischievous intelligence but did not always choose to apply it in the most judicious manner. Sometimes wildly overconfident, he was just as frequently paralyzed by debilitating self-doubt. Many of his troubles, though, were none of his doing. He experienced ordeals in his youth that no one should be forced to endure. They scarred him, I will argue, in ways that not only led him to that lonely outpost in the middle of the ocean, but, once there, shaped his approach to waging war—and dying.

In addition to the intrigue and spectacle of his emotional stumbles through life, Elrod gravitated from the very start toward the exciting new frontier of flight. As early as the 1910s and 1920s, as a high school student in Thomasville, Georgia, while his friends were buying the latest clothing styles or Victrola records, he walked through weeds to the outskirts of town to buy as many tickets as he could afford to fly with traveling barnstormers. Again and again, he went up in World War I–style, canvas-covered, two-seater biplanes to survey the cotton fields of south Georgia. Sometimes he paid a little extra for a "loop-the-loop."

As a newly minted private in the US Marine Corps in 1928, his first assignment placed him with a marine air squadron at North Island, San Diego, where he worked as a clerk and armorer with Curtiss OC-2 Falcons. These were observation aircraft, though still two-seater biplanes, with metal fuselages and canvas-covered wings. From there to flight school at Pensacola and onward to Quantico and Hawaii, Elrod flew every airplane the marines would let him taxi out to the runway, ending, of course, with the state-of-the-art Grumman F4F-3 Wildcat fighter, with which he sank a Japanese destroyer in 1941. His life story is therefore bound up inextricably with the story of interwar flight. As such, I have tried as much as possible, without losing sight of the main character, to explain how aviation history informed his experience of flying, both in peacetime and in war.

War itself changed in fundamental ways during Elrod's life, and that is part of his story, too. As an ROTC cadet in college, he studied Civil War–era cavalry tactics that required him to train on horseback. His early days as an enlisted member of an observation squadron's ground crew introduced him to the "Advanced Base" theory that guided marine operations in the 1920s. Yet over the next decade, marine strategists developed an increasingly sophisticated "Amphibious Operations Doctrine." Once he got his wings in 1935, Elrod participated in every Fleet Landing Exercise, or FLEX, staged by the marines until the outbreak of war, honing his skills in carrier-based takeoffs and landings, reconnaissance, bombing, fighter support for ground combat, the use of amphibious landing craft, and parachute drops. All of these exercises, moreover, were conducted on small islands very similar to Wake. By 1941, there was no pilot better prepared for the challenge of attacking or defending such a position. The marines moved him forward to Hawaii for this reason in 1940. And as the prospect of war with Japan became ever more likely in late 1941, the same logic contributed to the decision to move him two thousand miles farther into harm's way.

Lastly, it is important to say a word about the methods I employed in reconstructing some of the most obscure moments of a life that went largely without notice until it ended on Wake Island. As a college history professor who has taught and published for the last thirty years to earn my living, I have been careful to work within the constraints and expectations of academia. The book draws on primary sources and archival material, wherever possible, and I have labored to cite those sources accurately and to maintain objectivity. Yet, at the same time, this project is a bit of a departure for me. I am Elrod's great-nephew. My grandmother, Farrar Elrod Ramsey, was his little sister. So some of my information, especially concerning Elrod's early life, comes from family stories, especially hers. Many of them exist today only in my memory. As his adoring younger sister, moreover, my grandmother was not always impartial in her depictions of him. She was a fierce and loyal advocate. I have tried to take this into account. Her recollections, nevertheless, provide a crucial glimpse into his troubled childhood and adolescence.

My account also relies in some places on letters, memories, and diaries, the latter recorded by my father, William L. Ramsey Jr., and my uncle, Henry Elrod Ramsey. They grew up idolizing their "Uncle Talmage" and spent their adult lives gathering information that they hoped would become a book someday. The book they envisioned writing together never materialized, but they managed to produce a rough manuscript of about seventy-five typewritten pages that documented many of their discoveries and ideas.

While they were not always adept at recording names and dates, their energy and commitment led them to some remarkable information that has proven indispensable. My uncle Henry, for instance, managed to find Elrod's high school sweetheart in her golden years and copy a few excerpts from her diary. These provide the foundation for chapter 2. Henry also traveled to Virginia to speak with Elrod's widow, Elizabeth Carleson. Both brothers, meanwhile, attended reunions of the Wake Island defenders throughout the 1970s and 1980s, collecting stories about Elrod from anyone who remembered him. On a few occasions, they pulled me by the elbow in my teens to hear memories I had not yet learned to revere. These sources of information are not ideal for academic purposes, yet they have allowed me to tell the story of Hammerin' Hank Elrod more fully than I otherwise might. I am grateful to them for that foundation of knowledge.

Chapter i

1905–1920

In the late evening hours of Wednesday, September 27, 1905, the last visible crescent of the moon narrowed into almost nothing, and Henry Talmage Elrod took his first breath. The exact hour was not recorded. The state of Georgia required no official records of such things yet, and the small farming community of Pitts, in the southwest corner of the state, had no place to keep them if it did. According to the Irish poet William Butler Yeats, who may have been watching the sky that same night, only the "Hunchback and Saint and Fool" are born under the influence of the moon's last waning crescent. Henry Talmage Elrod, as things turned out, would never be mistaken for a saint, and the marines have not traditionally enlisted hunchbacks.

As for the last option, he was also no fool in the pejorative sense of the word. Yet if we take it to mean, as Yeats surely intended, a medieval-style jester, a clown, a performer of foolishness for the amusement of others, it fits perfectly. In his younger years, he was constantly in trouble at home and school for his pranks and playful humor. As an adult, there is plenty of evidence as well that, while it made him many friends, it may have held him back a little in his military life. He may have taken his name in part from his father, Robert Henry Elrod, but no one in later generations had a clue where "Talmage" came from. My uncle Henry used to speculate that he was named for the Georgia politician Herman Talmadge, who was reputed to have stopped by the Elrod household frequently in 1904–1905 to sell agricultural products. Perhaps his parents just fancied it. At any rate, this was the name he went by in the immediate household, Talmage, and most of his friends in high school called him that. As a married man, he signed his letters to his wife as "Talmage." By contrast, he was known exclusively as "Hank" to his fellow marines from 1927 onward. The nickname "Hammerin' Hank," by which he is typically remembered today, also came from the marines, but he heard it himself only in the final week of his life.

The first years of the twentieth century were heady times, not just for the Elrod family, but for south Georgia as well. While Pitts was not much to speak of as towns go, not even worth a mention in the census, it lay on the fringes of the fledgling community of Rebecca, Georgia, and Rebecca was officially incorporated as a township in 1904. Today, Rebecca has a declining population, and its main street is largely deserted. Abandoned storefronts present a quaint reminder of its glory days, which, in all likelihood, occurred about the same time as Talmage's birth, 1905, or the years just after. It had a functioning bank and general store back then, and a population of over 250. Even in its heyday, however, it was a remote, rural community devoted to agriculture. The federal census of 1910 lists the residents of Rebecca and Turner County as being engaged almost exclusively in the trade of "farmer."[1]

The year 1905 was an eventful one for the United States as a whole. It marked the beginning of Theodore Roosevelt's second term in office as president. He made a name for himself on the world stage this year by brokering a peace treaty between Russia and Japan. His niece, Eleanor, married a twenty-three-year-old Franklin Delano Roosevelt in New York City, and the Wright brothers made headlines again. Having invented human-powered flight only two years earlier, they improved on the original Wright Flyer by modifying the rudder, increasing the capacity of the gasoline tank, and adding two radiators to cool the engine in hopes of making longer flights possible. The 1905 Wright Flyer III did not look much different from the first one, but Wilbur and Orville Wright astonished the world by keeping it aloft for a whopping thirty-nine minutes.

Elrod's father, like most residents in the region, was listed as a farmer in the census, but he had received at least some education at the college level at Mercer University in Macon, Georgia. While it's unclear whether he ever received a degree, it was enough to qualify him to teach school in Turner County, which boasted an illiteracy rate of 24 percent. It was possible to farm and teach because the academic calendar was crafted to accommodate the seasonal demands of agriculture. Students, too, were expected to work on farms rather than study during the growing and harvesting months.

It might raise eyebrows today, but Elrod's mother was one of his father's former students. She was somewhere in her teens and he was twenty-six when they got married. It is hard to pin down her exact age, in part, because the Elrods appear to have misrepresented or misremembered it to a federal census agent when he stopped by their house in 1910. They told him that she was twenty-two years old and that they had been married for five years at that point. That puts her at about seventeen years of age in 1905, the year of Talmage's birth, and suggests that they were married that same year. Yet her birth date is listed as August 11, 1886, on her grave marker. If the tombstone is correct, she would have been nineteen years of age at her wedding. The marker also suggests the marriage may not have been her happiest memory in later life. She chose, for instance, not to be buried next to her husband in Thomasville, although there was (and is) space available, but rather in Ashburn, Georgia. In addition, she requested to be listed on the marker only by her original maiden name, Margaret Belle Rainey, with "Wife of R. H. Elrod" chiseled in small letters at the bottom.[2]

Talmage, too, carried scars from this household—quite literally, I argue—for the rest of his life. Maybe his mother shared a portion of the blame by being too reticent or retiring in times of trouble. Yet by all accounts his father played the dominant role in shaping their home life, with religion casting the brightest flames from the hearth.

Robert H. Elrod was a member of the Primitive Baptist Church and served periodically as a minister. *Primitive*, in this case, meant "original" or "old-style." Sometimes referred to as "Hard Shell" Baptists, they were committed Calvinists, even as they denounced John Calvin himself. As such, they embraced the doctrines of predestination and "Limited Atonement," the idea that Christ died only to save a limited number of souls, more fiercely than many modern Baptists. Indeed, a number of mainstream Baptist denominations reject these beliefs today. Primitive

Baptists did not practice infant baptism. Church membership was signified instead by baptism as an adult, either by immersion in the waters of a baptismal font within the church or, more often, in a nearby stream. They washed each other's feet in remembrance of Christ's example and foreswore the use of musical instruments in worship because they could find nothing in scripture to recommend them.

My only keepsake from Robert H. Elrod is a handwritten poem about the importance of observing the Sabbath. It is articulate, capably rhymed, and predictably devout. I have read it twice in the four decades that it has been in my possession, once when my grandmother first gave it to me and once when writing this chapter. I have no desire ever to do so again. Nevertheless, it confirms that he had some literary skill and was not messing around when it came to religion. Henry Talmage Elrod was given a heavy dose of his father's doctrines from the cradle onward.[3]

He was joined in the crib by a younger brother, Hubert, in 1906. While Talmage developed normally, experimenting with sounds and making words within his first year, it became clear early on that something was amiss with his little brother. Hubert was a lively, affectionate infant, but he could not hear. So the first words never came for him, and traditional schooling, such as his father taught, was out of the question. The Elrod family did their best to teach him to read and write and do his numbers, but the experience taxed everyone, especially Hubert. The frustration sometimes overwhelmed him, and he gave way on occasion to tantrums that traumatized the family.

It seems likely that Hubert was still struggling to read and write as late as December of 1915, for he did not submit a letter to Santa Claus to the local newspaper like his older brother. At ten years old, Talmage's letter was not a literary masterpiece itself, but he managed to get his message across. He asked Santa to bring him "just five things. The first thing I want is a coaster brake bicycle and a Winchester rifle and seven boxes of cartridges, a cowhide whip and some oranges." Hubert, age nine, would likely have appreciated a bike and a rifle, too, but he apparently had trouble communicating those wishes in a manner fit for publication.

I met Hubert in his later years, when he had mastered sign language and overcome the obstacles that had given him so much trouble as a child. He resembled his older brother in many ways physically. He was tall, thin, and loosely sprung. Hubert may also have shared some of his brother's personal traits as well. He was irreverent, impatient, and constantly alert to opportunities for comedy, even in situations that were not well suited to it. He was an old man when I knew him, but he always had a glint of mischief in his eyes that I feel certain he must have shared with his brother.[4]

My grandmother, Farrar, was the last of the Elrod children to be born in Pitt, in the Rebecca District. She arrived in February of 1910, as the family was considering a move. Her father ultimately purchased a sizable amount of land in Thomas County, near the bustling city of Thomasville. It does not appear to be a significant move on modern maps, only about a forty-minute drive by car, but in 1911 it must have been a grueling affair to move furniture and equipment by horse-drawn carriage along dirt roads. It brought the Elrod family into contact with a broader variety of social life than ever before. Thomasville was a regional railroad hub, with vibrant linkages to Savannah, Atlanta, and Birmingham, Alabama. Due to its location in the pine barrens just north of the Florida border and its easy accessibility by passenger rail, it developed a reputation during the Gilded Age as a temperate and healthy seasonal resort for wealthy Northerners seeking to escape harsh winters. The first visitors came for their health in the 1870s and 1880s, but others soon came for the abundant recreational opportunities of south Georgia, including hunting, fishing, and swimming. Glamorous hotels and resort accommodations sprang up around Thomasville by the turn of the century.[5]

Initially, the Elrods had little to do with this resort economy. Their new place lay just south of Thomasville, Georgia, by about eight miles. Highway 19, which runs between Thomasville and the next small town to the south, Monticello, Florida, was known as Monticello Road in the early 1900s. Most of the Elrod universe revolved for the next few years around a two-mile stretch of this dirt thoroughfare, taking in its side roads and paths. They occupied a modest four-room house with a long central hallway. At the height of his prosperity, R. H. Elrod owned about four hundred acres, devoted in large part to pasturage for horses and cows. At least some of these were milk cows, for Talmage's chores included tending to them. A good part of the farm was devoted to cotton farming, as well, though it is unclear how much. Two more sisters followed in due time: Mildred in April 1912, about two weeks after the sinking of the *Titanic*, and Kate, in 1923.

My grandmother's earliest memories came from this farmhouse in Thomasville. The first involved a litter of kittens that she loved to cuddle with and pleaded with her father to keep. He was determined to rid the farm of them, however, and placed them all in a burlap sack and plunged them into a pail of water until they stopped kicking. My grandmother, between four and six years old, squatted beside him the whole time, sobbing.

Traumatic as that was, the incident she discussed with me most frequently was a beating that her father dished out to Talmage in the front yard. She and her little sister Mildred huddled together on the front porch watching their father whale away on him. Talmage crouched in the dirt, taking blow after blow, some delivered with a stick, some with a clenched fist. The viciousness of what she witnessed remained with her the rest of her life. It was so bad, she said, that she feared for Talmage's life.

When it was all over, her brother at last stood up and staggered up to the porch and passed by the two terrified girls on his way into the house. He paused just then, surprised to see them there, and mumbled something like "It's awright," or "It's okay," or "It's all over." She noticed a trail of blood running down from one of his ears. This may be the event that caused what appears in later photographs to be a fractured orbital bone that never healed properly above his left eye. It can be seen clearly in his 1922 football team photo and his 1927 marine enlistment photo.

She remembered the incident with such detail because of the sheer terror it instilled, but also because she felt guilty. The punishment was administered because of her behavior, hers and her little sister Mildred's, while under Talmage's supervision. She had begged him to let her slide down the roof of the barn, a pastime that he had invented some time before and subsequently taught to his little sisters. They would climb up to the ridgeline of the tin roof, position themselves directly in line with the trunk of an oak tree that had grown jamb up against the edge of the tin sheeting, then slide down so that they grabbed the tree before flying off into the air. It was a dangerous and thrilling game, and their father had warned them to stop it. When he returned from a trip into town to see the two girls once again sliding down the roof of the barn, he flew into a rage. He parked Farrar and Mildred on the porch and pummeled their brother.

My grandmother could not remember the exact year of the incident. She and Mildred might have been anywhere from six and four years old, respectively, to eight and six, but no older, since they moved to a new house in 1918 when my grandmother was eight years old. That puts Talmage at between twelve and fourteen years of age, and the year, between 1916 and 1918. Woodrow Wilson was president, either way, and the world was at war.

The primary form of local transportation in the war years was still the horse-drawn carriage, although a growing number of "motor" carriages began to appear by 1918. These sported a variety of brand names that are unfamiliar today: Hanson, Comet, Revere, Tulsa, Paige, Oakland, Stanley. Most of them failed to survive the 1920s, when the Ford Motor Company rose to prominence. The Elrods may not have had an automobile just yet, but they certainly had one by 1922. We know because Talmage crashed it that year.

As head of the household, Robert Henry Elrod comes across as a stern and forbidding figure, as a drowner of kittens and beater of small boys. Yet other stories suggest that he allowed his children a good deal of latitude and freedom around the farm. Talmage was given a jet-black colt about this time, which he named Prince, and he spent a fair amount of time galloping through the fields around the house. The basics of horsemanship apparently came easy to him, and he soon began practicing more advanced techniques of rodeo-style maneuvering and roping. This was sometimes accomplished at the expense of his two sisters, who served against their will as targets for the lasso whenever they were spotted in the pasture. They were about the same size as small calves or pigs and could cut and change direction about as quickly. They were a little less fleet in straight-line speed of escape, but their genuinely terrified screaming and angry recriminations likely made up for that deficiency in his mind. Both Mildred and Farrar agreed in later recollections that their participation was not voluntary, but they also acknowledged that neither of them had ever been injured as a result of being chased down, roped, and hog-tied.[6]

Prince did not always serve as an engine of war in Talmage's hands. Up through the sixth grade, he rode Prince to McLean's Grammar School along a series of dirt roads and shortcuts through the woods. Mildred and Farrar tagged along on foot until they reached Hammond's Slough Creek, at which point he would stop and let them each take a stirrup for support. This story caught my attention as a child, and I asked many questions about the mechanics of the crossings. The girls would carry their shoes and socks across with their books while holding the stirrup to keep their balance in the rushing water. If there had been a hard rain or the stream was too high, they would each place one foot in a stirrup and cling to the saddle horn as Talmage rode them across.

The girls had to improvise a different way of crossing the creek beginning in the fall of 1918, because Talmage was sent away to a residential private school, the Norman Institute, at the start of his seventh-grade year. Perhaps the barn roof incident was the precipitating factor. Maybe Mr. Elrod simply hoped to provide his oldest son with a quality education. The promotional material for the school, published in the local newspapers, certainly made it sound like a superb opportunity for students:

1. Located in the most progressive section of Georgia, between Moultrie and Tifton, on A. B. & A.

2. It has excellent equipment, good facilities for teaching sciences, home economics, short-hand, book-keeping, piano, violin, voice, expression and teachers' course.

3. Large beautiful campus, basketball, track and football fields.

4. Two large dormitories, brick and cement, shower and tub baths, steam heat, electric lights, artesian water. All doors and windows just screened at cost of $1,000. . . .

5. New and excellent library, best magazines and reference books.

6. Five superb attractions from one of the best lyceum bureaus.

7. Health conditions are perfect. No illness in town or school caused by local conditions. Matron with two years hospital training in charge. Not a case of "flu" this year.

8. Faculty composed of college-bred men and women, who have had experience. All live in dormitories. All are Christians.

9. Thorough-work, high curriculum, supervised study, day and night, accredited by A-1 colleges.

10. Norman Institute's graduates succeed. They are leaders in their community, or are leaders in colleges.

11. State Supt. Brittain has granted the graduates of Norman Institute who take the one-year normal course, the license to teach two years without examination.

12. Rates as reasonable as efficiency will justify.

13. Girls wear uniforms consisting of college cap, white and navy blue middy suits. No uniform for boys.

14. No loafing on streets. Girls carefully chaperoned.[7]

So Talmage was packed off to the school, about thirty miles up the road toward Moultrie, Georgia. This was more than half the distance from his original home in Rebecca. In fact, the family probably passed by the Institute, and may even have discovered it, while moving to Thomasville. It had been established by Georgia Baptists in 1901 and boasted an imposing two-story brick academic building by 1917, surrounded by gender-segregated dormitories on a sixteen-acre campus. It originally offered primary, elementary, and high school classes, but later added college classes as well, in the 1920s.

One of the students who attended during Talmage's tenure at the school recalled that he got into a bit of trouble over the playing of his

Elrod at age twelve, while in seventh grade at the Norman Institute. Marine Corps Archives, Quantico, Virginia.

bugle. He had brought it from home and, even though the Norman Institute was not a military institution, decided without consulting the administration to walk out in front of his dormitory at the crack of dawn every day to play "Reveille." This apparently brought a flood of complaints from his fellow students and faculty (most of whom lived in the dorms), and he was warned by school officials to desist. Talmage nevertheless continued to sound "Reveille" every morning until his bugle was forcibly taken away by his fellow students. Despite this episode, Talmage was quite popular at the school and was voted captain of the football team. His friends returned the bugle to him at the end of his eighth-grade year in 1920, when it was clear that he would be returning home to enroll at Thomasville High School.[8]

His chores and obligations were more involved when he got home than they had been when he left. In the course of those two years, his father had taken on managerial responsibilities as the "superintendent" of two nearby "plantations," Sinkola and Pebble Hill. These were not farms in the traditional sense, but rather semi-recreational properties owned by Northern investors. They were intended to provide a seasonal distraction for their owners and guests during winter months and, at the same time, yield a marginal profit through a variety of enterprises. These included the raising of cattle and horses to be shown at regional agricultural fairs and contests, and, in the latter case, raced for prizes in northern Florida. Portions of each plantation were devoted to agriculture, with rental housing for migrant workers, while other portions were retained in a state of nature to provide a hunting preserve. Mr. Elrod assumed responsibility for all of these endeavors. The opportunities presented by the new employment persuaded him to build a new house on the property of Sinkola Plantation. Both Pebble Hill and Sinkola continue to operate in Thomasville today.

Talmage worked alongside his father whenever necessary and seems to have taken a special interest in the racehorses. Within a year or two, he was taking them to the racetracks in Florida on a regular basis. There is no evidence that he ever rode them himself in competition, but there can be no question that he would have been highly motivated to do so. It would, indeed, be surprising if he did not race as a jockey at some point, given his lifelong love of speed and excitement.

Speed and excitement showed up in Thomasville in another form that captivated Talmage in 1920. A traveling airplane pilot named George Keightley flew into town for a few days and began giving rides to anyone willing to pay the price of a ticket. Aviation technology had taken huge strides forward during the Great War. Whereas the Wright brothers were pleased to keep their Wright Flyer III aloft for thirty-nine minutes at a speed of about 30 to 35 miles per hour in 1905, Mr. Keightley's airplane could attain speeds of 100 miles per hour and fly for hours at a time. That was easily sufficient to circle about the city of Thomasville and tour the surrounding fields and even take a look at the nearby towns of Moultrie and Bainbridge and Monticello. Newspaper reports did not identify the model of the plane, but it may have been something along the lines of a two-seater Spad. An airplane of any sort was a rarity in south Georgia at this time, but a two-seater capable of taking up a passenger must have been seen as a true technological marvel. The price of a ticket was therefore considerable at the outset, and only the most prominent citizens appear to have gone up with Mr. Keightley. Their names were listed in the newspaper. Thomasville had no official airport, of course, but a parcel of land just outside of town was cleared and named the "T. L. Spence Jr. Field."[9]

After Keightley moved on to other venues, a pilot named Davis Winn began plying his trade in Thomasville on a more permanent basis. In October of 1922, he let it be known that "he had lowered the price of a ride in the airplane to five dollars . . . temporarily for the purpose of stimulating business." This may well have been the chance that Talmage had been waiting for. He had been watching the airplanes maneuver over the cotton fields with a keen interest and ultimately could not resist going up himself. He let his little sister Farrar tag along with him to Spence Field. She could not remember the exact year, but the memory of that day remained vivid for her until the end of her days.

If 1922 is right, then Talmage would have just turned seventeen years old when he left the ground for the first time and saw the world and its troubles diminish to a manageable size beneath his feet. The five dollars was probably well spent in his mind, for he returned from the flight so energized that he insisted Farrar should go up as well. She had not planned on going up herself that day and explained that she did not really wish to fly. It was dangerous. She was afraid. She was twelve years old. Talmage would not be deterred, however, and because she idolized him, she allowed him to strap her into the passenger seat. He stepped back a safe distance and gave her the thumbs-up and away she went. In the end, she found the experience just as awful as she had imagined. She threw up. The wind dried the vomit in her hair before landing. She never wanted to fly again. Talmage, on the other hand, wanted to stay in the air forever.[10]

CHAPTER 2

A Roaring Start to the Roaring Twenties

HAVING COMPLETED TWO YEARS AT THE NORMAN INSTITUTE, TALMAGE enrolled as a sophomore at Thomasville High School in the fall of 1920. This was his ninth-grade year, since high school only went through eleventh grade in those days. He seems to have established a niche for himself in his new school fairly quickly, and did very well in his biology course. The humanities were a different story. He received straight Cs in both history and English for the fall and spring semesters, and developed a reputation as a smart aleck along the way.

In October, his English teacher, Miss Houser, became frustrated over his lack of preparation on a particular poetry assignment and told him to stay an hour after school that day, "so you can tell me all about Edgar Allan Poe." Talmage responded by asking, "Will an hour be long enough?" In his spelling class, meanwhile, he asked Mr. Edwards, "What does 'hard-boiled' mean?" "Tough," said Mr. Edwards. Before spelling the word, however, Talmage insisted on using it in a sentence: "You sure are hard-boiled." Mr. Edwards finally lost his patience a few weeks later when Talmage was late getting into line with other students. "Stay in half an hour, Elrod," said the teacher. "I couldn't help being late," explained Talmage. "I had an accident. I bumped into the door."[1]

His classmates may have appreciated his cavalier attitude more than his teachers, for they elected him class vice president that fall. He contributed to virtually every athletic activity the school offered: football, baseball, and track. Whatever effort he withheld from the study of Edgar Allan Poe was devoted to sports. By his junior year, Talmage had become a mainstay on the Thomasville High School football team, moving from running back to tackle or guard as needed. He distinguished himself by intercepting a pass against Bainbridge High School in October of 1921. A few weeks later, he thrilled the home crowd with several long receptions while playing wide receiver. "To an observer," the newspaper reported, "it looked as though they would slip through his hands, but he pulled them in, getting about thirty yards every time."[2]

Thanks to the diary of a classmate, Talmage's senior year at Thomasville High School is one of the best-documented periods of his life. Emily Neal made regular and detailed entries that captured much of the flavor of that era. She had "bobbed" her hair just the year before, surely one of the first girls in south Georgia to adopt the fashion trends of the "flappers." As the "social editor" of the school newspaper, moreover, she knew virtually everyone and had access to all the latest news and developments. Most importantly, Emily Neal had caught the eye of Talmage Elrod sometime just before the start of the school year in September, 1922. As a result, their eventful journey together through eleventh grade left her diary filled with references to phone calls, football games, gifts of flowers, silent films, and fusses.[3]

It was a whirlwind of flirtation and upheaval and soul searching. For Emily, it likely went in the record books as one of the most eventful years of her life. For Talmage, on the other hand, it was all par for the course. He had experienced this level of turbulence prior to 1922, and it would follow him for most of his adult life.

Several themes emerge from Emily's diary. First, Talmage possessed a winning personality that brought him many friends and much popularity. This, too, was not limited to Thomasville High School but would be a lifelong characteristic. Second, the penchant for jokes and high jinks that made him so popular among his peers also regularly got him into trouble. In fact, "regularly" may be an understatement. There was almost a timetable for it. He could only go so long, it seems, before doing something that called forth some type of disciplinary action.

Emily Neal's diary also bears early evidence of another theme that became a decisive influence on Talmage's life: his persistent desire to run away and enlist with the United States Marine Corps as a way of escaping his recurring hardships.

There is no record of their first meeting, but Emily and Talmage were on friendly terms from the very start of their senior year. Just a week or two into the fall term, September 22, they attended a Friday-night showing of the silent film *Nice People*, starring Wallace Reid, Bebe Daniels, and Conrad Nagel. Emily did not describe it as a "date," necessarily, but it was just the two of them. Talmage was allowed to use the family car for the occasion, and on the way home he gave her a turn at the wheel. She bragged in her diary later that night: "I think I can drive it better than he can."

Whether it ranked as a date or not, the relationship was not exclusive or serious at this point. In fact, Emily appears to have had some reservations about him. When Talmage rang her up to ask for a formal date a couple of weeks later, she was not enthusiastic. She declined the invitation on the grounds that she already had a date for that Friday night. "Thank Goodness!" she wrote, after hanging up.

But the danger had not passed. This setback only seems to have inspired him to rejoin the pursuit with greater creativity. Three days later, he called again to offer a compliment about how pretty she looked driving her father's Buick around downtown Thomasville that afternoon. He had only heard about it from friends, he confessed at length, since he had been out hunting, but he had "a good imagination." Another three days and he was on the phone again, claiming now to have discovered a mysterious secret about her. Talmage refused to divulge it over the phone but promised to spill the beans that Friday night if she went on a date with him. For good measure, he wagered that he would score higher than her on the French test they both had coming up that Thursday. He even bet her a "yankee dime" on it.

It is unclear what effect this gambit had on her feelings toward him, but it definitely piqued her curiosity on one level. Date or no date, Emily confronted him about the secret at school the following day. It was only, he said, that he had learned through a certain unnamed source that she had not actually had a date at all the previous Friday. He expressed disappointment, no doubt with a bit of dramatic flair to drive the point home, that she would "treat him that way." Taken aback, Emily pressed him for his source. It took a fair amount of "wheedling," but he finally named a mutual friend: "W. M." This must have carried some weight with her, for later that evening she continued to "wonder how W. M. came to tell him that?"

Feeling guilty, perhaps, she at last relented and agreed to go to another film with him. Even so, she took care to arrange for her friend Anabel to come along for safety's sake. Their night out must have gone well, for they returned to Emily's house and listened to some music on the Victrola. On taking his leave, Talmage asked her to keep the record on the turntable until the following Friday. The French exam, meanwhile, must have been exceedingly difficult. Only Emily and one other student (not Talmage) even managed to finish it within the time allotted. She was proud to have scored a 97, and Talmage Elrod said no more about the "yankee dime."

I don't mean to suggest that it was smooth sailing for the two of them after that. Nothing was ever smooth sailing for Talmage. But he had broken the ice, as they say, and Emily began attending his football practices on a regular basis. He was not by any means the only point of interest for her there. She also seemed to have a high opinion of W. M., the young man who had spilled the beans about her not really having a date. W. M. was a starter on the varsity football team and a popular senior. The roster lists a William Mays for that year. He and Talmage seem to have been "two peas in a pod." Prior to one of their games, for instance, they suited up before the rest of the team had emerged from the locker room and climbed a tree while waiting. The sportswriter for the *Thomasville Daily Times-Enterprise* found the incident so amusing he described it at some length:

Messrs. Mays and Elrod have gone back to the primitive. Imagine the surprise of the other members to find these two supposedly sound young men sitting in the top of a tall pine tree when they came out on campus. Elrod was hung by his toes from a limb and Mays was chanting "I'm a bird, cockle-doodle doo."[4]

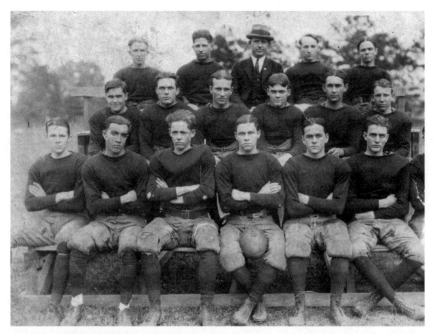

Thomasville High School football team, 1922. Elrod is third from the left in the first row and William Mays is directly to his left, with the football in his lap. Collections of the Thomasville Historical Society.

It must have been difficult for Miss Neal to choose between two such alluring candidates. Yet Talmage occupied her thoughts more and more. When the rosters for the game against Moultrie's high school appeared with a typographical error for Talmage's age, listing him as 116 rather than 16, she found herself chuckling secretly about it all day long. By the end of October, things may have begun to get a little more serious. On a Monday-night outing just the day before Halloween, Talmage brought her a bouquet of roses, and the two of them drove into town to watch the romantic drama *Blood and Sand*, starring the great lover himself, Rudolph Valentino. As chance would have it, they "sat right in front of W. M." during the film. Emily may have felt a bit awkward about the situation, but it was probably no accident, if Talmage had had any say in choosing the seats. Afterward, they sat on a bench outside the theater under the soft glow of the marquee and "talked . . . a long time."[5]

Maybe things were going a little too fast for Emily's liking. She attended a Halloween party with him the following night and agreed to another date after his football game on November 3. She agreed to that one, however, mainly because he had suffered a knee injury and been knocked unconscious in the game (on two separate plays) and felt sorry for him. "I'm too soft-hearted," she complained in her diary.

Thereafter, her resolve began to stiffen. When he called a few days later to invite her to attend a party with him in nearby Albany, Georgia, she told him she was already "going with somebody else." She astutely neglected to tell him that it was her friend Martha and not a rival. Talmage would have learned as much for himself had he been patient enough to wait until that Friday to attend the party, but the suspense was too much for him. Rather than walking straight to school the following morning, he budgeted a little extra time to make his way toward Emily's place and hide beside the road. As she walked along with Mac (short for Maxine), another of her closest friends and editor of the school paper, he jumped out "from behind a tree," directly in front of her. "I was never more scared in all my life," she wrote, "for he was not in the back part of my head."

She already knew he was unpredictable and prone to trouble, but this incident seems to have raised new concerns for her. He called for a date that Friday, November 10, and was rebuffed. Emily was not the only one to notice that he had a bit more of an edge to his personality than most. His class voted him "meanest" at the end of their senior year and presented him with a "powder puff" as an award. It served him well on the football field, where violence and the infliction of pain were virtues. It sharpened his wits in the woods when he went hunting, with life and death balanced on his trigger. Whatever it was, it brought him to grief in his private life on many occasions, in spite of his good qualities.

Yet Emily could not help liking him. On November 11, Talmage drove his mother and little sisters into town to watch the parade commemorating the armistice of the Great War. He parked by the curb in downtown Thomasville and the three of them waited for the show. Emily attended as well and waved to them from where she was standing across the street. Mildred, Farrar, and Mrs. Elrod waved back, but Talmage was slouched down in the driver's seat, reading a newspaper, and "never looked up." Surely his little sisters poked him on the shoulder from the back seat and giggled as they delivered the news that his girlfriend was standing right there, but he continued reading. Emily cast a few more glances his way to ascertain just how long his distraction would endure and was relieved, after some time, to see that "Talmage finally happened to be looking & grinned."

There was no telephone call that night or the next, but a few days later he arranged for a mutual friend to carry a chocolate ice-cream cone out to Emily's house as a peace offering. He called her that night, and they "talked a long time." The conversation must have allayed some of her concerns, for she accepted his offer to go and see *The Prisoner of Zenda* that Wednesday. They had to walk to the cinema because the Elrod family's car was in the shop, but otherwise things seemed to be back on track. Their plans to take a drive in the country once the car was fixed were scratched when a hard rain set in on Sunday, November 19. Nevertheless, Talmage surprised her by showing up anyway. He jogged out of the storm and leapt up the steps of her front porch, dripping wet, to bring her a bouquet of white japonica flowers.

At school the following week, he loitered awhile outside the classroom where she was stuck in her Wednesday-afternoon "study hall" with Miss Smith, then casually walked by the open window next to Emily's desk and tossed in a box when Miss Smith was looking the other way. It turned out to be a box of candies. She ate some herself, then circulated it surreptitiously among her friends.

The two began talking by telephone almost every day at this point, with some of the conversations lasting an hour or more. A call from Talmage sounded different from other calls, she noted, because there was always a strange buzzing noise in the background. She could tell it was him as soon as she lifted the receiver, before either of them had said a word, when she heard that peculiar buzzing. This was due to some troubles between Talmage and his father about which there is little surviving evidence. Perhaps it was a simple issue of fair usage for other family members or neighbors, since Talmage's daily marathon conversations were monopolizing the line. Remember, these were "party lines," in which several households shared the same service. In those days, you could pick up the receiver, if you had a mind, and listen to your neighbor's business. This meant that only one call at a time could go out or come in. So neighbors, too, may have become a little irritated with all the love talk.

Whatever the source of the disagreements, they ended with Mr. Elrod forbidding his son from using the household telephone. But there were other ways to make a telephone call in 1922 if you were Talmage Elrod. He bought himself a surplus telephone receiver (with only the cord attached), scaled a nearby telephone pole, scraped the insulating material away from the wiring with his penknife, pressed his receiver cord against the freshly exposed telephone wire, and tapped into the network as an unauthorized user. It worked like a charm. The operators couldn't tell the difference. They asked who he wanted to be connected to, Talmage told them, and they plugged the jack into Emily's network. The quality of the sound was not optimal. It carried a static buzz that never went away. So while Emily lounged in a chair, or leaned back against the wall in her house, laughing, listening, chiding him by turns for hours at a time, Talmage was usually perched on top of a telephone pole.

In addition to the ban on telephone usage, there were a few other signs of possible friction within the Elrod household, as well. Talmage was in the habit of staying over for the night about this time with several of his friends from the football team. It is clear that some of these stays ran for two or three days, suggesting that he might have been trying to avoid a situation at home. The pattern became so conspicuous that some of Emily's friends began to joke around about her father maybe making a room available for Talmage, too. To make matters worse, Talmage wrecked the family car on his way home from a late-night cane grinding (for sugarcane) in early December. Emily was in the car with him at the time. No one was hurt, but the car could not be driven, so they had to hitch a ride back into Thomasville, where they spied Mr. Elrod standing on the sidewalk waiting for them. Emily concluded that diary entry with "Oh my."

That yuletide began a season of troubles for Talmage, most of them, as usual, of his own making. When Emily came down with a fever and had to stay home from school, he climbed up a telephone pole and called to see how she was feeling. He promised he would get out of his last class early the next day and carry her Latin book out to her.

True to his word, he showed up the next day at about three o'clock, toting the book. As they chatted, though, he let slip that in fact he had cut classes for the whole day and gone hunting. To make the day a complete wash, moreover, he said he would also skip football practice that afternoon if she would go to a movie with him. Although she must have had some misgivings about this type of dereliction of duty, not to mention a lingering fever, she took him up on the offer. They went to see *The Old Homestead*, while the Thomasville football team practiced without its starting tackle.

Next morning, she lifted the receiver to hear that familiar buzzing sound. Talmage said he'd taken a horse down to the racetracks in Tallahassee, Florida, and had decided not to go to school that day either. When he brought her books to her that afternoon, she tried to rein him in by telling him he shouldn't skip football practice for a second day in a row. He "said he was, tho."

His reputation for rebellious behavior sometimes landed him in troubles that may not have been his fault. In early February of the following semester, 1923, the French teacher, Miss Lucie, arrived in class just in time to see a piece of chalk hit the chalkboard and shatter into dust and fragments. As she surveyed the mess, she discovered the debris of several other pieces of chalk littering the floor. Miss Lucie ordered the girls to depart and stand in the hallway. Then she closed the door and turned back to deliver a stern lecture to the boys about personal responsibility. She concluded by demanding that the individuals involved in throwing pieces of chalk identify themselves immediately and receive their deserved punishments.

After an agonizingly long silence, a student named Russell finally stood up next to his desk and confessed that he had thrown a piece of chalk. Miss Lucie thanked him for his honesty and sentenced him to a half-hour of detention after school. Russell sat back down again, and Miss Lucie waited for the other culprits to come forward. No one else said a word. As she scanned the classroom for evildoers, her gaze came to rest on the face of Talmage Elrod. Had he thrown a piece of chalk?

No, he assured her. Miss Lucie, however, found it hard to believe that the immense mess she now beheld on her classroom floor could have been fully achieved without the unique talents of this exact student. So she gave him two hours of detention. The extra time was added, in all likelihood, as a punishment for his stubbornness in not confessing.

His lengthy detention was supposed to be served in two separate hour-long periods over the course of two days, but he did not show up for the first one. He didn't seem too worried about it all. Yet as he explained the situation to Emily after school that day, she became concerned. She knew he was developing a bad reputation and asked him to "promise not to do anything to get expelled." He promised, and he must have kept it that time around, for there were no further repercussions.

By this time the two of them were so close that Talmage proposed a telepathy experiment during one of their calls. As soon as they hung up, Emily was to think of something and write it down on a piece of paper and seal it in an envelope. He would then tap into the unseen universe of thought waves from the top of his telephone pole to figure out what it was. In the cool winter night, high above the Georgia cotton fields, the wind whistled over the wires. He closed his eyes, and, sure enough, a clear thought came to him. Perhaps he knew right then that it was his alone, not hers. They compared notes the following day, but Emily never recorded the results. Memories of the chalk incident began to fade, at any rate, and they got back into the usual routine, with outings to movies and parties and daily telephone conversations.

But this was Talmage Elrod. Nothing stayed routine for long. In late February, he skipped a couple of study halls. The evasion was transacted so smoothly that no teachers seemed to be aware of it, but Maxine (the same "Mac" who had been walking with Emily when Talmage jumped out from behind a tree) was fed up with it all. She walked into principal Mr. Mahler's office and spilled the beans. Talmage was promptly "shipped," or expelled. It was not a mere suspension, since there was no return date given.

His popularity with his peers manifested itself when the news became public. There was an outpouring of sympathy and support for him, matched by a wave of anger and criticism directed at Mac for having turned him in. The general opinion was that Mac should at least have given him some warning that if he kept skipping study halls she would tell, rather than simply sinking him as she did. So pronounced was this sentiment that Mr. Mahler felt obliged to give a speech to the assembled student body, in which he praised Mac "for doing her duty & standing for the right rather than popularity."

Talmage had clearly thought about his next move beforehand. He had already spoken to Emily and other close friends about his desire to join the US Marine Corps someday. With his high school graduation now postponed indefinitely, there seemed no reason to delay his enlistment any longer. When his usual phone calls did not come, Emily feared he might already be on the road, headed to the nearest recruiting station. It was a fear shared by other friends, who conferred with each other to figure out where he was. Finally, he called on February 26 and told her he would meet her on her way home from school. She wrote in her diary that she felt "so relieved to find him still here." During that walk, he told her he was indeed planning to go, perhaps as soon as that very night. He promised to give her a call to say good-bye before he left.

She waited that night, but the call never came. As she listened for the phone to ring, she heard the rain start up and hoped that meant he would not be "going off" that night.

Whether it was the rain or his own second thoughts, Talmage stayed. He worked with the cows and horses at Pebble Hill Plantation, where his father was the manager, in the mornings and early afternoons, and then he met Emily for movies and small talk after she got out of school. As his anger began to fade, he found himself, perhaps to his own surprise, missing school. In early March, he decided to swallow his pride and ask to be allowed to return. Principal Mahler agreed, on the condition that Talmage would apologize to Mac personally and present a speech before the whole school, confessing all that he had done. He was told to conclude the speech with a public acknowledgment that he thought "Maxine was an influence for the good at Thomasville High School." All this was duly accomplished. The speech took place during chapel on March 5, 1923, his first day back in class. His high school transcript recorded a total number of sixty-five days absent during that spring semester.

Talmage appears to have worked hard academically to make up for lost time, but there was more wrong with his life than just grades. He and Emily were always together, and she knew better than anyone that something was amiss. Walking home with him from a friend's birthday party near the end of March, she tried to talk some sense to him, but it didn't go well. "I had a hard time," she wrote, "trying to get Talmage started right in straightening his tangled affairs."

On April 26 they went with a number of friends for a day's outing at Lake Miccosukee in Florida. They had a grand time, rowing boats, walking in the woods, talking. Talmage took out his penknife and carved their initials in a tree. Yet only two weeks later he was in distress again. He ambled through their date on May 11 "glum as Hector," without speaking. By the time they got home he "looked as if he was ready to blow up," so she asked him what he was so mad about. He said he was mad at himself "& said everything he did was wrong." He tried to explain further but words failed him. He just "walked up & down & tried to say something & couldn't." After a while, Emily had had enough of this and told him she had to go to bed.

It was a trying time, and Talmage increasingly wore his heart on his sleeve. Emily complained that she now had "to treat him as if he were a rare piece of china." On top of it all, the possibility that he might take off at a moment's notice to become a soldier was never far from her thoughts. When he did not show up for school, Emily started asking friends for information. One of them reported "that Talmage told him yesterday he was going to join the Marines." So she persuaded someone to call out to the Elrod place to check. It turned out that he was just out sick.

Even on their graduation day, June 1, 1923, she worried about it. When he didn't come straight into the auditorium after dropping her off at the door, she "thought Talmage had run off [for] sure." She spread the word, and in a short while all the boys from their graduating class, dressed in their finest suits, were "running around looking for him." He finally turned up, but that appears to have been the last straw for Emily. God knows, she had accumulated a sizable collection of them by that time. She broke up with him that night.

"I wasn't mad at all," she remembered, "& I think he realized that." The most painful part of the breakup, from her perspective, "was making him take back his little gold football I'd been wearing. . . . When I went to get it, he went & got in the car but I went out there & talked to him quite a while & finally in desperation dropped it in his hat that was on the back seat & ran into the house."

It was not a clean break. There were a few more calls, even a few more dates, more talks by the car, where they "argued things out all over again." But Talmage Elrod was not meant for Emily Neal in the long run, or she for him. He was not, for that matter, meant for Thomasville, Georgia, or the state of Georgia, broadly speaking, or any particular place. His destiny called him elsewhere—not away from the cotton fields, necessarily, but up above them, above the tops of the telephone poles, above the cottony clouds. When he finally found his place, in the cockpit of an airplane, the combination of speed and altitude somehow transformed him. The personal qualities that had always caused him so much trouble on the ground eventually crystallized into "conspicuous gallantry."

CHAPTER 3

College Years, More or Less

THE SUMMER OF 1923 WAS A HOT ONE, ESPECIALLY IN JUNE, WHEN TEM-
peratures rose a little above average. Mercifully, there were no extended
heat waves, and July turned out to be a little cooler than expected. Regular rains helped to cool things off. Newspaper headlines that summer
focused on the roiling scandal of the Teapot Dome investigations, which
involved various cabinet members of the Warren G. Harding administration in a scheme to accept bribes from oil companies. The biggest news
came in August, when Harding died in office of a heart attack and was
succeeded by his vice president, the moderate and unremarkable Calvin
Coolidge. Out on the West Coast, the iconic "Hollywood" sign was
erected, but life continued apace in Thomasville, Georgia. A new baby
girl, named Kate, joined the Elrod household. Talmage continued to
work with the horses and cattle at Sinkola and Pebble Hill Plantations,
but he had broader ambitions as well.[1]

Despite the turmoil of his senior year at Thomasville High School,
he managed to gain admission to the University of Georgia for the fall
of 1923. He joined a freshman class of seventy-eight young men and
ten young women for the start of classes in September. The big man on
campus was William Tate, already a senior, who would go on to become
a fixture in Athens as an English professor and dean of young men in
the coming decades. According to my grandmother, Talmage lived at the
YMCA for both years he was enrolled at Georgia.

As a freshman, he was kept humble by a variety of routines and
traditions. He was required to attend church on campus and perform

community service. On September 28, he marched with the rest of his class along Milledge Avenue to the Lucy Cobb Institute, a finishing school for young ladies that functioned as a sister college to the university. Once there, the freshmen serenaded the girls and then performed requested maintenance around the grounds.[2]

He may well have arrived in Athens on horseback, for he promptly joined the cavalry division of the newly formed ROTC. World War I had taught the United States how important it was to develop a trained reserve of officers, even in peacetime, as a matter of national security. So the Reserve Officer Training Corps was reconfigured under the National Defense Act of 1916. Ironically, many of these prospective officers, Talmage included, continued to be trained in the old cavalry tactics of the nineteenth century in spite of the harsh lessons of trench and chemical warfare. His habit of riding down and roping his little sisters must have served him well as a member of Troop A, but would have had little application in actual combat. These old cavalry tactics were soon to give way to more modern methods by the end of the decade.

ROTC participation was mandatory at most American colleges and universities, but it remained voluntary at the University of Georgia until the late 1920s. The most advanced tactical training was reserved for the seniors. Freshmen like Talmage spent their first year in basic training. For the cavalry units, this involved a considerable amount of work on horseback. They practiced twice a week during the semester and wore blue uniforms that cadets derided as "bellhop" outfits.[3]

Talmage devoted the rest of his afternoons and weekends to the freshman football team. In those days, the varsity squad was restricted to sophomores and upperclassmen, with freshmen serving on what amounted to a scout team or scrimmage unit. The "Bullpups," as they were known, provided practice opposition for the upperclassmen, but they also played their own official schedule of games against other freshman teams around the Southeast. Although he had played both offense and defense in high school, he appears to have been moved exclusively to defense at Georgia. Under Coach Bachman, the Bullpups won six of their seven games in the fall of 1923, most of them by a comfortable margin.

The defense in particular, with Talmage playing tackle, proved formidable. Talmage and his fellow freshmen kept Clemson, NC State, and Auburn scoreless, and gave up only two field goals in a victory over the hated Florida Gators in Jacksonville. Their only loss of the season was a closely fought battle with the Crimson Tide of Alabama, which was decided by a single touchdown. The defeat was difficult to swallow, in part, because the final score resulted from a heated dispute between Coach Bachman of the Bullpups and the referee, which ultimately handed the victory to Alabama.

The Bullpups and the Bulldogs played on a field very close to, even overlapping, modern-day Sanford Stadium. When they gathered there for a team photograph at the end of the season, Talmage knelt on the left side of the middle row. He was distracted momentarily by something of interest to his left, and, as a result, appeared in the yearbook forever after as the only player who did not look directly at the camera.[4]

In addition to his regular academic work, Talmage began reading a new work of fiction by Percival Wren in 1924. *Beau Geste* told the story of three orphaned brothers who ran away to join the French Foreign Legion. The story of their struggle to maintain personal and military honor in the face of overwhelming hardship struck a chord with him, and it quickly became his favorite book. His younger sister Farrar also read it, probably at Talmage's urging. She immediately recognized the qualities of Michael, the oldest and most dynamic of the Geste siblings, in her own brother:

> . . . known as "Beau" Geste by reason of his remarkable physical beauty, mental brilliance, and general distinction. He was a very unusual person, of irresistible charm, and his charm was enhanced . . . by the fact that he was as enigmatic, incalculable, and incomprehensible as he was forceful. He was incurably romantic, and to this trait added the unexpected quality of a bull-dog tenacity. If Michael suddenly and quixotically did some ridiculously romantic thing, he did it thoroughly and completely, and he stuck to it until he was done.[5]

Farrar thus began calling him "Beau" whenever he returned home from college. He seems to have embraced the moniker, and identified with the character so thoroughly that he expressed a desire to be worthy of a Viking funeral at the end of his life, just like Beau Geste. Talmage returned the favor of the new nickname by calling his little sister "Esmeralda," after the free-spirited gypsy girl in Victor Hugo's *The Hunchback of Notre Dame.*

He completed two full years at the University of Georgia. Not surprisingly, his highest grades came in Military Science, ranging from a 93 his freshman year to a 97 at the end of his sophomore year, in the spring of 1925. He received his lowest grade, an 82, in Botany. These were yearlong courses, split into three quarters (with summer quarter off). Half of them were As, and half were Bs. It was an adequate performance, but not a sterling one. Nevertheless, at some point in his sophomore year, Talmage became fixed on the idea of transferring to Yale University. In later years, his sister Mildred remembered the daughters of the Pebble Hill Plantation owner as having encouraged him to try his hand in the Ivy League. He must have written one heck of an application essay, considering the mediocrity of his grades at Georgia. Perhaps to his own surprise, he was accepted as part of the class of 1928.[6]

It was likely the first time he had left the state of Georgia. It was certainly his first encounter with the North and the broader currents of global culture. Excerpts from his letters to Emily Neal, his star-crossed sweetheart from high school, showed him to be in obvious distress over the transition. "I am having the most dreadful existence," he confessed, "that you can possibly imagine." He felt overwhelmed by the whole experience. He even feared for his future at Yale "if the work is as hard as the getting settled down is."

Added to the difficulties of homesickness, relocation, and a whole new level of academic challenge, Talmage also found himself at odds with his own personality. "I dream and idealize too much," he confessed, "and I have always been about the most imperfect of the more or less imperfect." Such pronouncements became more dramatic as the semester wore on. A week before final exams, he wrote that he was "fighting hard to overcome myself and my propensities." "I am more helpless," he explained in one of his final letters, "in this turbulent sea, which my ship of life is just entering, than the drifting piece of flotsam out on the mid-wide ocean."[7]

Just as troubling, the curriculum at Yale appears to have exposed him to religious ideas and concepts that he had not considered previously. He had listed his church affiliation at UGA as "Baptist" in 1923, and there is nothing to indicate that he had come to question his views or very much else before leaving for Connecticut. Yet he had questions aplenty by the end of his first semester at Yale. In coursework designed to prepare him for a career in medicine, he encountered material that challenged the fundamentalist religious orthodoxy of his father's Primitive Baptist faith. Darwin's theory of natural selection and geological discoveries that extended the age of the Earth billions of years beyond the generational chronologies of the Old Testament were undoubtedly a part of this. It is clear enough that Darwin, at least, was on his mind, because, when he fantasized about throwing in the towel at New Haven, he saw himself escaping "to the Galapagos or some other far away place." "It is cruelly frightful," he observed, "to see one's pet beliefs and closest thoughts manhandled by the tyrannical creeds of science." In the same letter, he expressed a desire "to always be a child—to never grow up."[8]

Talmage gave expression to his new doubts and misgivings in a heated conversation with his father during the Christmas break of 1925, when he returned to Thomasville. The exact manner in which he expressed himself, the context, and the occasion remain unknown. Indeed, no member of the family ever spoke of it afterward. In all the stories my grandmother told me about Talmage, this incident was never discussed. Never. I find this striking, since there is a better-than-average chance that she was sitting right there listening. We know of the conversation, and that it did not go well, only because Talmage himself talked about it. His account was apparently so engaging that it captured the imagination of a writer, who chanced to run into him in New Orleans, Louisiana, the following year. Seeing the opportunity for a catchy headline, the journalist wrote it up with the title "Modernist Son Leaves Fundamentalist Father." Thus packaged, the story of Talmage's fateful run-in with his father was eagerly picked up and published in a handful of newspapers clear across the country in late November 1926.[9]

The author depicted Talmage as part of the nationwide youth rebellion of the 1920s. "Another story of youth's revolt," the article began, "against the beliefs of his father was revealed here [New Orleans] when Talmage Elrod, twenty-one years old, a former Yale student, was discovered working as a day laborer." Whether he was genuinely part of it or not, that revolt had set the generations against each other in a way the country had not seen before. Automobiles gave young people a nearly unlimited ability to escape the prying eyes of their elders. Young women, known as "flappers," flouted traditional gender roles and boundaries by cutting their hair short, wearing skirts above the knee, and smoking cigarettes in public. All of this, moreover, was set to the frenetic tempo of Dixieland jazz, which found its keenest expression in the illegal "speakeasies" where Americans gathered to defy the prohibition against alcohol. The author argued that Talmage, too, had "assimilated the beliefs of the moderns" while attending Yale.[10]

There were plenty of opportunities for those beliefs to find expression back in Thomasville, even if Talmage had intended to keep them under wraps. Since his father was a Baptist minister, he would have been expected to attend services, and these, of course, were more involved and demanding during the Christmas season. At some point, anyway, he "aired [his] views before the family fireside." A discussion with his father naturally ensued. It is not hard to guess the questions the old man put to the undergraduate, once his skepticism had revealed itself. Do you not believe that the Earth was created in six days, as the Bible teaches us? Do you not believe that man was created from clay on the sixth day in his present form, in God's own image? No transcript of the conversation exists, of course, but in a short period of time it "progressed into an argument." Suspecting Yale to be the likely root of this spiritual evil, Mr. Elrod ultimately proclaimed that he would not pay for his son to continue at the university if he persisted in his disbelief. Talmage struck back in kind by refusing "to go back to college on the money furnished by his father."[11]

And that was that, according to Talmage. He lit out for New Orleans, lured by "glamorous tales of romance" about the city, and began working to save up money to go back to Yale without his father's assistance. The journalist who wrote the article knew a good angle when he heard it. It was an engaging tale, one that likely found many interested readers, but there was a bit more to it than Talmage let on. Some of it was surely true, make no mistake. Talmage was definitely in New Orleans, for instance, in November 1926. He was no longer attending Yale. His father was no longer paying for him to continue at the university. No question about it.

But there were other reasons beyond the argument with Talmage. Mr. Elrod was no longer paying for much of anything that November, to the very great distress of the entire family. He had been dead for over eight months at that point, having shot himself in the head around 5:30 p.m. on Monday, March 8, 1926. Some Black children walking home from school along the "Tallahassee Road" (modern-day Highway 319) between Pebble Hill and Sinkola saw him slumped in the car, bleeding from the head, and reported the incident. He had parked on the side of the road apparently to consider his options and, having made his decision, survived for only a few hours after his body was found.[12]

A report of the incident, published in the *Atlanta Constitution*, speculated that "poor health" may have factored into Mr. Elrod's thinking, but it also hinted at mental illness by observing that "his nerves were shattered." The Thomasville newspaper provided further detail, reporting in a front-page story that R. H. Elrod was widely known to be suffering from a "nervous affection, which seemed to worry him greatly." According to the reporter, Mr. Elrod "talked several times of his condition in a way that led to the fear that he was irrational." He had even "been away a short time for treatment," raising the possibility that he had been placed in an asylum or even attempted suicide at least once before.[13]

Talmage's version of events, told to a reporter in mid- to late 1926, throws valuable light on his relationship with his father, but it also makes it difficult to establish the real sequence of events that year. It seems clear enough that the rupture occurred while Talmage was home for Christmas break, with his sojourn to New Orleans commencing soon after. But when? How soon?

A book given to me by my grandmother, *The Poems of Sydney Lanier*, offers a glimpse of family life at this moment. The following inscription was written on the front endpapers: "To Papa from Talmage / Happy

New Year '26." My uncle Henry inherited three other books with the same inscription and date. Before I discovered the newspaper article about the argument with his father, I had often wondered why Talmage gave these gifts on New Year's rather than on Christmas Day, as is customary. Now I have come to suspect it may have been an effort to make amends, or even a farewell gesture. In any case, he hit the road at the turn of the year.

A departure in early January 1926 would not have raised any eyebrows, since he was expected to return to Yale for the spring semester. To all outward appearances, his surviving family members still believed that he had done so. As they prepared for Mr. Elrod's funeral services in March, the Elrod family informed the local newspaper that Talmage was still "away at Yale." It is possible, therefore, that Talmage and his family were each telling the truth, as they understood it at that moment. If the final stages of the argument, in which Mr. Elrod had refused to pay any more tuition, were known only to the two men, the rest of the family may simply have assumed that Talmage was leaving for school as usual when in fact he was running away. In this permutation, Talmage traveled westward to New Orleans rather than north to New Haven, and may not have known for a very long time that his father had subsequently killed himself. It is easy to see him under these circumstances giving a tell-all interview about the incident that he would later come very much to regret.[14]

Our family history holds few clues about his departure from Thomasville, and these may well have been conflated with a later departure in 1927. Essentially, he left by hopping a train. His younger sister, Farrar, then sixteen years old, went with him to the train tracks on the west side of town. She could not remember the exact date, but the event remained one of her most vivid memories for the rest of her life. Talmage took a knapsack of clothing and incidentals, and the two of them lay in the tall grass and scrub waiting for a freight train to come around the bend. When it did, he took off running alongside it. He grabbed the open door of one of the boxcars and climbed inside. He never said good-bye, never waved, never even looked back. That's the way the story always ended.

Talmage likely sat for some time catching his breath, watching the Georgia clay and pine trees roll past for the last time. If New Orleans, Louisiana, was his intended destination from the start, he had his work cut out for him. No railroad lines ran directly from Thomasville to the Crescent City in 1926 or 1927. He either traveled westward into Alabama or southward through Florida first. Any route he chose, however, would have forced him to jump out of that freight car and find a different route in cities such as Pensacola and Mobile. It is possible he spent a few days knocking about in one or more of these junction cities before continuing to Louisiana. Then as now, westbound trains came into New Orleans by skirting the southern shore of Lake Pontchartrain to arrive at Union Station on South Rampart Street. Talmage climbed down from his boxcar into the bustling life of New Orleans' Central Business District, about a six-block walk north from the famous French Quarter. The city had a long tradition of entertaining and housing transient populations, including sailors, soldiers, musicians, and merchants. So Talmage had his pick of cheap and ready accommodations, some more restful (and reputable) than others. Perhaps he simply stretched out on a park bench for his first night in town. That, too, would not have been terribly uncommon in New Orleans.

After some hot food and a good night's sleep, his first order of business was to scan the classified section of the *Times-Picayune* newspaper for work. A new "skyscraper," designed by local architect Emile Weir for the Canal Bank and Trust Company, was just then going up in the Central Business District. It was not a tall building by the standards of New York or Chicago, only projected to reach nineteen floors upon completion the following year, since the sandy soils of the Mississippi floodplain made it hard to stabilize the foundation. Yet it was the biggest project in New Orleans in 1926, and the only skyscraper under way.

Talmage made his way to 210 Baronne Street and introduced himself to the foreman. He was able to cite nothing more than "two years of college" as qualification, but the foreman needed able-bodied men. The journalist who wrote about him followed Talmage on one occasion to the upper reaches of the construction site, where "your correspondent hugged a steel upright with one arm and clenched an Alpine stock with the other, getting this story. Elrod can be seen," he wrote, "walking on girders high above the street with the nonchalance of an inveterate girder walker." When the reporter expressed his concern about the extraordinary danger of the job, Talmage "smiled benignly" and responded with a shrug: "I prefer this work to office employment."[15]

A twenty-one-year-old college dropout does not typically attract a great deal of media attention. It seems unusual, therefore, that a seasoned journalist, one who knew enough to syndicate the story to multiple publications, chose to write about Talmage in 1926, much less follow him to the uppermost girders of the Canal Bank and Trust Company building. Perhaps they met at one of the numerous smoke-filled speakeasies around the French Quarter, where construction workers and writers rubbed elbows after work. Such a conversation could have started in a thousand ways, but here's one possible scenario: An Ivy League–educated writer sits at a bar on Royal Street, nursing his Dixie beer and smoking a Lucky Strike. In the mirror behind the counter, his attention is drawn to a white shirt with a blue "Y" on the front, worn by a tall, thin fellow with flyaway hair at a table just behind him. The writer swivels on his barstool, beer in hand, to face the fellow.

"Yale?" he asks.

When Talmage nods in the affirmative, the next logical question is, "What class?"

A little drunk at that point, Talmage raises his beer, smiles "benignly," and shouts out "1928!" What reporter worth his salt could resist investigating this mystery—a member of the Yale 1928 class walking girders in New Orleans in 1926?

Regardless of how the dialogue began, it is fair to assume that the idea of publishing the story came from the writer and not from Talmage. If the interview took place during his first arrival in the Crescent City, before his father's suicide—or, at least, before he knew of it—he may be entitled to a little latitude, or even pity. Yet if he told this story knowing full well the awful truth of things in Thomasville, it presents a more complicated psychological portrait.

He was clearly not ready to give honest answers to some of the questions he was asked, especially about his father. Shame and guilt were surely part of it, yet if the stages of grief held true in his day as they do in ours—denial, anger, bargaining, depression, and acceptance—Talmage was still very much in denial. In public it was easier for him, even eight months after the fact, to describe an angry and ongoing rupture between two living men than to own the fact that his father had not found life worth living. He may have wrestled with it more earnestly in his private thoughts. In one of his last letters to Emily Neal, he discussed the issue of suicide, albeit without specific reference to his father. "Sometimes," he told her, "I admire the one who commits suicide." He explained his position by appropriating lines from the commemorative poem by Brian Hooker, written to honor Yale veterans of the Great War: "We who must live salute you / who have found strength to die."[16]

Talmage eventually learned of the awful news by means that are lost to history, and hastened back to Thomasville. The family desperately needed his help. Mr. Elrod's death meant they had no money coming in, but it also meant they would have to move out of the superintendent's residence on Sinkola Plantation. They squeezed as best as they could into a small apartment in downtown Thomasville. Then Mrs. Elrod turned her attention to trying to feed the family. Swallowing her pride, she appeared before the Thomas County Court of Ordinary on May 4 and requested that public support be provided for the family for a period of twelve months. She listed Talmage as one of the "five minors" she had under her care. The public humiliation of the Elrod family was broadcast even further when the *Thomasville Daily Times-Enterprise* published a legal notice inviting anyone who was opposed to Mrs. Elrod's request for charity to appear and testify at the June meeting of the court.[17] No one appears to have done so.

The family was awarded $5,000 for the period of one year, but they received slightly less than $2,000 of this due to outstanding debts that had been left by Mr. Elrod. Any hope Talmage may have harbored of finishing his degree was necessarily put on hold. In addition, he qualified as a "minor," entitled to public relief, for only a few more months. He turned twenty-one years old on September 27, and must have begun to think early in the summer about how he might find work to support himself and help the family. This was not an easy task in south Georgia, where opportunities were limited, even in the best of times. New Orleans offered better chances. Perhaps his old high school dream of joining the marines began to revive at this point.

Three significant developments may have converged in 1927 to move him closer to a sea change in his life. The first of these was the release of the movie version of his favorite book, *Beau Geste*, starring Ronald Colman as Beau. The film first appeared in New Orleans theaters in January and became such a hit that it continued to be screened at multiple venues through the end of the year. At some point Elrod surely bought himself a ticket, and was reminded of all the reasons he had loved the story of the fatherless Geste brothers who overcame personal shame through the fearless pursuit of military honor, unheralded though it was in the public eye. He knew the story so well that he barely needed to read the dialogue of the silent film. Second, the news of Charles Lindbergh's daring solo flight across the Atlantic Ocean stirred his memories of soaring above Thomasville in a two-seater biplane. His passion for aviation may in turn have been rekindled. And lastly, construction work on the Canal Bank and Trust building was completed, and he found himself looking for new opportunities.

He had come close to running away to join the marines on a couple of occasions in high school, only to think better of it, or to be talked out of it. There was nothing stopping him now. He presented himself at a marine recruitment office in downtown Denver, Colorado, on November 25, 1927. No surviving records exist to indicate how he got from Louisiana to Colorado. Perhaps he had enough money saved up to travel as a paying passenger this time around. There was, after all, a direct train route from New Orleans to Denver. Perhaps the decision was not made in New Orleans at all, but somewhere along the line as he considered his next destination.

The recruiter was curious about some of these same questions in 1927. He couldn't help but wonder why a young man who listed his hometown as Thomasville, Georgia, would travel all the way out to Colorado to enlist. Since recruits from east of the Mississippi River were typically sent to Parris Island to be enlisted and trained, he wanted to be sure that Talmage had not already tried to join and been rejected by the Marine Corps back east. In addition, Talmage had shown up with no identifying information at all, so a telegram was dispatched to his mother in Thomasville: "Please telegraph collect date birth your son Henry Elrod has he ever been in Army Navy or Marine Corps or married was he ever rejected by Marine Corps at Parris Island South Carolina." She responded the same day to the satisfaction of the recruiter, and the following day Talmage signed his name to enlistment papers committing him to four years of general service in the US Marines.[18]

CHAPTER 4

Enlisted, 1927–1931

THE DENVER OFFICE WASTED NO TIME SHIPPING THE NEW RECRUIT westward by rail to the Marine Corps Recruit Depot (MCRD) in San Diego, California. Henry Talmage Elrod was officially enlisted as a private, given a uniform and rifle, and signed his service record book on December 1, 1927. Calvin Coolidge was president, and the US economy and stock market were, to all outward appearances, humming along nicely.[1]

His physical examination listed him at five feet, eleven and a half inches tall and 168 pounds, with brown eyes, brown hair, and a "ruddy" complexion. As testimony to the active life of athletics and construction work that had occupied him previously, the exam also recorded a wealth of scars on his arms, legs, back, and buttocks. At least four of these were clustered around his left knee, suggesting that perhaps he had undergone surgery at some point to repair the ligament or cartilage damage that slowed him down a step in his senior year of high school football.[2]

The Marine Corps base at San Diego was in its first decade of regular operation when Elrod came through in 1927 and 1928. The parade grounds were still not paved, but most of the infrastructure was complete. The administration building had been finished, along with seven barracks, officers' quarters, a power plant, ice house, machine shops, and a bakery. The facility was designed to echo the Spanish mission heritage of Southern California. The same themes were put to work in the construction of the naval air station just across the channel on North Island as well.[3]

Enlistment photo, December 1927. National Archives and Records Administration, Washington, DC.

The new recruits began their training with a three-week session of classroom and field instruction. They were introduced to Marine Corps history, traditions, and customs in the administration building and then went outside to the parade grounds to practice the manual of arms and other foundational drills. By January of 1928 they were ready to move on to the rifle range and more advanced tactical training, some of which involved trips off the base. In the midst of this, Elrod spent a week in early January as a "messman," serving dinner to the officers. He was deemed worthy of this special duty in part because he had two years of college under his belt. He then worked in the kitchen as a cook for the rest of the month. The final two weeks of basic training saw instruction in the use of the bayonet and company-level drills. Ceremonies for graduates were held in early February, 1928.[4]

Napoleon Bonaparte once said that the best preparation a soldier could receive for military life was poverty. Although he had not grown up "poor," Henry T. Elrod had certainly seen his share of hardship and deprivation since his father's death. He doggedly continued to identify himself as a "student" in his enlistment papers, but in truth he was two years removed from any college classroom at that point. Those years had seen him riding freight trains and doing dangerous manual labor to make ends meet. There is a better-than-average chance, moreover, that he was homeless or living at the YMCA when he showed up at the Denver recruiting office in November of 1927.

By contrast, the amenities available to him at the Marine Corps Recruit Depot in San Diego must have seemed like manna from heaven. In addition to room and board, he had access, free of charge, to several motion picture screenings each week. Tennis and handball courts could be reserved during off-hours, and there were even organized team sports available on the base. Elrod embraced this opportunity to relive his glory days as a star athlete at Thomasville High School by participating in several team sports. He was even a member of the second string of the marine basketball team that won the Pacific Coast championship later that year. In the evenings there were often performances by bands, along with social gatherings and dances. Most importantly of all, perhaps, he encountered for the first time male authority figures he could admire and seek to emulate. His drill instructor was harsh and demanding, but he was predictable and clear in what he expected. Proper conduct yielded proper outcomes, a marked contrast with the painful memories of his father.[5]

For these and other reasons, Private Elrod found the home he had been searching for in the Marine Corps, and he behaved as if he knew it. The same young man who had made a name for himself in high school for talking back to teachers and missing class became a paragon of discipline in the marines. To be fair, he was occasionally given average marks for "military efficiency," especially at the start of his basic training, but he received perfect scores from the beginning to the end of his enlisted career in the categories of "obedience" and "sobriety."[6]

Just as significant, his presence at MCRD allowed him to explore his interest in aviation. Perhaps he had done his research in choosing to enlist west of the Mississippi River. Perhaps, for once in his life, he just got lucky. For a young man interested in flying, however, there were few places in the United States more auspicious than San Diego. Across a sparkling channel of water known as the "Spanish Bight," easily visible to the recruits as they drilled and exercised at the Recruit Depot, lay North Island. By the time Elrod arrived in 1927, it had become the launching point for many of the United States' most significant aeronautical developments.

Most of these had occurred, in fact, within the previous two decades. The aviation pioneer Glenn Curtiss first identified North Island as a promising airfield in 1910. He began training the first naval aviator there in 1911, and by the mid-1910s the navy had established an air station on the northern corner of the island. The US Army, meanwhile, laid claim to the southern half of the island for its air corps. In the early 1920s, about the same time that Elrod was making his first trip into the air as a paying passenger back in Thomasville, Georgia, daring pilots routinely broke world endurance records in the skies above North Island. In 1923, as they considered ways of overcoming those endurance limits, aviators and mechanics on North Island developed techniques that allowed them to perform the first air-to-air refueling maneuver in aviation history.[7]

Upon arrival at basic training, Elrod surely heard stories about North Island's most famous visitor, Charles Lindbergh. Only six months earlier, Lindbergh had been a regular sight at the naval air station. While he waited for his airplane, the *Spirit of St. Louis*, to be built at a nearby factory, he trained for two months with the naval aviators. They tutored him on methods of "dead reckoning," by which a pilot could determine his progress and geographical position when flying over open water. This was, of course, the most important skill he needed in order to make his transatlantic flight from New York to Paris, when he would have no opportunities to verify his position with visual landmarks. He had never had much call for it as an airmail pilot.

At its most basic level, dead reckoning simply calculates the progress of the airplane based on its speed and elapsed time from a fixed starting point. The North Island aviators, however, had taken it several steps further by developing trigonometric formulas to account for barometric pressure and prevailing winds. They had even set up a test range at sea, identified for several miles by marker buoys. Lindbergh spent many hours running the course to test his accuracy with dead reckoning. At length, he took off in the *Spirit of St. Louis* from North Island on May 10, 1927, on the first leg of his journey across the country to New York.[8]

Inspired by such stories, Private Elrod made it clear to his commanding officers as basic training was coming to an end in early 1928 that he wished to be involved with the naval air station on North Island. Under ordinary circumstances, the preferences of a freshly minted private would not have carried much weight, but the Fourth Regiment of marines had been deployed from San Diego in 1927 to help protect the American Embassy in Shanghai, China. As a result, the MCRD and North Island Naval Air Station were severely understaffed. Elrod had arrived at just the right moment to fill that void. As soon as he finished basic training, he was assigned to work with Squadron VO-8M at North Island.[9]

Each letter of the squadron's designation held significance. The "V" signified that the aircraft it flew were "heavier than air," meaning that they depended on the shape of the airplane's wings and the thrust generated by its engine to take flight. In this sense, the "V" functioned as a sideways "greater than / lesser than" symbol. It was necessary to make that distinction in 1928 because the future of aviation seemed just as likely to involve "lighter than air" craft, such as the *Graf Zeppelin*, which made use of hydrogen or helium to gain lift. The *Hindenburg* disaster was still nine years in the future. The North Island Naval Air Station, in fact, had just constructed a hangar for dirigibles when Elrod showed up. The letter "O" identified the squadron as an "Observation" detail, meaning that its primary function in case of deployment would be reconnaissance of enemy artillery, naval, and troop locations. The letter "M" identified it as a Marine Corps squadron. VO-8M had about seven airplanes in 1928. Its pilots were drawn from commissioned marine officers, but about sixty enlisted men, such as Elrod, took care of the airplanes. This involved all forms of maintenance of the engines, wheels, wings, and armaments, along with refueling and storage.[10]

"Observation" was one of the three basic functions expected of marine aviation. "Fighter" squadrons (designated with a "VF" prefix), by contrast, were trained to engage enemy aircraft in the sky and establish air supremacy for US naval forces and marine operations. Finally, some squadrons were trained to provide direct combat assistance to marine ground troops through dive-bombing and machine-gun strafing. Each of these squadron specialties supported the Marine Corps' fundamental purpose within the navy, as it was understood at the start of the twentieth century: to function as an "advance base force," capable of seizing and holding targets of value to naval operations even when the navy itself was not yet able to reach them. Marine airpower thus aimed to be integrated with ground tactics in a way that naval aviation was not. In addition, the Marine Corps worked hard to make sure that marine pilots and aviation support crews understood themselves to be part and parcel of the service, rather than a separate or superior branch.[11]

Private Elrod worked as the operations clerk for Squadron VO-8M from February 1928 until March of 1929. The marines did not distribute such titles lightly, so it was undoubtedly meant to communicate his specific duties within the unit. Unfortunately, the Marine Corps Manual in use during his period of service did not list that job title. Most positions that included the word "clerk," however, such as "pay clerk" and "quartermaster clerk," entailed a significant involvement with paperwork. So it is possible that Elrod's increasingly legendary two and a half years of college, which had already garnered him time in the officers' mess, now landed him in the squadron operations office updating and keeping track of inventories of spare parts, muster rolls, flight schedules, and any other documentation generated by the squadron.

If so, the job probably took up a good portion of his day, since most military activities generated a sentence or two of official typewritten correspondence that typically needed to be copied and distributed to as many as five other command offices. Even so, there must have been numerous occasions that saw him out on the sandy runways of North Island, running out to airplanes with a clipboard to collect the signatures of pilots on the flight logs, placing chocks in front of airplane wheels, or standing on wings and cranking flywheels to get engines to turn over and start.[12]

Those sandy runways were supposed to be carpeted with grass, but the number of takeoffs and landings had risen to such a volume by 1928 that the grass could not be maintained. As a result, great clouds of dust and fine sand rose up and hovered over the base during periods of intense traffic. Even clerks like Elrod were summoned out to help tamp down the sands, as best they could, with rollers and water. Sometimes they applied stabilizing agents like motor oil. Their efforts met with only limited success. Another solution, of course, was to reduce the number of airplanes operating out of North Island, especially during the busy summer months. This was done in 1928 by shifting all marine squadrons northward to Mathis Field near Sacramento for "maneuvers." Elrod thus followed VO-8M there from June to August. He probably spent a good deal of his time, even as a clerk, filling in potholes and clearing weeds, since the field had not been used for several years.[13]

If Elrod was not already passionate about airplanes that summer, he could not have resisted the allure of flying when the marine squadrons returned to San Diego in the fall. There were big developments under way, and the North Island marines were in the middle of most of them. The first was the dedication of San Diego's Lindbergh Airport in August, 1928. The marines participated in a mass flyover of more than four hundred airplanes. Then the navy's crackerjack aerobatic unit, known as the "Three Sea Hawks," put on a performance for the ages. Flying Boeing F2B-1 fighter planes, they stunned the spectators with airborne stunts such as "looping the loop while flying in formation, wing overs while flying 10 feet apart, upside-down flying, cartwheel loops, true Immelmanns and slow aileron rolls."

Elrod must have stood, like thousands of others, with his face turned to the sky in wonderment. By the end of 1928, their harrowing maneuvers had earned them the unofficial nickname of "The Suicide Trio." The Three Sea Hawks are often cited by modern scholars as the first iteration of the Navy's "Blue Angels" performance team, and they generated a similar level of awe and national pride in the late 1920s. Because they were posted to the naval air station at North Island, moreover, Elrod could do more than simply marvel at them in the sky. He could stand with other airfield support staff and pilots by the runways and listen to the legendary Sea Hawks plan their shows and discuss the technical challenges of particular feats. Perhaps he gazed past them on occasion at the Boeing fighters parked a few yards away and imagined, if he were a pilot himself, how he might adjust the flaps to minimize the drift or "slide" of the aircraft in a tight turn.[14]

Just then, Hollywood came to North Island. The Metro-Goldwyn-Mayer company sent director George Hill to make a movie about navy pilots training at the naval air station. The film's production staff and stars held a joint press conference with high-ranking navy officers at the Hotel del Coronado in late August to publicize the event. The reigning heartthrob of 1928, Ramon Novarro, was to star in the movie, along with Ralph Graves as his comedic foil. Actress Anita Page was their joint love interest. The plot followed a group of friends as they struggled to win their wings as naval aviators.

From late July through September, Private Elrod and other airfield staffers had to work around the stars and their production crews, taking care not to walk through scenes unawares. Needless to say, the film enlisted the aid of the Three Sea Hawks for an extended segment of aerial performances. They executed all their signature maneuvers flawlessly, but when close-ups of the pilots' faces were spliced into the sequence later in the editing phase, Ramon Novarro and Ralph Graves appeared to be at the controls. Many other pilots and airfield workers were "impressed as actors" by director George Hill as needs arose. Private Elrod may have made a small "bit" appearance in this capacity, but it is impossible to identify him with certainty. The working title of the movie was originally *The Gold Braid* during the production phase at North Island, but it was released to theaters in January of the following year as *The Flying Fleet*.[15]

Inspired perhaps by this whirlwind of aviation-related activities, Elrod appears to have applied himself with renewed vigor to moving up in the ranks. He completed an armorer's course, which qualified him to work on and operate the machine guns and other weaponry carried aloft by Observation Squadron Eight. This carried with it a modest raise in monthly pay, along with a designation as "specialist fourth class," and an "air artillery badge" to be worn on the left lapel of his dress uniform. It may have allowed him to escape some of the paperwork of his clerk position, but, more likely than not, it simply added to his existing responsibilities. At about the same time, Elrod demonstrated his accuracy with a pistol on the firing range and was qualified as a "Marksman."[16]

Above all, however, he wanted to fly airplanes. As chance would have it, the marines were in desperate need of new pilots. They preferred to draw aviators from their pool of commissioned officers, but with so many deployed in China and Nicaragua, the Corps decided to experiment for the first time with training enlisted men in late 1928. Elrod immediately placed himself at the front of the line for this new opportunity.

As part of the application process in October, he was subjected to an extensive physical examination. Film critics at the time were unimpressed by the love triangle plot of *The Flying Fleet*, yet, in spite of its dramatic shortcomings, the movie succeeded in creating a valuable real-time historical record of the naval (and marines') flight training program at exactly the moment that Elrod was going through it. As depicted (to humorous effect) in the movie, Elrod too was spun in a barber's chair to determine his resistance to vertigo. His eyes were tested for 20/20 vision, because, as the silent movie's dialogue screen explained, "Bad eyes don't belong in the air."

Since pilots did not have oxygen masks in 1928, aspiring aviators were tested for their ability to function under natural atmospheric conditions at high altitudes. The applicant's nose was closed with a padded clip and a scuba-like hose and mouthpiece placed in his mouth. As the oxygen feeding into the hose was steadily reduced, he was scored on his ability to place an electrified stylus into appropriate receptor sockets labeled by numbers and letters, according to verbal instructions. When the applicant could no longer insert the stylus into the appropriate socket in a reasonable amount of time, the mouthpiece was removed and the subject revived. Based on the final ratio of oxygen to other gases when the student had lost effectiveness, the doctor calculated the altitude at which he could be expected to operate for extended lengths of time. At the end of it all, Henry Talmage Elrod was judged to be "physically qualified and temperamentally adapted for aviation training involving actual control of aircraft."[17]

Instruction got under way for those selected during the first week of December. Two-seater seaplanes were used as trainers during the first weeks of instruction, since landing on water was more forgiving than on traditional airstrips. The student typically sat in the rear while the instructor sat in front. Most airplanes were not yet furnished with radio equipment, so the instructor communicated by means of rubber tubes that ran from his mouthpiece back to the earholes of the student's helmet, a low-tech solution that worked quite well. The full course of training to create a functional pilot could take as much as a year, but only the first phase was to be conducted at North Island. Students who successfully completed the introductory-level courses were then to be recommended for further flight training at the Pensacola Naval Air Station in Florida.[18]

Judging by this measure, it is difficult to assess the outcome of Elrod's early flight training. He was not transferred, at any rate, to Pensacola, nor is there any evidence that he was allowed to fly airplanes by himself at this time. He seems, nevertheless, to have impressed his instructors enough to merit promotion to specialist third class in early January, 1929. At the end of the month he was promoted to private first class and transferred from VO-8M to the Headquarters Squadron. It is unlikely that this carried any change of actual duties, since he continued to be listed as an operations clerk.

By spring, however, there were clear signs that Elrod was making meaningful strides forward. He was promoted to corporal on April Fools' Day, a coincidence that must have occasioned a fair amount of ribbing among his peers. This carried with it a "probationary technical warrant for aviation duty." The probationary period ended one month later when he was officially "detailed to duty involving actual flying in aircraft" on May 6, 1929.[19]

The language of that order suggests that he was not the pilot but rather the second member of an airborne team who handled matters of navigation (or "avigation," as pilots liked to call it), observation, and, in combat, use of the side-mounted swivel machine gun. The marine squadrons of the North Island Naval Air Station were flying Curtiss OC-2 "Falcons." These were, for the most part, two-seater biplanes. They were among the first military airplanes to have a metal fuselage and could reach speeds in excess of 200 miles per hour. The aviation duty for which Elrod was detailed must have been very limited in scope, for the authorization was revoked at the end of the month "by reason of completion of duty." His orders did not give any specific information about what it entailed, but it is not hard to guess.[20]

Against all odds, another Hollywood production crew arrived on North Island to make a movie about aviators in May of 1929. Ralph Graves was again one of the co-stars. He was joined in the limelight by the alluring Lila Lee and veteran Hollywood leading man Jack Holt. This time, however, their focus was not on naval aviators in general but exclusively on marine pilots, and the US government cooperated by placing the marine squadrons of North Island and two companies of marines at their disposal.

Frank Capra, later to become famous for films such as *It's a Wonderful Life* and *Mr. Smith Goes to Washington*, directed the movie, released later that year under the title *Flight*. It was one of the first "talking" movies produced. Capra recognized the value of the government's assistance and made extensive use of aerial photography to capture the marines in flight. Elrod's brief authorization to fly must have been a part of this unusual activity. If so, he probably appears in the film as one of the helmeted figures in the rear seat of a Curtiss Falcon as they fly in formation to provide assistance to marine ground troops. He may also have been caught on film as an extra in several scenes, though it is hard to identify him with certainty. The most likely of these fleeting glimpses occurs when the students are gathered together waiting to take their solo flights. They are shown leaning against the wing of a naval training biplane, wearing black trousers, leather jackets, leather helmets, and goggles that have been pushed up to rest on their foreheads.[21]

This is the same outfit, I now realize, that he wears in a cherished family photo that has rested on my father's piano for decades. No one in my family ever knew exactly when that photo was taken, but it must have been in 1929. The squadron number on the fuselage behind him confirms it: 7-O-4. Observation Squadron Seven was operating out of North Island Naval Air Station in 1929, and two of its aircraft can be identified by number in the Capra film. It may have been one of the perks the marine aviators received for their otherwise-unpaid participation in the movie: a professional photo by one of the cameramen on staff. Another appearance occurs toward the end of the film, when an airplane swoops down over the tent of the "operations office," scattering papers. Five startled clerks, one of whom appears to be Corporal Elrod, stumble out of the tent and gaze skyward in a befuddled manner, a truly immortal moment in the history of Marine Corps drama.[22]

As it appeared in theaters, the film's climactic scene showed marine airpower providing strafing and bombing support to a courageous band of two hundred ground troops besieged by an overwhelming force of Nicaraguan rebels. Most of the flying in that scene had been completed in early and mid-May in the neighborhood of North Island or the adjacent California coast, and the ground battle, ostensibly in Central

Elrod as a student aviator at North Island, ca. 1929. Photo in author's possession.

America, was actually staged on the outskirts of San Diego on May 22. Elrod must have been part of the marine ground forces that day, since all available hands were mobilized for the shoot. From the perspective of the marines, after all, there was no difference between air and ground personnel. They built a small palisaded fort and took up positions along the walls, awaiting attack. For the besieging rebels, Frank Capra hired a diverse assortment of over one thousand extras whose main qualification was that they did not require much money and appeared to be vaguely Nicaraguan when wearing a straw hat.[23]

Capra armed both sides with powder charges for their guns (no bullets, of course) to produce a respectable bang for the sound equipment and a satisfying puff of smoke for the cameras. They were instructed to stop firing within twenty feet of the opposing side, since the cartridges, even without bullets, could inflict painful burns at close range. Yet as the scene neared its conclusion, a sizable contingent of "Nicaraguan rebels" lost their composure in the heat of battle and rushed forward to the stockade. They thrust their rifles through the cracks of the fort and fired point blank at the marines who, having been given their orders, took the rolling barrage with not a single step backward for the better part of two minutes. The result was a thrilling finale for American moviegoers.

The ticket-buying public never knew that after Mr. Capra had shouted "Cut," the marines had carefully stored away their rifles, assembled at the makeshift gate of the fort, unlatched it, and charged forth in anger to attack their fellow extras. The resulting melee took several hours to subside. The *San Diego Union* newspaper, which reported the incident, claimed that despite their immense numerical advantage, a far greater proportion of rebels than marines had required medical treatment or hospitalization afterward. It is quite possible, therefore, that the revocation of Corporal Elrod's detail to aviation duty one week later had something to do with his participation in this unique performance.[24]

By the time *Flight* was released to theaters in September, Elrod was back to his usual routine as operations clerk in the Marine Air Headquarters of the West Coast Expeditionary Forces. Perhaps his coursework for aviation training continued, but there is no clear evidence that he took to the air again during the remaining two years of his enlistment term. Even so, the marines had invested time and money in grooming him for greater responsibility, and they found themselves facing the same dilemma encountered by the navy: Investments made in training enlisted men were lost in relatively short order if the soldier could not be persuaded to reenlist. That fateful horizon was coming up in January of 1931 for Elrod.

In his case, however, another term of enlistment was not the only way around the problem. A bachelor's degree was the standard prerequisite for commissioned officers, but the marines had a number of merit-based options by which enlisted men without a diploma could obtain their commissions. Exceptional enlisted service was one of them. And while Elrod may have taken a step or two backward as a result of the unfortunate brawl on the set of Frank Capra's movie, he had for the most part proven his mettle to his superiors at North Island. As he himself must have pointed out, moreover, he had made it halfway through college. He was thus encouraged to apply for admission to Officer Candidate School. If he succeeded in graduating, he would be commissioned as a second lieutenant. The marines would then be able to continue reaping the rewards of their investments in him, and Henry Talmage Elrod would have more than a four-year stint as a leatherneck. He would have a "career."

CHAPTER 5

Commissioned

ELROD BEGAN LAYING THE GROUNDWORK TO APPLY FOR OFFICER CAN-
didate School in the late summer of 1929, just as Babe Ruth was chasing
the five-hundred-home-run milestone in his legendary baseball career.
Herbert Hoover had been inaugurated president in March, and the
country was feeling optimistic about the prospect of having achieved
permanent economic prosperity. "Unemployment in the sense of distress
is widely disappearing," Hoover assured Americans. "We in America
today are nearer to the final triumph over poverty than ever before in the
history of any land."[1]

Sure enough, the Babe did it! He became the first player in the history of the game to hit five hundred homers in August in a game against
the Cleveland Indians. The sky really was the limit, it seemed, and Henry
Talmage Elrod's ambitions were no exception.

As occurred when he first enlisted, poor Mrs. Elrod was summoned
again to testify "that he was borned [*sic*] on September 27, 1905," this
time under oath before a justice of the peace. When asked for corrobo-
rating evidence, she had nothing but her own memory. The boy's father
was "deceased," she said, and "the physician who attended me at his . . .
birth is now dead, also the midwife who attended me at his birth is now
dead. And at that time the laws didn't require the birth of children being
registered as it is now."[2]

The rest of the application process was complex and rigorous, and it
produced a significant amount of paperwork for historians who may wish
to delve more deeply into the topic. It does not strike me as the stuff from

which a compelling biographical narrative is made, so for the present I will summarize briefly and move forward. Elrod was asked for three endorsements from his commanding officers within the Marine Corps, three character reference letters from individuals outside the military, and academic transcripts from high school and college. He then underwent a mental and physical evaluation and completed examinations in history, algebra, trigonometry, geometry, grammar, and physics.

Strangely, *very strangely*, Elrod reached out to the principal of Thomasville High School for one of his reference letters, the very man who had expelled him from school for two months during his senior year. Mr. H. R. Mahler, to his credit, did his best to type some positive words about his former charge. "While in this school," he said, Elrod "showed ability above the average and quite a bit of ambition." Toward the end of the letter, though, he could not help reminiscing about the unbridled nature of that ambition: "Though Talmage sometimes got into disciplinary troubles, I have always found him frank and truthful and willing to mend his ways." It is the sort of reference, I would judge, that a young man seeks out only if he has pathetically few reputable connections in the civilian world on which to call for help.[3]

Fortunately, Elrod's commanding officers had seen enough of him in action to endorse his candidacy without such caveats. He was approved on June 7, 1930, to begin studies at the Officer Candidate School in Washington, DC. Even so, the examining board ended its approval letter with a warning that he should "devote particular attention" during his upcoming studies to the subjects of algebra and trigonometry, in which his scores had been marginal. He was awarded a ten-day leave to enjoy himself before boarding a train for the cross-country trip.[4]

What did Corporal Elrod do with himself for those ten days of glorious leave? He packed his belongings and got things squared away with the paymaster so that his $25-per-month allotments ended in San Diego and resumed in Washington. He closed his account at the Bank of Italy. And while there is no hard evidence of it, there can be little doubt that he made another trip or two (or three) south of the border to whoop it up in Tijuana, Mexico, or "Tia Juana," as the marines of North Island preferred to spell it. One of the greatest attractions of Tijuana was that it lay outside the American judicial and recordkeeping system, so there was no readily accessible paperwork to follow one home as proof of gambling losses or profits, fights or incarcerations, marriages or divorces. Another of its great attractions was alcohol. As the United States entered its tenth year of federally enforced sobriety in 1930, the beer, wine, and tequila were still flowing in the streets of Tijuana.

"Satan's Playground," as it was known, was only about a ten-mile drive from downtown San Diego, accessible through a United States customs checkpoint at the border that was so understaffed and nonchalant in the 1920s and 1930s that cars were often waved through without even coming to a complete stop. With so much temptation so close and so easily enjoyed, it is hard to imagine that Elrod did not make a habit of visiting Tijuana. Although there is no evidence that he did so as an enlisted man from 1927 to 1930, he made many such journeys south of the border during his second assignment to North Island, from 1938 to 1940. He was known, during those years, to pile into the backseat of a southbound car almost every other weekend. Of course, making assumptions about early behavior based on later patterns is not always wise. It is possible, for instance, that something happened in the years between his first term of enlistment and his later life as a commissioned officer that changed him from a teetotaling non-gambler into a freewheeling lover of good times, but I very much doubt it. All the evidence I have come across suggests that Henry Talmage Elrod was a lover of good times from start to finish, from Thomasville, Georgia, to Wake Island in the middle of the Pacific.[5]

The allure of Tijuana became even more irresistible when the Agua Caliente horse-racing track opened in December, 1929. Elrod had always loved horses. He was a capable rider himself, and had spent many happy days playing hooky in high school in order to take horses down to the tracks in Tallahassee, Florida. He would not have missed the races in Tijuana or the chance to bet on the winning horse. Obviously, there was only so much wagering one could do on $25 per month, and his accounts indicate that Elrod left the West Coast no richer or poorer than when he first arrived. The chance was the thing! The singer Al Jolson presided over the opening ceremonies that December, and Hollywood celebrities were always in attendance thereafter. The Agua Caliente complex also included a sumptuous casino, bars, restaurants, and extensive floral gardens.[6]

After ten days of unsupervised "rest and relaxation," Elrod probably spent much of the train journey to Washington, DC, sleeping. He was accompanied by another corporal, August Larson, who had also been approved to move up from the enlisted ranks to become a commissioned officer—contingent, of course, on successful completion of Officer Candidate School.

Once in Washington, the two men reported to the Marine Barracks and began a six-month sequence of college-level courses. After all his forlorn boasting about once having been a college student, Elrod was finally back in the classroom as an actual student again. He appears to have seized the opportunity with both hands, if his final exam scores are taken as a measure. In the two subjects that he had been warned about in his qualifying exams, algebra and trigonometry, he received almost perfect scores. Based on this performance, the Marine Examining Board concluded on January 12, 1931, "that Corporal Henry T. Elrod, U.S. Marine Corps, has the physical, mental, moral, and professional qualifications to perform the duties of the grade of a Second Lieutenant."[7]

He was formally discharged as an enlisted corporal on February 25, 1931, and signed his commission and oath of office as a second lieutenant the following day. The marines sent him to the Navy Yard at Philadelphia, Pennsylvania, for his first active-duty assignment. It is unclear what his specific duties were initially, but he may have been working on the rifle range. By April of 1931, however, he had managed again to enroll himself in training "as a student naval aviator." It must have been an introductory-level course, because it lasted only from April 27 to May 15. Elrod remained active in team sports during this period as well, for he was listed as playing for the marine rugby team that defeated the Harvard University Crimson squad in March and the Columbia University Lions in April. It was probably his first exposure to the sport, but he seems to have caught on to it quickly. *Leatherneck* magazine praised him for "playing a fast game at the breakaway."[8]

All of this was really just a way of passing time until the start of Basic School in August. The Officer Candidate School had been designed to assess whether the student was suitable material for commissioned status. The Marine Corps Basic School, on the other hand, exposed the newly commissioned officers to advanced classroom and field training to equip them with the knowledge they would need to lead soldiers in a variety of situations. Between August 1931 and June 15, 1932, Elrod studied a bewildering range of complex topics: First Aid and Military Hygiene, Naval and Military Law, Drill and Command, Administration, Interior Guard Duty, Land Operations, Marksmanship, Military Field Engineering, Naval Ordnance, Signal Communications, and many more. Each one of these topics, moreover, included a similarly broad range of subtopics. A qualifying score for Signal Communications, for instance, required Elrod to demonstrate mastery of visual signals, field telephones, switchboard installations, radio code, radio procedure, and cipher devices. He passed Signal Communications with an average exam score of 84.25 percent, but seems to have wilted badly under the ponderous weight of Naval Law. After scoring well on "Charges and Specifications," Elrod sank lower and lower in this litigious subject area until he reached an embarrassingly low 72 on his exam for "forms of evidence." On the bright side, this disappointing result was soon counterbalanced when he moved on to the study of weapons, earning scores ranging from 92 to 94 percent for various techniques of "laying" machine-gun fire. This, Elrod might have argued, could be viewed as a "form of evidence" in its own right under the proper circumstances.[9]

Somehow, in the midst of all this, he also found time to play baseball for the Philadelphia Marines, the "Philly Nine," in the fall of 1931. He was now twenty-six years old, but he had not lost many steps at second base. According to *Leatherneck*, the marine infield was "well protected by the limber Lieutenant Elrod, who in early innings of an important league contest, handled three hot chances with consummate skill."[10]

After a year of intensive study, he graduated in July of 1932. There were thirty-five graduates that year. Their families came from far and wide to witness their achievement. Even if Elrod told his family about it, he knew they could not afford the trip to Philadelphia. His sister Farrar had just gotten married and was starting a new life in Atlanta, Georgia, and his mother still had no permanent address in Thomasville. In addition to the family's hardships, the Great Depression was taking an economic toll on all Americans. In short, no one appears to have made the trip to Philadelphia to help him celebrate the moment. Major Benjamin H. Fuller, the commandant of the Marine Corps, gave the commencement address and presented each officer with a certificate. Second Lieutenant Elrod was assigned to the Marine Base at Quantico, Virginia.[11]

This was the point at which newly commissioned officers began to diverge from one another in their training. They were allowed to request further specialized instruction to work with ground, naval, or air units. Although Elrod was initially assigned to the "Rifle Range Detachment" at Quantico, he wasted little time in requesting assignment to aviation duty. Within a few weeks of arriving at Quantico, he had lined up four endorsements from his superior officers and filed a formal request to be selected for the "Flight Preparatory Course" at the Naval Air Station in Norfolk, Virginia. Once again, he presented himself for a thorough physical and mental examination to determine his fitness for the training. As at North Island, he was again spun around in a barber's chair, again deprived of oxygen while poking letters and numbers with an electrified stylus. Upon receipt of a positive report, his request was approved on September 1, and he was ordered to report to Norfolk "not later than September 20."[12]

He was given routine work to do at the Norfolk Naval Air Station until the course got under way on October 3, 1932. It must have been very similar to the one for enlisted men that he had already completed at North Island: familiarity with instrumentation, safety checks, taxiing, takeoffs, landings, basic maneuvering, navigation, and so forth. This course, however, was only for officers. It was the standard gateway for aspiring pilots. The official title—Flight Training Elimination Course— revealed much about its objectives. It was intended to weed out marines who, despite their courage and enthusiasm, were simply not suited to combat aviation. Instruction lasted for only four weeks and concluded with a solo flight.

Elrod completed the course without incident. On the day of his solo test, he took off from the Norfolk NAS runway, flew out a few miles over the waters of Hampton Roads, where the *Merrimac* and *Monitor* had

Elrod as second lieutenant, 1931. National Archives and Records Administration, Washington, DC.

fought seventy years earlier during the Civil War. He demonstrated his ability to fly at different speeds and maintain prescribed altitudes, then turned back. He circled the airfield several times, so that his instructors on the ground could assess his use of different drag configurations during the descent, and landed.[13]

There was no great fanfare, unless it occurred privately among Elrod and his buddies that evening. A naval message was sent to his commanding officer with the news that "Second Lieutenant H. T. Elrod, U.S.M.C., successfully completed Flight Elimination course." He was given the chance to request leave time at this point, but he was so eager to continue on to the next level of training that he declined it. Accordingly, orders were issued for him to be detached from the Quantico marine base on November 7 and proceed to the Naval Air Station at Pensacola, Florida, "for aviation duty and instruction as a Student Naval Aviator." This was the official flight training that he had been gunning for since his first encounter with aviation at North Island, San Diego. He had hit all of his career targets in the Marine Corps thus far, but Pensacola was about to test him at a whole new level. As the next chapter will argue, the second lieutenant tested Pensacola right back.

CHAPTER 6

Pensacola, 1932–1935

PENSACOLA, FLORIDA, HAD SERVED AS A NAVAL BASE SINCE THE EARLY days of the United States' possession of Florida in the 1820s. The harbor was a natural asset, and its location gave the US Navy access to major trading lanes in the Gulf of Mexico. The first naval aviators began to learn their trade there during World War I. When Elrod arrived in 1932, it was still the navy's only full-fledged aviation training program. Student aviators worked through a twelve-month course of instruction that earned them, if successful, their wings as pilots. In Elrod's day, the program produced on average one hundred graduates per year.

Elrod had acquired an automobile while in Virginia, and he initially requested that he be allowed to drive it to Pensacola with a five-dollar-per-day allowance for fuel and food. This was approved but later crossed out in his transfer papers, so it's unclear exactly how he made his way to Florida. A road trip of that length in 1932 would have been a rigorous undertaking, involving many unpaved country roads that sometimes led to rivers where there were no bridges yet. In such cases, one relied on local ferry services. There were not, moreover, many reliable maps of roads, bridges, and ferries in the rural South. It is therefore possible he reconsidered his original request and simply sold the car.

Whether he went by car or train, the journey would have taken Elrod straight through, or very close to, his old stomping grounds in Thomasville, Georgia. Yet he seems to have passed through very quietly and contacted few if any of his family or friends. The local newspaper, the *Thomasville Daily Times-Enterprise*, prided itself on providing information about such visits. When Elrod's sister, Farrar, had traveled from Atlanta to visit some friends the previous winter, it merited a full paragraph upon her arrival and another on her departure. Had the editors known that the former high school football star Talmage Elrod, now a respectable second lieutenant in the US Marine Corps, had rumbled through town on his way to flight school in Pensacola, they would surely have published that story. Yet nothing at all was said. Perhaps the memory of his father's death led him to plot a course that took him the long way around.

Elrod presented himself to his commanding officer at the Pensacola Naval Air Station on November 15, 1932. After two weeks of classroom instruction, he took to the air to begin a prolonged course of "dual instruction." This involved flight time with an instructor who assessed the student's execution of specific types of maneuvers.

Lieutenant Voit accompanied Elrod on his first flight on November 29, and he was not impressed. He complained in his log entry that Elrod was "too tense" throughout the flight and performed "mechanically." In addition, he judged the student to be "slow entering spirals." The following day, they went aloft again and ran through the same routine. Once they were back on the ground, Voit wrote "No improvement" in his log.[1]

Lieutenant Voit served as Elrod's primary instructor for the next two months, logging an average of ten to twenty hours of air time each week. The tenseness he observed in their first flight continued to manifest itself at unexpected moments from that point onward. By the first week of December, Voit judged him to be "stiff on the controls." They worked on overcoming that problem the next day. Yet, on December 8, he repeated the criticism and added that Elrod "yaws some takeoffs and spirals." The following day, he wrote "No progress" once again.

Elrod was due to make a five-hour solo flight in early January as part of the standard progression of the course, and Lieutenant Voit clearly had some misgivings about it. The student, he worried, was "not at ease as much as he should be for the amount of time he has had." Nevertheless, he gave his consent for Elrod to make the flight. Without an instructor present in the cockpit to critique his performance, he appears to have risen to the challenge and even impressed observers on the ground. As soon as Voit strapped himself in the following week, however, the nerves returned. Once they were back on the ground, an exasperated Lieutenant Voit wrote in his logbook that Elrod was "sloppy. Slipped into turns and spirals. Slipped some spirals. Some landings levelled off too high. Not as good as he was at 5 hour solo."[2]

The main problem, Voit had come to believe by February 1933, was that the "student is high strung." Taking that into consideration, he mercifully judged Elrod's work at the controls to be on the whole "fair to good" with an "average" aptitude for flying. It was not a ringing endorsement, by any stretch of the imagination, but he felt that once Elrod was up in the air, alone, he would probably be fine. In one of his last entries on the matter, Voit predicted that Elrod "should pass a fair final, if he does not get excited."[3]

Well, what do you know? He got excited. Yet there was more to the story this time than simple nerves.

A week or two after Voit had written this entry, just as Franklin Delano Roosevelt was being inaugurated president, Elrod attended a dance at the naval base. There was to be plenty of food and a live band. Duke Ellington's big hit "It Don't Mean a Thing (If It Ain't Got That Swing)" was still wildly popular with American audiences. Alcohol remained illegal until later in the year, when the Eighteenth Amendment was at last repealed, but there were ways around that for courageous marines who had studied offensive tactical operations in Basic School. Best of all, there were women.

Elrod had likely seen his share of such dances and such women, many of them very upstanding persons in all likelihood. He was, after all, a veteran of Tijuana. This dance, this night, however, was destined to be different. As he chatted with friends, he noticed a beautiful young woman who did not seem to fit in with the festivities. Elizabeth Hogun Jackson did not, in fact, appear to want to be there at all. She was leaning against a wall, arms crossed, refusing to dance or engage in small talk, when their eyes met. Nothing more is known about that evening; perhaps they never even got around to dancing together. But they did talk, and the more they learned about each other, the more they wanted to find out.[4]

Elizabeth was there, it turned out, only because her uncle was in town visiting his old navy buddies. She had no choice but to cool her heels at the dance while he made the rounds, slapping backs and exchanging jokes. Rear Admiral Richard H. Jackson had retired three years earlier, but only because a congressional law mandated it for top-level commanders at the age of sixty-four. He still itched to be in the middle of things, and given his experience as former assistant chief of naval operations and commander in chief of battle fleets (let that title sink in for a moment), his base of knowledge and professional connections were so extensive that naval officers from coast to coast still coveted his insights and favor. He had hired Elizabeth in 1924, when she was just nineteen years old, to manage his vast network of associates and host professional receptions when he was in Washington, DC. Now, at the same age as Elrod, twenty-eight, she continued to function as chief of staff in the admiral's hectic "retirement."

"Betty" Jackson lived with her uncle in Florence, Alabama, on the Tennessee River. Today, it is a six-hour drive by modern interstate highway from Pensacola to northern Alabama. The dirt roads of 1933 undoubtedly made that distance an even more forbidding obstacle to romance, yet somehow they found ways to visit. The admiral appears to have taken temporary lodgings in Mobile in order to facilitate his frequent trips to Pensacola, so the distance was not insurmountable.

Within a week or two of that first meeting at the dance, the two had fallen in love. It did not affect Elrod's performance in the air at first. He continued to have up and down days. His new flight instructor, P. A. Putnam, judged his work to be "fair enough" on March 11. He passed his written examination on the navy's N-2 flight manual and flight rules a few days later and made a second successful solo flight on March 15.[5]

Yet there were clouds on the horizon. As the affair with Ms. Jackson commanded more and more of his attention on the ground, Elrod began to be distracted in the air. The first sign of trouble came on March 21, when he was written up for having made unauthorized landings at two airfields in Mobile, Alabama. He probably thought he could make a quick stop to see her without anyone spotting him, but someone at the airfield noticed. They sent a report to Pensacola. As a result, he was grounded for two days by the superintendent for aviation training. When he was allowed back in an airplane, he knew he was under scrutiny, and his nervousness returned in full force. Several different instructors flew with him in late March and early April to compare notes. C. W. Crawford reported "a poor ride in practically all respects" on April 3. His full comments did not pull any punches:

> Handled plane roughly in taxying. Stalled and yawed on takeoffs. Skidded turns and spirals badly. Emergencies indifferent. Missed five out of five circle shots. Landings poor. Leveled off with too much speed and tried to fan it on. Student appeared nervous and jerky throughout.[6]

On a scale of 1 to 3, Lieutenant Crawford rated Elrod's precision landings at an unacceptably low "0.0." The following day, First Lieutenant P. K. Smith was a little more forgiving, but still rated him as "barely passable."[7]

By the first week of April 1933, the flight instructors at Pensacola had seen enough. Elrod was called before a hearing of the base commanders and informed that he had not made adequate progress in the program. He was presented with a complete record of his flight logs, including the ratings given by each instructor. When asked if he had any complaints about how he had been treated, he answered "No, sir." When asked if he had anything to say in defense of his poor performance, Elrod tried to explain his dilemma:

> My failure to measure up to the required flying standard was due to an excessive anxiety to fly perfectly with the check pilot. I earnestly believe that I will be able to overcome this tenseness and fly as smoothly and calmly with a check pilot as I do with my regular instructor or as I do alone.[8]

His primary instructor, Lieutenant Putnam, agreed with this assessment. "This student's failure," he told the board, "is due directly to over-anxiousness to please." He felt certain that Elrod could be taught to relax during test flights and that additional time for instruction would enable him to complete his training. The board again asked Elrod if he had anything further to say. "No, sir," he responded, "except that I love flying and I want to be a naval aviator and I know that I can do it." The board granted him two additional hours of instruction and one hour of solo time in order to prepare for another round of test flights to determine his fate.[9]

The additional flying time did nothing to mitigate or control his stress. If anything, it worsened it. With the stakes now higher than ever, his nerves frayed completely. Under the piercing gaze of the check pilots, Elrod stalled and yawed his takeoffs, leveled off too high on landings, then fanned it on at the last moment. He circled the field too widely, missed his circle shots over and over, skidded turns, and slid into spirals. When presented with emergency scenarios, he panicked, second-guessed himself, and made matters worse. In rating Elrod's handling of emergencies, the check pilot on April 11 rated his "judgement poor in nearly every case." One week later, it nearly cost him his life. He "froze on [the] throttle in one emergency when throttle was needed in a hurry; barely missed hitting trees." Elrod tried again to explain that his mistakes were "due to over-anxiousness to pass checks," but it was too late. The advisory board met again on April 17 to review his most recent blunders, and they wasted little time in ruling that he had demonstrated a "lack of ability ever to acquire the proficiency required of a naval aviator."[10]

It was brutal, final language, and Elrod must have turned the phrase over and over in his mind: "lack of ability ever to acquire the proficiency . . ." He had time to think about it, since he was promptly "dropped from naval aviation training" and did not yet have a new assignment. The marine commandant immediately requested that Elrod be detached from Pensacola and transferred elsewhere.

As he waited to learn where he would be headed next, he probably shared a few beers with his best friend, Second Lieutenant James T. Wilbur, who had also been washed out of the program. They may have met before their arrival in Florida, since Wilbur had come through all the same places as Elrod: Basic School in Washington, DC, and the Flight Training Elimination Course at Norfolk Naval Air Station in Virginia. Wilbur's dream of becoming a pilot had ended six months earlier, but he continued to serve at the Pensacola Marine Barracks in other capacities. He likely reassured Elrod that life would go on, and that the honor of being a marine was still untarnished.

Both Elrod and Wilbur took pride in being marines first and foremost. Despite the disappointment over flight training, there were no sour grapes for these two. Later, during World War II, Wilbur would distinguish himself with marine ground forces in some of the most bitter fighting of the "island-hopping" campaign in the Pacific. Later still, he would lead marines in combat in the Korean conflict, and ultimately, once retired from the military, teach as a professor of naval science at the University of California. He was fully committed to the service in whatever role the marines chose to use him. If anyone could talk Hank Elrod out of his depression, it was Wilbur.[11]

To his surprise, perhaps, Elrod also found another sympathetic ear in retired rear admiral Richard Jackson. As his courtship of Elizabeth Jackson flourished, he found himself on increasingly good terms with her uncle. Elrod was no budding professor of naval science, like Wilbur, but thanks to Officer Candidate and Basic School, he was sufficiently knowledgeable about naval operations, tactics, lore, and procedure to serve as an engaging audience for the admiral's endless stories around the dinner table.

By the same token, Elrod's flight training ordeals struck a nerve with the admiral. He knew better than anyone that artificial test conditions and mastery of formal curriculum could not always predict how well a soldier would perform in actual combat. Admiral Jackson had been a poor student at Annapolis. "Poor" was, in fact, an understatement. The admiral was at the very bottom of his graduating class—if not dead last, close to it. As a result, he did not initially receive a commission in the navy. He enlisted, nevertheless, and served with such distinction that a petition campaign convinced the US Congress to reconsider. Once given his ensignship, he rose to the highest levels of naval command.

Although neither Elrod nor Admiral Jackson left a written record of their developing friendship, it emerges clearly in photographs of the two of them. They appear together on the beach, playing with the admiral's dogs, and hunting. Following a successful quail hunt, Elizabeth took a picture of them joking around. Elrod cradles a shotgun in his right hand and a clutch of quail tied with string in his left. Admiral Jackson, meanwhile, has strung his birds around his neck like a necklace and is leaning over to hug his dog. Elrod's quizzical expression suggests a moment of humor or whimsy. The two men clearly enjoyed each other's company.

There must have been a moment in which Admiral Jackson leaned back in his chair, sizing up the second lieutenant across the table, and came to the conclusion that he was looking at a younger version of himself. At the same time, Elizabeth may well have asked him to intervene on her husband's behalf. Nothing else explains the bizarre turn of events that followed.[12]

Everything proceeded as might have been expected through mid-May of 1933; at least, there are clear and rational sequences of cause and effect that can explain the story up till then. Elrod had been reassigned to other duties within a day of being dropped as a student naval aviator. He requested to be transferred either to the Marine Barracks in Washington, DC, or Quantico, Virginia. Instead, on April 27, he received orders that he would be detached from Pensacola on May 15 and was thereafter to "proceed overland" to report to the Naval Operating Base at San Diego, California.

At this point, he and Betty appear to have made some very quick decisions about their future together. Perhaps they discussed the issue of marriage in a calm and deliberate manner and arrived at a mutual decision. Perhaps Elrod surprised her with a grand romantic gesture, as his favorite fictional character, Beau Geste, would have done. Either way, they got married. Elrod arranged for a five-day leave from May 8 until May 12. They traveled to Mobile, Alabama, and exchanged vows at 4:00 p.m. on May 10, in St. John's Church. Betty "wore a sports frock of white crepe, a corsage spray of gardenias and carried a prayer book." Although her father was still alive and living in Alabama, Admiral Richard H. Jackson walked her down the aisle. Elrod's best man for the occasion was Second Lieutenant James T. Wilbur. Mr. and Mrs. Elrod then departed for a two-night honeymoon, probably at a beach on the Florida Panhandle.[13]

Elrod and Admiral Richard H. Jackson joking around, ca. 1933–1935. Marine Corps Archives, Quantico, Virginia.

Henry T. Elrod and Elizabeth H. Jackson in Mobile, Alabama, on their wedding day, 1933. Marine Corps Archives, Quantico, Virginia.

Upon returning to Pensacola on May 12, Elrod sent a standard request to the Naval Department for additional per diem expenses for his new wife on the trip to California. He also requested fifteen extra days before being required to report at San Diego. The telegram was marked as sent from Pensacola at 11:03 a.m. and was stamped as having been received and processed in Washington, DC, at 11:50 a.m.

From this point onward, mysterious forces working at the highest levels of the Naval Department began to take an unprecedented interest in the career of Henry T. Elrod. Before that working day was finished, at 1605 hours (4:05 p.m.), the following message was telegraphed to Pensacola: "SECOND LT HT ELROD ORDERS TWENTYSEVEN APRIL TO SAN DIEGO REVOKED."[14]

The marines had no particular need for Elrod any longer in Pensacola, but the lieutenant was not going away, so duties of an unspecified nature were found or manufactured for him. And there were more surprises to come. A little over a week later, on May 23, Major General Commandant of the Marine Corps, General B. H. Fuller, sent a letter to the commander of Pensacola Naval Air Station, Ralph Wood, asking if Lieutenant Elrod's "records on file at your station . . . warrant his reassignment to the course of instruction as a student aviator, in the class commencing on or about 1 August, 1933."

Captain Wood must have been thunderstruck. He had just finished signing the papers terminating flight training for Elrod four weeks earlier. Wood had been careful, moreover, to send the report to Washington with a complete record of the miserable dual instruction logs and check flight reports as evidence of the student's unfitness. Now, however, the Marine Corps wanted to know if Elrod could start all over.

Captain Wood answered no. He put together another report, highlighting the most critical aspects of the original judgment, reminding the commandant general that the student had "stalled and yawed" and "skidded," "missed five out of five circle shots," and "barely missed hitting trees." He concluded the report by repeating the most brutal line of all: Elrod's "progress to date indicates a lack of ability ever to acquire the proficiency required of a naval aviator." In case his report left any doubt, Captain Wood added one last numbered observation: "It is rec-ommended that Lieut. Elrod not be reassigned to aviation training."[15]

Given this firm response, the Marine Corps did not press the issue. The fall aviation class commenced in August, with Second Lieutenant Elrod still serving on the ground. Commandant Wood, however, was merely an "acting" office holder, and a new commandant, F. R. McCrary, took the reins of the training program in September. Elrod must have felt that the new leadership would look more kindly on his persistence. He may also have begun to surmise that his new father-in-law was capable of mobilizing support for him at the highest levels of naval and marine leadership.

So on October 18, he filed a formal request to be readmitted as a student naval aviator. McCrary's endorsement was tepid, at best, but at least he did not dredge up the awful language of his predecessor. "Should the department find it advisable to return students who have failed for further instruction," he wrote, "the case of 2nd Lieut. Elrod may merit reconsideration." With the door thus left slightly ajar, General B. H. Fuller, Commandant General of the Marine Corps, thrust Elrod through it. The second lieutenant was ordered to report for a physical exam with the flight surgeon in December and received official notifica-tion on January 11, 1934, that he had been reassigned as a student naval aviator.[16]

Few marines receive the second chance that Elrod was granted in 1934. Even fewer seize it as fiercely as he seems to have done. His old troubles with nervousness did not disappear altogether; in fact, he never entirely overcame them. Many of his instructors commented on the con-tinuing struggle. When he first took to the air again in January 1934, his instructors noted again and again that he seemed "overanxious to please." That phrase appeared at least four times from two different observers between January and April. Knowing that he was prone to such nervous-ness, perhaps, his instructors may even have begun to study his manner-isms a little more closely than those of other students. When flying with him on August 6, John Young observed that Elrod "jiggles [the] stick too much most of the time." Henry Bellman, meanwhile, became increasingly concerned that Elrod "looks in [the] cockpit too much," repeating the criticism in at least three dual instruction log entries between November 1934 and January 1935. There were good days and bad days, but over the course of the year Elrod seems to have gained at least enough mastery over his nerves to become functional as a naval aviator.

His marriage to Betty may have settled him down a bit. There is a good chance also that his check flight examiners, knowing that he had acquired friends in high places, may have softened the edge of their criticism or even offered some encouragement. Just as important, Elrod had spent a lot of time in the air by the spring of 1934. It was hard-won knowledge, to be sure, but he knew better what he was doing the second time through. He was promoted to first lieutenant in October, 1934, and successfully completed his training as a naval aviator in April of 1935. His final report showed respectable scores in all areas. Ironically, he scored lowest in the categories of fighter planes, dive-bombing, and fixed gunnery, the very weapons he would rely on most, six years later, in the fight for Wake Island.[17]

There is a species of albatross native to some of the Pacific islands, especially Midway and Wake, that is embarrassingly clumsy when taking off. Because its wings are so long, it stumbles and falls repeatedly when trying to gain speed on the ground. Yet once it is airborne, it becomes a master of the sky. It is hard to avoid drawing a comparison between the gooney bird, as it is sometimes called, and Hank Elrod. He had a world of trouble earning his wings at Pensacola. Some of his instructors even doubted his "ability ever to achieve the proficiency required of a naval aviator." He knew better, and once he was in the air, he quickly became one of the most accomplished pilots in the Marine Corps. He requested service in either San Diego or Quantico and was granted the latter, with a generous thirty days' leave before he was to report for duty.

CHAPTER 7

Quantico, Virginia, 1935–1938

IT HAD TAKEN HIM THREE YEARS TO DO WHAT MOST MARINE PILOTS did in one, and much had changed in those years. When Lieutenant Elrod first arrived in Pensacola in 1932, Franklin Delano Roosevelt was just beginning to consider how he might solve the nation's problems. The most pressing of these involved the economic hardships brought about by the Great Depression, but the president's reforms included the reorganization of defense forces as well.

For the marines, this involved a sweeping reconfiguration of command structure. Within the first year of his administration, Roosevelt discontinued the old designations of West and East Coast Expeditionary Forces. From 1933 onward, the marines were to be organized into two Fleet Marine Forces. The Atlantic division of the Fleet Marine Force was headquartered in Norfolk, Virginia, and worked as part of Naval Fleets in the Atlantic Ocean theater of operations. The Pacific Fleet Marine Force was headquartered in San Diego and operated as part of the fleets in the Pacific Ocean. The marines are still organized this way today, except that the headquarters for the Pacific Fleet Marine Force was moved to Pearl Harbor after World War II.[1]

The era of Prohibition also ended in 1933, with the repeal of the Eighteenth Amendment in December. Roosevelt's National Industrial Recovery Act was passed that year to encourage shorter working days and fair wages. By 1935, when Elrod reported for duty at Quantico, the nation's unemployment rate had dropped from 33 percent to about 17 percent. Hard times were still the order of the day, but there was reason to hope that the worst of it was in the past. Roosevelt himself did much to convey that optimism in a series of radio addresses known as "Fireside Chats." More and more American families purchased radios in the 1930s, not only to hear the president but also to enjoy an increasingly broad variety of entertainment. The most popular programs in 1935 were *The Bob Hope Show* and *Flash Gordon*.

Yet for those paying attention to foreign affairs, there were ominous developments afoot. In Germany, Adolf Hitler had gathered the reins of political power in his hands as führer by 1935 and began revealing his military ambitions. In violation of the terms of the Treaty of Versailles, he announced in March the creation of a German air force, or Luftwaffe, and initiated conscription in order to increase the size of the army. He had made no secret of his racial and territorial ideas in *Mein Kampf*, but most Americans had never read it. They had enough problems of their own to think about. So the US Congress passed the first of several Neutrality Acts in 1935 to make it clear that Americans would not allow themselves to be dragged into European disputes.[2]

On the other side of the world, the Japanese Empire was also arming itself, and had taken meaningful steps to increase its geographical footprint. There, the ambitions of the United States began to be challenged in significant ways in the 1930s, and American military leaders appear to have recognized the potential for future conflict much earlier than they did with Hitler's Germany. Japanese leaders had never resigned themselves to the US annexation of Hawaii in the 1890s, and they submitted a whole new set of complaints when President Roosevelt granted Pan Am Airlines a contract to establish landing bases on the Pacific islands of Midway, Wake, and Guam. Responding to these tensions, the US Navy staged a massive defensive simulation in 1935, officially called "Fleet Problem V," around the Hawaiian Islands to prepare for the possibility of Japanese attacks. The marines, functioning as Fleet Marine Force, Pacific, were a vital part of the exercises.[3]

Elrod reported to the Marine Air Station at Quantico for duty on May 29, 1935, and was assigned to Squadron VO-7M. The "V" continued to signify their use of heavier-than-air vehicles. The *Hindenburg* disaster was closer now, but still two years in the future, and a significant portion of flight training for new naval aviators related to balloons and zeppelins, so it remained a necessary distinction. The "O" identified it as an observation squadron, devoted to reconnaissance and patrol activities.

When Elrod joined its ranks, marine observation squadron VO-7M was in the process of upgrading to newer Vought O3U-6 airplanes, known as "Corsairs." With a cruising speed of about 164 miles per hour, they were not significantly faster than the old Curtiss Falcons that Elrod had first worked with in San Diego. They were two-seater biplanes, like the Falcons, but they sported many other improvements. The Corsair could carry more fuel than the older airplane and climb to higher elevations, about 16,000 feet. Operating at this altitude for any length of time required the use of an oxygen mask, which now became standard equipment. In addition, the Corsair could carry a heavier bomb load than previous airplanes and sported a heavy-caliber front-mounted machine gun that was connected by a timing belt with the engine so that it could fire in sequence through the rotating propeller. It still featured a swivel machine gun mounted on the rear cockpit for the navigator's use. Over the next few years, it became the quintessential marine observation platform.[4]

The new Corsairs were among the first US military planes to be fitted with radio equipment. This gave pilots and navigators the ability to transmit vital information and reconnaissance immediately. The radios also aided in navigation and allowed naval pilots to land by instruments alone when heavy clouds or fog enshrouded the landing field. This was done by Jimmy Doolittle for the first time in 1929, but it was still an advanced technique in 1935. A radio marker beacon was set up at the end of the runway, and pilots judged their distance from the field by that signal. Used in conjunction with other instruments, such as a directional gyro and altimeter (to measure height above sea level), they could descend safely, even if they had no visual cues, to what was called the "Decision Altitude." This was the lowest height at which pilots were expected to be able to establish visual contact with the runway, usually about 200 feet, in order to make a safe landing. If they still could not see the landing strip at that altitude, they would have to decide quickly whether to circle the field and try again or reroute to another field entirely. To protect this equipment, the front cockpit had a canopy that could be slid forward to enclose the pilot. The navigator, alas, remained exposed to the elements in the rear.[5]

Elrod had already received instruction on radio protocols and navigation at Pensacola, but, given Squadron VO-7M's increasing reliance on the new technology, he wisely enrolled in an intensive radio course at the Marine Corps Institute that summer. One of his first jobs was to ferry the new Corsairs from the naval aircraft factory in Philadelphia back to the Marine Barracks at Quantico. He and another first lieutenant from the squadron, William Willis, were given railway tickets and a six-dollar-a-day allowance for food to travel to Philadelphia to pick up two brand-new Vought O3U-6s. They inspected the Corsairs in the hangar and then put them through their paces on the flight home to make sure they were fit for service. Once back on the ground at Quantico, the planes were painted and detailed with the squadron designation and Marine Corps insignia.[6]

Elrod took on many responsibilities in addition to his primary role as naval aviator over the next few years. His coursework in radio technology led to his appointment as communications and radio officer for his squadron. He was also appointed as its welfare officer. This was a position that dealt with many diverse issues involving the quality of life of his fellow aviators and support staff, both commissioned and enlisted. Those issues could variously require him to work to secure specialized medical treatment, educational opportunities for dependents, and religious accommodations.

As appears to have happened at every stage of his life, Elrod's personality earned him a great deal of goodwill that extended well beyond the personnel of his home squadron. As a result, he was ultimately appointed recreation officer for "Aircraft One," the entire aviation wing of the Atlantic Fleet Marine Force at Quantico. This was closely related to his welfare role within the squadron, but also required him to actively arrange and manage entertainment and leisure activities for all squadrons. Based on his performance reports, he displayed an unusual talent in this field. Whereas he typically received evaluations of "Very Good" or "Excellent" for his other duties, he was consistently given the highest rating of "Outstanding" as recreation officer.[7]

Several of those roles converged in November, 1937, when one of the new Vought 03U-6 airplanes went down in Chopawamsic forest about eight miles away from Quantico's Brown Airfield. Elrod's observation squadron was practicing instrument-only flying, with the front canopy "hooded" in order to deprive the pilot of all visual cues. The second pilot in the rear open cockpit had the ability to fly the airplane as well, but something went wrong. Flying at a relatively low altitude of only two thousand feet, the hooded pilot became disoriented and flew the plane straight down into the ground before his instructor could take control. Both were killed on impact.

Elrod may or may not have been in direct radio contact with the pilot at the time of the tragedy, yet as communications and radio officer for the squadron, he was surely involved in the effort to recover the radio equipment from the wreckage and assess whether a malfunction of some sort had contributed to the disaster. This entailed the grim work of extricating the mangled bodies of his friends from the debris. Both marines, Sergeant Cleo Bowers and Sergeant Herman Williams, were considered experienced pilots. Both men, moreover, were married, so it was Elrod's job as welfare officer to help their widows and families make arrangements for the funerals and assist with insurance paperwork and housing.[8]

Perhaps the best illustration of Elrod's genuine concern for the lives and well-being of the men he served with involved his response to a deadly fire. His friend Frank Tharin, also a marine pilot, told a story of how he and Elrod rushed into the heart of the flames to save marines trapped in the burning building. Unfortunately, the fire advanced so quickly behind them that they could not escape by the same route they had entered by, and all the windows were covered with steel bars. Elrod gripped the bars across one window, he said, and "with the strength of a madman" ripped them out so everyone could escape.[9]

Elrod and Betty lived in an apartment complex on the base set aside for families and married officers. They had no children of their own, but the family amenities available at Quantico struck him as a good environment for his little sister Kate, just turning fourteen years old back in Ashburn, Georgia. Elrod had been sending money home to his mother as best he could since he'd first enlisted in 1928, but it was still hard for his unemployed and widowed mother to raise a teenager all alone. Inviting Kate to live with them would relieve some of that pressure, he thought, and she would have access to good health care and an excellent education. He proposed the idea to his mother first, who then shared it with her daughter. Kate, according to family recollections, was easily the most free-spirited and lively of a very spirited family. She jumped at the invitation and was put on a train to Virginia in the summer of 1937. About this time, Elrod also arranged to have a portion of his monthly pay diverted to a new life insurance policy that named his mother and four siblings as beneficiaries.

Living in the married housing complex brought the Elrods into contact with other young couples on a regular basis. They developed a broad network of friends, but the closest and dearest of these were marine pilot Frank Tharin and his wife, also named Betty. The four of them spent many happy hours drinking beer and mulling over the day's, or the week's, developments. Betty Elrod remembered these regular conversations taking place for the most part in one another's kitchens, sitting around the table.

Elrod and Tharin were virtually inseparable from this point forward, until they parted ways forever at Wake Island. They developed nicknames for each other that became standard for the next few years. Elrod was "Baron," after the German World War I flying ace, because his skill as a pilot had become so exceptional by 1937. Tharin was known as "Duke," perhaps because he liked John Wayne movies, or reminded Elrod of the movie star. Such nicknames were an essential part of a pilot's identity in marine aviation. In one squadron photo from this period, Elrod wrote the nickname of each pilot in quotation marks over his image: "Pops," "Bigshot," "Mac," "G," "Purry," "Doc," "Soupy," and the like. Elrod is seen standing to the left of the airplane's cowling, a position he always preferred in squadron photos. He wrote no nickname for himself.[10]

In addition to the positive developments, new friends like the Tharins and the addition of his sister Kate to the household, 1937 also brought a new wave of aviation-related troubles.

On May 6 the *Hindenburg* airship was scheduled to arrive at the Lakehurst Naval Air Station in New Jersey, so a detachment of marine aviators and ground crewmen from Quantico were sent to assist. There is no evidence that Elrod was among them, but he likely helped organize the detachment. The airship had departed from Frankfurt, Germany, only three days earlier on the first leg of a round-trip transatlantic commercial

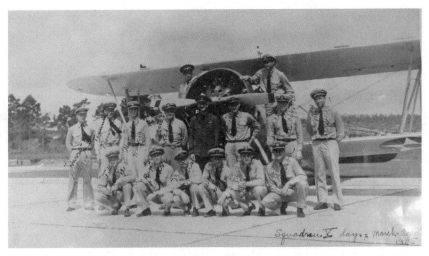

Observation squadron at Quantico, Virginia, 1935. Elrod is standing to the left of the airplane's cowling. Marine Corps Archives, Quantico, Virginia.

flight. Its progress dominated the newsreels, and ten more round-trip flights were scheduled. Many of those were already booked to capacity.

The future of lighter-than-air passenger travel seemed as promising as ever until 7:25 p.m. that evening, when witnesses on the ground reported seeing some of the fabric flapping near the top of the rear tail-fin. Within a few seconds the elegant ship burst into flames, and its rear section began sinking slowly to the ground. Many passengers and crew members were able to leap to safety, but thirty-six lost their lives. The disaster was broadcast live on the radio, and recordings of it were aired nationwide throughout the next day. The marines from Quantico were deployed to control the crowds that began to form around the crash site.

The operators of the *Hindenburg* had made a fatal mistake in choosing to use flammable hydrogen gas rather than helium. It was an error that could easily have been corrected in future flights, but the spectacle of the ship's demise at Lakehurst instilled such horror that potential passengers worldwide withdrew their support. The history of aviation thereafter belonged entirely to heavier-than-air technologies.

Nearly two months later, the world was once again transfixed by an aviation mishap. In her attempt to fly around the world, Amelia Earhart disappeared on July 2, 1937, somewhere in the vicinity of Howland Island in the South Pacific. Nearly three hundred naval and marine pilots were dispatched to the USS *Lexington* aircraft carrier to undertake an exhaustive search of the islands and atolls between Papua, New Guinea, her last known location, and her destination. They flew from morning to night for slightly over two weeks. Naval and marine resources around the country were also mobilized to provide analysis of radio signals and assess how prevailing winds and ocean currents might affect the trajectories of wreckage and survivors.

Earhart and her navigator, Fred Noonan, were never found. Nevertheless, the search reinforced American awareness of two fundamental challenges confronting naval operations in the Pacific: First, although the Japanese navy provided welcome and meaningful assistance in the search, their help underscored the extent of Japan's pervasive influence in the Pacific Rim. In some areas, the United States was forced to rely exclusively on Japanese forces for information because American ships and airplanes were not allowed access.

Second, the Earhart search emphasized anew the importance of joint training and operations between the various branches of the military. The Unites States had already begun to consider how best to address these challenges through a series of staged war games, known as Fleet Problems, that had been under way for many years when Earhart disappeared. They were designed to test the effectiveness of US naval responses to a variety of hypothetical situations.

In 1924, when the first Fleet Problem was run, the scenario was drawn from a relatively simple textbook template and took less than three days to execute. By 1937, Fleet Problem scenarios were often modeled explicitly on perceived threats from Japan, and the scale of the forces and theaters involved had grown to gargantuan proportions. Fleet Problem XIX in 1938, for instance, unfolded over the course of forty-six days. Ironically, in trying to anticipate and prepare for every possible eventuality, the problems had become so complex by the late 1930s that military experts had difficulty digesting the results of the maneuvers in order to identify areas of strength and weakness.[11]

Even so, amphibious landings emerged as one of the most glaring areas of weakness. Not surprisingly, the marines were the first to draw attention to it, since they were called upon to establish beachheads and advance bases. Marine strategists did more than merely complain about the problem; they solved it by developing a coherent landing theory that integrated every facet of the Corps' capabilities. It was published for the first time in 1934 under the title *A Tentative Manual for Landing Operations*. Although, as the title suggests, its authors considered it "tentative" at the time, many scholars now regard it as one of the twentieth century's most important advances in military science.

In order to test the ideas set forth in the manual, the navy organized a more specialized and smaller-scale version of the Fleet Problem. The first of these operations, known as Fleet Landing Exercise No. 1 (or FLEX 1), took place in early 1935, just prior to Elrod's arrival at Quantico. Six more Fleet Landing Exercises were conducted prior to the Japanese attack on Pearl Harbor, and Henry Talmage Elrod participated in most of them.[12]

In January 1937, Elrod led fifty-five airplanes from Aircraft One at Quantico, Virginia, to participate in Fleet Landing Exercise No. 3 at San Clemente Island, off the coast of California. This represented the bulk of the marine aviation wing at Quantico and included pilots from all squadron designations: observation/scouting (Elrod's own squadron), fighting, and bombing. Meanwhile, over one thousand marine ground troops of the First Brigade made their way to the exercise site by means of the USS *Wyoming*, a retired battleship that had been relegated to training, and other transport vessels. Once there, the Quantico marines were joined by a similar number of planes from Aircraft Two from San Diego and roughly one thousand soldiers from the Second Marine Brigade. Their objective was to capture San Clemente Island, where a regiment of the US Army had been stationed as defenders. Army personnel set up encampments, supply depots, and artillery emplacements just as they would have done to meet an actual threat to the island, complete with camouflage and attempts to deceive the enemy's aerial reconnaissance. In this case, that was Elrod's Quantico-based observation squadron.

According to the *Tentative Manual for Landing Operations*, the first step in any attempted landing was the gathering and analysis of aerial reconnaissance information. For Elrod and his squadron members, this included two levels of data: strategic and tactical intelligence. *Strategic reconnaissance* focused on understanding the enemy's general disposition, numbers, capability, supply lines, and topographical considerations. This information guided decisions about which specific targets should be attacked. *Tactical reconnaissance*, in turn, provided very detailed information about those proposed battle sites.

In each case, the information was gathered by a single airplane flying at a high altitude—the Vought O3U-6 Corsair that Elrod had flown for the first time two years earlier. The Corsair's relatively slow cruising speed, 164 miles per hour, was less important as a reconnaissance craft than its ability to operate at the upper limits of the enemy's antiaircraft defenses. Elrod therefore wore an oxygen mask for most of his work above San Clemente. In actual combat, if the defenders mounted an aggressive challenge in the air, the rest of the squadron or fighter planes from other squadrons would be expected to provide support and cover for the observation plane.[13]

There was no attempt at secrecy or surprise with respect to strategic reconnaissance. In the *Tentative Manual*, the marines had concluded that "adequate and timely information regarding the hostile defenses, and the number and suitability of landing beaches and approaches, [were] far more essential to the success of the landing than . . . any benefits derived from attempted surprise without such knowledge."

Tactical reconnaissance, however, still depended quite a bit on the element of surprise. The enemy would surely know, for instance, that the island of San Clemente was about to be attacked, since it had been surrounded by the US Navy. They would not yet know, however, which beach or bay or inlet or river to concentrate their defensive efforts on. That was a tactical matter. For this reason, Elrod was instructed not to fly too frequently above the areas he judged most suitable for a landing. Instead, he tried to fly conspicuously over regions that had already been ruled out as targets while taking long-distance photos of the actual landing site. In this way, it was hoped, the enemy could be tricked into positioning

Lieutenant Elrod makes the most of chow time. Marine Corps Archives, Quantico, Virginia.

its defenses in places that did not really need to be defended and fail to defend the places that really mattered.[14]

The island was sufficiently remote—about sixty miles directly west of San Diego—to allow the use of live artillery rounds during training. Several live-fire zones were thus marked out on the island that would come into play during the amphibious landing attempt. In addition to identifying appropriate landing targets, therefore, Elrod's reconnaissance work was judged on his ability to identify the locations and types of artillery placed within these zones and, just as important, recognize attempts to camouflage and conceal defensive assets. Today, satellite imagery of San Clemente Island reveals a moonlike wasteland riddled with craters in these areas. Some of the bombardment that produced this virtual moonscape was done from a distance by shipboard naval artillery, attempting to degrade defenses prior to the landing. Much of it, however, was done by marine dive-bombers acting in close support of ground troops as they landed and attempted to establish beachheads.

During Fleet Landing Exercise No. 3 at San Clemente Island, the marines experimented with solutions to several problems that had been identified in the previous two exercises. Even the most precise aerial reconnaissance, it was discovered, could miss essential details. So they practiced sending small clandestine squads ashore by night to provide more detailed ground-based reconnaissance just prior to the landing. Landing forces also experimented with using cargo nets hung from the sides of transport vessels so marines could climb down into landing boats. These "scramble nets" proved effective and were subsequently used by the marines throughout the island-hopping campaigns of World War II.

The most vexing problem by far, however, involved landing craft. None of the small naval boats available in 1935, 1936, and 1937 were suitable for transferring soldiers from battleships and transports, anchored in relatively deep water, through shallow reefs and inlets to the even shallower drop-off points near shore. Four different prototypes of landing craft were tested in FLEX 3, with none of them doing the job adequately. All were variations of a traditional ship-to-shore craft, with soldiers disembarking in shallow water by jumping over the sides of the boat.

QUANTICO, VIRGINIA, 1935–1938

The marines expressed their disappointment to the navy's Bureau of Construction and Repair, but they also went a step further by initiating discussions with a New Orleans–based boatbuilder named Andrew Higgins. The marines explained the specific issues they had encountered in trying to land men on beaches in FLEX 1, 2, and 3: inadequate engine power, taking on water as a result of high waves and surf, lack of cover from enemy fire, among others. Higgins, in turn, designed a shallow-draft boat, known as the "Eureka" boat, for testing the following year, 1938, in Fleet Landing Exercise No. 4.

At the conclusion of FLEX 3 in early March, Elrod quickly shifted roles from pilot to recreation officer. As part of the entertainment committee, he organized a dinner dance for the officers and spouses of both Aircraft One and Aircraft Two at the Rosarito Beach Club. In 1937, it was still a rather remote resort, located thirty miles south of San Diego, though it had gained a reputation for hosting movie stars. About two hundred people attended the event.

Elrod and the rest of the Quantico squadrons, fifty-four planes in all, then made their way across the country by air. After refueling in Montgomery, Alabama, they split into two groups of thirty-eight and sixteen planes. The smaller unit proceeded straight to Fort Bragg, North Carolina, which was to be the last refueling stop before reaching their home base in Quantico, Virginia. Curiously, the larger group of thirty-eight planes made a short jog of only about 160 miles to Atlanta, Georgia, where they stopped to refuel at the US Army hangar there. Perhaps this unit included airplanes whose maximum range was not sufficient to reach Fort Bragg in a single flight. At the same time, however, it is possible that Elrod lobbied for the stopover in Atlanta so that he could visit for an hour or two with his sister Farrar and meet his three-year-old nephew, William L. Ramsey Jr., for the first time. If so, she probably drove out to the airport, since the squadron took to the air again that same afternoon to rejoin the rest of the planes at Fort Bragg.[15]

These two themes—the FLEX maneuvers and his little sister's growing family in Atlanta—would become increasingly important over the next year.

Lieutenant Elrod at about the time of the San Clemente exercises. Marine Corps Archives, Quantico, Virginia.

CHAPTER 8

FLEX 4 and an Unauthorized Flight, 1938

UPON RETURNING TO QUANTICO, ELROD'S AIRCRAFT ONE AND THE rest of the Atlantic Fleet Marine Force incorporated new exercises to work on the numerous difficulties of amphibious landing operations they had encountered at San Clemente. Fleet Landing Exercise No. 4 was already scheduled for January, February, and March of the next year, 1938, and the marines were expected to have some proposed solutions ready to test out.

Later that summer, First Lieutenant Elrod, Betty, and Kate gathered around the phone to share some exciting news with sister Farrar in Atlanta. In addition to the FLEX preparations and his regular duties, Elrod had spent much of that spring and early summer assembling paperwork and sitting for examinations for promotion. He learned in June that he had qualified for promotion to the rank of captain.

Farrar had always idolized her older brother and was overjoyed to hear he was finally receiving the rewards and recognition she felt he deserved. As it turned out, she had some news of her own. She was expecting a second child, she told them, due sometime the following March. In those days, parents had no advance knowledge of the baby's gender; it was always a surprise at birth. Yet Farrar had done a good deal of thinking about what she wanted to name the child if it happened to be a boy. She kept those ideas to herself until it came time to fill out the birth certificate.[1]

Elrod took his oath as captain in December, 1937, with the rank being retroactively in force since September. His squadron was occupied all that month preparing airplanes and personnel for the fourth fleet landing exercise. It was shifted from the West Coast to the Caribbean this time, to guard against the possibility of Japanese espionage. Ground troops debarked by transport ships from Norfolk, Virginia, but Aircraft One was scheduled to make a mass flight directly to San Juan, Puerto Rico, on January 21. This was delayed by two days because a dense fog boiled up from the Potomac River and reduced visibility at the Quantico airfield. Elrod and Squadron VO-7M, along with the rest of Aircraft One, stood by all day long waiting for the weather to break. Conditions did not improve until January 23, at which point they all scrambled into the air between about 10:00 a.m. and 12:40 p.m., before the fog returned. The size of the formation—composed of fifty-two airplanes, forty-seven officers, and seventy enlisted men—and the fact that it flew nonstop over open water to Puerto Rico, made it a milestone event in aviation history.[2]

The main focus of the exercise was to be an integrated naval, land, and air assault on the southern shore of Puerto Rico in March of 1938, but the marines spent much of January and February honing their skills on the small island of Culebra. Designated as a National Wildlife Refuge by President Theodore Roosevelt in 1909, Culebra was about eighteen miles east of the main island of Puerto Rico. Roosevelt had encountered Culebra during his time with the Rough Riders in 1898 and recognized it at once as a natural treasure. It was only about three miles long and two miles wide, but it offered sanctuary to several rare species of sea turtles and birds. Because the president had placed the Culebra National Wildlife Refuge under the protection of the Department of the Navy, moreover, naval and marine forces had full access to the region for war games and exercises.[3]

Elrod's promotion in rank probably made his role in FLEX 4 a little different than his role in FLEX 3. The rank of captain is the highest of the "Company" grade ranks within the Marine Corps, which usually entails the command of an entire company of soldiers. This unit level of command authority was not immediately bestowed on him at Quantico, where he continued to carry out his junior officer duties as recreational

Captain Elrod on Culebra. Marine Corps Archives, Quantico, Virginia.

officer, welfare officer, and communications and radio officer for Scouting Squadron One through the spring of 1938. In the context of a fleet landing exercise, however, where new tactical configurations and approaches were being tested out on a daily basis, there must have been occasions that called on him to organize and deploy forces on a grander scale than he had previously done.

His scouting squadron was at the forefront of early activities, but the Culebra exercises incorporated several new wrinkles in addition to traditional information gathering. First and foremost, the marines had come to believe that carrier-based operations would be the key to amphibious landings in the future, so they engaged in extensive training for taking off and landing on aircraft carriers. Elrod's promotion to captain probably put him to work in this training more than anywhere else, and he appears to have gained some recognition for it. For the next few years, his superiors consistently praised his familiarity with carriers, citing his experience at Culebra.

Second, the marines wanted to add a ground-level intelligence component to their aerial reconnaissance. This was done by sending four-man squads ashore in rafts by dark of night. These were launched as close to the island as possible from a submarine. The squads were to reconnoiter through the night, remain in hiding the following day, then row back out to rendezvous with the submarine the following night. Their information would then be analyzed together with data from Scouting Squadron One. This approach bore mixed results at Culebra, due in part to rough weather conditions that made it difficult for the squads to land and return. One squad, embarrassingly, was captured while on shore by a National Guard unit which had been placed there as one of the token "defenders."[4]

The marines also tested several new prototypes of landing craft during FLEX 4, including the Eureka boat designed by Andrew Higgins. During an integrated landing on the beaches of Culebra, the landing boats proved to be an improvement over previous equipment. Yet the marines reported continuing problems. The boats were still underpowered when confronting rough seas and headwinds. Marines also pointed out that disembarking over the high sides of the vessels wasted time and

Elrod's tent on Culebra. Marine Corps Archives, Quantico, Virginia.

exposed them to enemy fire. Higgins took this last criticism to heart and set to work creating a drop-down landing ramp at the front of the boat. It was not Higgins's own idea, it should be noted. Marines had seen a Japanese landing vessel with this feature in the South China Sea the year before and had suggested that Higgins ought to consider it. This was tested to rave reviews at fleet landing exercises in 1939 and 1940, and ultimately became the quintessential American landing craft of World War II.[5]

As FLEX 4 began to wrap up in early March, Elrod was given "advance information" that he would soon be detached from Quantico and transferred to the Naval Air Station at San Diego, California. As a newly minted captain, it was only natural that his duties and command responsibilities would change, and his participation in FLEX 4 probably served to bring his name to the attention of the marine commandant. It is unclear when he received this early notice, but he acknowledged it on March 14 in a formal letter to Marine Headquarters. He made a few requests in that acknowledgment, as well. He asked to be detached from Quantico on May 10 and given a forty-five-day leave before reporting to San Diego. He concluded by informing the commandant that he would be bringing two dependents with him: his wife Betty and his sister Kate.[6]

Five days later, in the predawn hours of March 19, his sister Farrar gave birth to her second son in Atlanta. In all her stories, my grandmother never told me how she conveyed this information to the rest of the family. I presume my grandfather jumped on the telephone and circulated the news later that day. Maybe he shared the baby's name in that call; maybe my grandmother did it herself in a subsequent call.

Captain Elrod, at any rate, was stunned to learn that the boy's first and middle names were to be Henry Elrod. He appears to have taken this honor deeply to heart. An invitation to the christening ceremony arrived a few days later. The date of that christening, or baptism, is lost to history, but it typically took place about two to three weeks, or even a month, after birth. So in this case it probably occurred between late March and mid-April 1938. The most auspicious date, of course, would have been Easter Sunday, which fell on April 17 that year. Elrod had never done much visiting or socializing with family back in Georgia, but he now became determined to go and see this little boy take on the heavy burden of his name, Henry Elrod Ramsey, before the eyes of the world.

The captain's appearance in the Ramsey household that Sunday became the stuff of family legend forever after. He piloted a Marine Corps airplane from Virginia to the Atlanta Naval Air Station early enough on Sunday morning to attend the church service with the entire family, then stayed on for dinner, perhaps reluctantly. He brought no luggage and no change of clothing. By all appearances, he intended to return to Quantico that same day. He had managed, however, to bring a present for the baby. He pulled a cloth marine cap out of his flight jacket. On its inner lining, he pointed out, it was stamped "Henry T. Elrod" in black ink. Little Henry didn't understand what a treasure he had until he was older, but his four-year-old brother Bill knew as soon as he saw it. He wanted one, too. He never remembered crying or fussing about it at the time, but Elrod must have seen it in his eyes. He pulled his own cap off and tossed it to him. Bill checked the inner lining and, sure enough, the name was there.

By hook or by crook, my grandmother somehow prevailed on him to spend the night. Our family owned and lived in a large boardinghouse on North Avenue that rented rooms and served meals in order to make ends meet. Unfortunately, there were no available rooms that night, so Elrod stretched out on the wicker sofa in the living room where the baby's crib was located. Both boys still slept in it together, and Bill could see his "Uncle Talmage" through the slats. He slept in his clothes, my dad remembered, with his boots on. Brown boots. He was just a little under six feet tall, longer than the couch, so he propped his feet over the armrest at the end and slept that way all night.

"His face was almost as brown as his boots," my dad often told me. It struck my father as curious at four years old, but it makes sense, as Elrod had just spent two months on the beaches of Puerto Rico and Culebra.

As soon as the dawn began to brighten, Elrod was up before anyone else. He walked to the crib and peered over the side, probably to take one last look at the baby. Big brother Bill was already awake and staring back at him. "Always be a good marine," Elrod said, then turned and headed for the door.

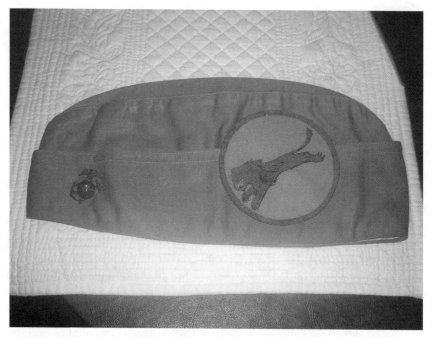

Marine cap, pin, and squadron insignia given to William L. Ramsey Jr. by Captain Henry T. Elrod between 1938 and 1940. Photo in author's possession.

Bill scrambled out of the crib and followed quietly after. Elrod tried to shut the screen door as softly as he could, but the click of the latch brought Farrar running down the stairs. By the time she got to the door, still pulling on her robe, he was already far down the sidewalk. The two of them, mother and son, stood there watching him through the screen. All the way down to the corner, then up toward Ponce de Leon Avenue, until he passed from sight, he never turned. He never waved.

My grandmother was not surprised. That was the way, after all, he had jumped on that freight train to leave Thomasville back in 1926. She had stood on a weedy hillside then, watching the cars curl westward, the same way she stood inside the screen door now, waiting in vain for some type of farewell.

Yet he may have had good reason to be preoccupied this time around. When his newly christened nephew, having grown to manhood, desired to know more about his famous uncle, he called up Aunt Betty, Elrod's widow. This was long after World War II, around 1986. Elizabeth Jackson Elrod had since remarried, another marine pilot named Roger Carleson, and was in her eighties. It had been four decades since she'd stood before the commandant of the Marine Corps to receive Elrod's posthumous Medal of Honor. It was a "cold call," moreover, with no forewarning or introduction, and he worried that she might not remember, or might not want to remember, events so distant and painful. So when she answered the phone, he simply led off with his name: "Hi, Mrs. Carleson, this is Henry Elrod Ramsey." Without hesitation, she said "You were born in 1938." Once he had confirmed that he was indeed that same baby, she added, "Oh, he got into big trouble for that. It was an unauthorized flight."

"Big trouble" is probably an understatement for the likely consequences of such an act. It could have been a career-ending sort of trouble, if his commanding officers had been inclined to really hold his feet to the fire. They apparently were not. His personnel file contains no paperwork suggesting that he was subject to any type of formal disciplinary action at all. Discipline, though, is not always meted out by formal procedures. The marines have several methods of punishment that do not leave a visible bruise on an officer's official record. One such method involves a public dressing-down in front of other officers, not enlisted men, followed by a conspicuous assignment to some humiliating chore. For marines who have no prior pattern of misbehavior, as was the case with Elrod, this communicates the basic message without risking the permanent loss of a valuable leader. If this is what happened, there is no way of knowing exactly what it entailed.

Nevertheless, there are some clues in his record that suggest a dressing-down may have come from the very top of the Quantico command structure. The legendary marine pilot Colonel Roy S. Geiger, who was serving as overall commander of Aircraft One at the time, had always graded Elrod very favorably on his semiannual fitness reports. These grades related to a broad range of character traits and behaviors, such as "Military Discipline," "Loyalty," and "Physical Fitness." In fact, Geiger had never given Elrod anything less than a rating of "Very Good" in any category for the previous three years, with most rising to the level of "Excellent" or "Outstanding." It is striking, therefore, that he suddenly changed his mind about the captain's "Judgement and Common Sense." In the report for May 7, 1938, filed about two weeks after the unauthorized flight to Atlanta, he lowered his rating of Elrod's "ability to think clearly and arrive at logical conclusions" several grades, to the lowest mark of his career: "Fair."[7]

He must have known he would be roasted by Geiger and others if he were found out. Maybe he hoped, against long odds, that he could make the run to Atlanta, attend the christening, and return to Quantico before sunset without raising any eyebrows. That hope began to dim when he agreed to stay for dinner with the family. It went dark altogether when he propped his boots on the arm of the sofa and stayed the night. In this light, his hasty departure in the morning looks less like callousness and more like the behavior of a man who knew he had some hell to pay. The fact that he was willing to pay it is a testament to his love for and devotion to his family.

CHAPTER 9

Westward to California, 1938–1940

I IMAGINE THAT SCENE SOMETIMES THE WAY IT WOULD HAVE LOOKED from Elrod's perspective, had he paused at the corner to look back: his sister gazing after him through the top half of the screen door, my four-year-old father gazing through the bottom. He was the greatest hero either of them ever knew. Not that they knew that many. They didn't know much about the world beyond that door, either, but it was a world in desperate need of heroes. And Henry Talmage Elrod was walking right into the middle of it.

The German annexation of Austria, the so-called *Anschluss*, had just been finalized, and the United States government, in keeping with the general pattern of appeasement of Hitler's behavior, unfortunately extended formal diplomatic recognition of the maneuver on April 6, 1938. As Elrod boarded the Ponce de Leon trolley and made his way back out to the Atlanta Naval Air Station that morning, Nazi forces were already rounding up tens of thousands of Austrian dissidents. The number of German concentration camps nearly tripled that spring, and Hermann Göring issued an ominous warning for all Jews to depart Austria. The Empire of Japan, about that time, hosted a delegation of Nazi emissaries and Hitler youth, as the two countries explored ways of cooperating to achieve their national ambitions.[1]

Elrod's collision with the Japanese Imperial Navy was still three years away. His primary concerns, once back at Quantico, were, first, to weather the disciplinary storm for his unauthorized flight and, second, to begin preparing for the move to San Diego. The marines had originally planned to send him aboard a naval vessel, but he requested permission to make an overland trip in his own car. This was granted. Forty-five days of leave was more than enough time to make such a journey, even in the days before interstate highways.

His little sister Kate had lobbied to go along. She had flourished at Quantico, completing ninth grade and making admirable use of the base's movie theater, library, concerts, and tennis courts. Betty genuinely enjoyed her presence in the household. Elrod even listed her as a dependent along with his wife on the car trip, but that was as far as the plan got. When they called Mrs. Elrod in Thomasville, Georgia, she was not at all happy about it. Virginia was only a day's train ride away, she said, but California was on the other side of the country. Betty remembered Mrs. Elrod also being worried that it might not be a wholesome influence on an impressionable teenager. So the first leg of their epic journey west turned out to be a long bumpy swing through south Georgia in order to return Kate to her mother. None of them knew it at the time, but it was a fateful visit: Kate would never again leave the state of Georgia, while Captain Elrod would leave it forever.

Their next stop was Florence, Alabama, where they spent a week or two catching up with Betty's beloved uncle, retired rear admiral Richard Jackson. They stayed with him for a week or two and then set out on their grand adventure across the country. The journey could take as much as two weeks or more, with the legendary Route 66 the likeliest way through most of the Midwest and West. Thanks to the continuous labors of thousands of young men enrolled in the Works Progress Administration, beginning in 1933, the road had been completely paved from Chicago, Illinois, to Los Angeles by the time they set out in 1938. The Elrods no doubt had to suffer through many dirt roads in Mississippi and Arkansas, but once they linked up with Route 66 in Oklahoma, it was a relatively smooth ride all the way to San Diego. They appear to have made the most of their opportunities, stopping at a variety of tourist attractions along the way. At Flagstaff, Arizona, for instance, they took a right off of 66 and drove northward through the desert for the better part of a day to view the southern rim of the Grand Canyon.[2]

Betty Elrod and pet dog on the road. The Elrods were traveling in what appears to be a 1936 Ford convertible. Marine Corps Archives, Quantico, Virginia.

At length, they arrived in San Diego, and Elrod reported for duty on July 5 at the Naval Air Station on North Island. It must have been an emotional moment. This was where he had begun his career in the marines as an enlisted private more than a decade earlier. Back then, he was thrilled to crank the engines for the pilots and file their paperwork. Now he was a commissioned officer and a pilot himself.

His second stint in San Diego was destined to be different in several ways. One unexpected difference involved his social standing. He would have been due a good deal more respect as a captain in 1938 than he enjoyed as a private in 1927, but his marriage added something unusual to the mix. He and Betty had probably discussed the possibility of visits from her uncle, Admiral Jackson, when they visited him in Alabama. He had not spent much time with them at Quantico, but San Diego was a different matter. This was a hotbed of naval activity. The retired admiral had many friends and contacts there, and he was eager to be back in the middle of things. So the Elrods made sure to rent an apartment in Coronado with an extra room for the admiral and enough living area to entertain his guests.

Admiral Jackson's first few visits were advertised in local newspapers as major events, and Betty hosted receptions at the apartment that drew in the top echelons of naval command. The success of those initial events apparently convinced the admiral that San Diego was a more auspicious locale for his retirement than northern Alabama. By December 1939, it was announced that he would be moving in with the Elrods "for the winter." The move turned out to be permanent, and the receptions continued on a regular basis through most of 1940, with visits by dignitaries and officials noted by local media. In many ways, Betty resumed her former role as the admiral's chief of staff.[3]

This was a level of notoriety that a marine captain could never have hoped to achieve on his own merits, and there are indications that it went to Elrod's head for a time. Betty remembered two questionable purchases, in particular, that led to some heated conversations between the two. In order to keep up appearances in the heady swirl of receptions and visitors, Elrod bought a brand-new dress uniform from the USMC shop, complete with a body-length cape. It cost several hundred dollars, which he could only afford by agreeing to pay in monthly installments. Betty acknowledged that he "looked awfully good," but explained to him that such outlays needed to be discussed beforehand with one's spouse.

Even so, when other officers of Aircraft Two invited him to join the marine polo team, he jumped at the chance. Polo was an upper-class sport, and Elrod, raised on a farm and never having finished college, must have seen it as an irresistible opportunity to further establish himself as one of the social elite. Once again, he arranged for a substantial line of credit so that he could buy a horse—again, without consulting his wife. His early training in horsemanship in Thomasville served him well on the field, and he turned out to be quite good. A *San Diego Union* sportswriter even praised him by name for his offensive play in the summer of 1939. Yet, as Betty had feared, they could not really afford to carry the additional payments for a horse. In the end, rather than permanently joining the ranks of elite polo society, Elrod suffered the humiliation of defaulting on his loan and having his horse repossessed.[4]

This concern with display and upward social mobility was fleeting, and not merely because he no longer had a horse by 1940. It was simply not in his nature. Every surviving personal recollection of Henry Talmage Elrod emphasized his blue-collar personality and lack of pretense. Although he had risen to become a commissioned officer, he always identified and associated with enlisted soldiers. Betty observed that on those occasions, which were not infrequent, when he rode down to Tia Juana to kick his heels up with fellow marines, he always jumped in the backseat with his enlisted friends and left the officers in the front. One of the members of the VMF-2 ground crew, Strimple C. Coyle, who claimed to have "strapped him in for many a flight," remembered him as being "very close to the enlisted men of the squadron, having come from the ranks himself." His nickname too, "Hank," reflected this informality. It had probably followed him from his earliest days in the Corps, but it only appears in the records from 1939 onward.[5]

The fanfare associated with Admiral Jackson's presence in the household was a novelty and, perhaps, a bit of a distraction. By far the most significant change in Elrod's life had to do with his new squadron designation in San Diego: VMF-2. This was a newly created fighter

Captain Elrod's polo horse in San Diego, early 1940, prior to the horse being repossessed for missed loan payments. Marine Corps Archives, Quantico, Virginia.

squadron, only about a year old when he came on board in the summer of 1938. This in itself represented a significant departure for him, since he had thus far served with an observation squadron in Virginia. All of his previous training and duties had involved reconnaissance and scouting. Now he was to focus exclusively on aerial combat and dogfighting. It was a sign that his growing skill as a pilot was beginning to be recognized. VMF-2 was packed from the very beginning with some of the best aviators in the service. In addition to Elrod, two other future Medal of Honor recipients were in the air with him: Robert Galer, and Gregory "Pappy" Boyington, later to win fame as leader of the "Black Sheep" in the Pacific. His best friend from Quantico, Frank "Duke" Tharin, joined in 1938 as well. This all-star squadron flew under the insignia of a red "diving" lion, depicted against a solid green background. It was painted on the tail sections of all their planes. Elrod made sure to mail a pair of official cloth patches to his two little nephews in Atlanta.

Membership in VMF-2 was not the only indication that he had been identified as a top-notch pilot. Official assessments of his performance

Squadron VMF-2 at San Diego, 1940. Elrod is standing above everyone, as usual, by the airplane cowling. Frank Tharin is immediately to his left, also a head taller than everyone else. Gregory "Pappy" Boyington of Black Sheep fame is closest to the camera on the left. Marine Corps Archives, Quantico, Virginia.

typically rated him as being exceptional, but they sometimes also included reservations. Major Vernon E. Megee, for instance, conceded that Elrod was a "very good pilot," but judged him to be only an "average unit leader." Major C. L. Fike, meanwhile, rated him as an "excellent" pilot, but cautioned that Elrod could be "somewhat daring" in the air. His participation in various navy and marine flying exhibitions at air shows and races around the United States also suggests that his abilities were held in high regard. Neither the navy nor the marines maintained a permanent exhibition team prior to World War II. In the late 1930s, rather, flying teams were assembled as the need arose, with pilots drawn from active squadrons. Even the Three Sea Hawks, who had achieved fame in the late 1920s, were selected in this manner.

The Blue Angels were not established as a permanent team until 1946. Records of these early temporary rosters are difficult to find in the archives, but Elrod's wife Betty remembered that he participated in many exhibitions. The earliest occurred at Quantico in 1937, when he led a marine exhibition team to the Great Lakes Exposition in Cleveland. He served in a dual role on that occasion, performing as both a pilot for aerial demonstrations and as coach of the Quantico baseball team. After posing for pictures with local dignitaries, Coach Elrod and the baseball team were escorted by motorcade to the Cleveland stadium, where they played a series of exhibition games. After the transfer to North Island, Betty specifically recalled him being in the Miami All American Air Maneuvers, one of the nation's largest air shows. The naval/marine team appeared there every year in the late 1930s and early 1940s. In January 1940, the only year that Elrod's schedule would have allowed him to participate, they gave three demonstrations of "formation flying" over the course of a three-day show. They flew in the classic V formation, did low-level flyovers of the observation stands, and then landed in formation.[6]

Frank Tharin was also assigned to some of those exhibition teams. He remembered at least one occasion when he and Elrod had been put forward to represent the marines in an air race. These were competitive events in which pilots raced against one another on a fixed course to record the fastest time. Some courses began in one city and ended in

Elrod is at center with hands clasped over each other as marine exhibition leaders are greeted by local dignitaries at the 1937 Cleveland Air Show. Marine Corps Archives, Quantico, Virginia.

another and could take several days to complete. The Miami show featured a race of this type, with the starting point in New York City and the finish line in Miami. Spectators saw only the end of this one, when the winner landed on the exhibition field to receive a trophy.

Other races took place on a smaller course around pylons placed several miles apart. The pilots circled the pylons a fixed number of times, jockeying with one another for position, to determine a winner. This is the sort of race in which Elrod and Tharin participated. They started off with a strategy that called for Tharin to take the inner line on the pylons while Elrod flew just outside to secure his position against other teams. According to Tharin, they had done relatively well in the qualifying rounds and moved into the final phase of the competition. He was satisfied with how things were going, but Elrod expressed frustration that Tharin was not seizing the initiative fearlessly enough on the turns and might, thus, be in danger of losing the advantage on some laps to other pilots. Tharin suggested that maybe Elrod should try taking the interior line in the upcoming rounds. In telling the story years later, Tharin laughed at this point and shook his head, as if amazed by what he had seen. He never told us whether they won that race or not, but he said that Elrod had cut the angles around the pylons so close that "his wingtips dug up dirt."[7]

Moving from an observation squadron to a fighter squadron meant that Elrod had to learn to handle a new type of airplane and new combat tactics. VMF-2 was flying a Grumman F3F-2 when he arrived. Sometimes referred to as "the flying barrel" because of its thick fuselage, it was one of the last biplanes used by the marines, sporting a fully enclosed cockpit and a front-mounted machine gun. It had a top speed of about 255 miles per hour in level flight and could operate comfortably at 12,000 feet. Its speed was made possible in part by a retractable landing gear that required the pilot to reach down and manually crank a wheel on the right side of the cockpit floorboard, both to raise it after takeoff and lower it prior to landing. The wheels folded up flush to the fuselage when in flight. This system made the airplane more aerodynamic, but it had some drawbacks in practical usage. Pilots sometimes experienced difficulty in getting the gears to "lock" properly prior to landing, and the narrowness of the wheel base, located as it was directly under the fuselage, could make the F3F-2 unstable when landing in high crosswinds or on the moving deck of an aircraft carrier.[8]

The principal mission of fighter squadrons was "clearing the air of hostile planes" during the various phases of an amphibious landing. Tactical training thus focused for the most part on maneuvers for aerial combat and methods of targeting an airborne opponent. At the same time, they were expected to be fully conversant with other activities so that, if they were no longer being challenged in the air, they could shift their attention to dive-bombing and close support of ground troops.

Elrod applied himself to learning the new material with his usual alacrity. In fact, he sometimes struck his fellow pilots as too enthusiastic.

During one exercise, conducted several miles away from the California coast, then second lieutenant John F. Kinney, who would rise to the rank of brigadier general later in life, worried that Captain Elrod's pursuit of perfection might be placing his life in jeopardy—not to mention his airplane. The pilots were practicing low-level bombing approaches that required them to release a small-caliber bomb toward a wooden target that was being towed behind a boat. Kinney remembered Elrod repeatedly holding his bomb "until he was about to fly right into the low target." Elrod scored many direct hits with this method, but it made observers nervous. It may be worth noting that this turned out to be precisely the approach that yielded impressive results for him in actual combat two years later.[9]

Kinney regarded Elrod as "one of the most aggressive" pilots in VMF-2, and his harrowing approach to target practice was not the only reason. When presented with the theoretical problem of scrambling fighter planes as quickly as possible to meet an enemy attack, for instance, he remembered Elrod proposing that they practice taking off in two-man teams. Rather than having pilots take off one by one, Elrod suggested that they practice taking off in tandem, with one plane hugging the left edge of the runway and the other hugging the right. That way they could get everyone in the air in half the time.

Elrod and Lieutenant David Kliewer went first and ran into problems. Elrod managed to get airborne, but Kliewer was forced off the runway. Either Elrod had drifted too far toward his teammate, as Kinney proposed, or the prop wash from his propeller was so powerful that it lifted the interior wingtip of his partner's airplane up and drove the outer wing into the runway. It nearly flipped over before finally skidding to a stop. Kliewer was unhurt, but the airplane's wing, landing gear, and propeller were damaged.[10]

If Elrod's prop wash was indeed a factor in that incident, it may be significant that his habit of gunning the engine was noted in other situations as well. A member of VMF-2's ground crew, Corporal Strimple Coyle, confirmed that "Elrod was very rough on his airplanes; he'd gun it, then jerk it around." Coyle remembered a specific incident on the USS *Saratoga* aircraft carrier.

Elrod may have been an old hand at carrier-based operations, but the squadron as a whole was still in the process of getting its carrier

A wrecked F3F-2 from Squadron VMF-2, which appears to be the one flown by David Kliewer when practicing tandem takeoffs with Captain Elrod. Marine Corps Archives, Quantico, Virginia.

qualification in 1939. Pilots began their takeoff run at the stern (rear) of the vessel and went airborne over the bow (front). When landing, they came in over the stern. The ground crew then pushed the plane, with its engine still running, to the bow of the ship for temporary storage so that other planes could land on the stern. Once everyone had landed, they pushed them all down to the stern again so they could take off and repeat the exercise. It made for an exhausting day for all concerned.

Well, Coyle recalled that in this particular incident, Captain Elrod, serving as a section leader, led two other fighter planes in for a landing without a problem. Elrod brought up the rear, watching to make sure his pilots landed safely before touching down himself. The ground crew pushed the airplanes forward to the bow, with one positioned on the right-hand (starboard) side of the deck and one in the middle. Elrod's plane was supposed to be pushed into line with them on the left-hand side of the deck, the "port" side, but his tail wheel got stuck in one of the grooves between the steel plating.

Coyle, at that moment, happened to be standing by the left wingtip of Elrod's F3F-2, just a few yards away from the port edge of the deck. "Instead of being patient and allowing us to lift the plane out of the rain gutter," Coyle recalled, "he gave it full power. He blew me off the deck of the carrier. It was about fifty feet down to the water, but there were nets spaced [alongside], and fortunately he blew me into a net."[11]

If Captain Elrod was "rough on his airplanes," he was just as rough on himself. On days when he was under the weather, he reported for duty nonetheless. As long as he was not too feverish, he flew through common colds as a matter of routine. He must have endured immense pain on occasion. Anyone who has been forced to fly with nasal congestion, even on a modern passenger jet, knows how agonizing the experience can be, especially in the descent phase of the flight. The closed canopy of an F3F-2 fighter plane offered far less comfort in 1938, since it was unpressurized. This caught up with him at last in December of that year, when a cold that would not go away "settled in [his] left ear." This was the same ear his father had beaten bloody when he was a boy. Perhaps it was a mere coincidence; perhaps not. A ruptured eardrum remains permanently weaker and less elastic along the site of the tear, even after it has healed. There is no telling how long he had forced himself to fly in this condition before it became unbearable on December 18, when he finally presented himself, probably at Betty's insistence, at the Naval Hospital in San Diego. He was diagnosed with "catarrhal fever" and admitted for treatment.[12]

Doctors today no longer use the term *catarrh*, which refers to an inflammation of the mucous membranes. These may be located in a variety of locations, including the lungs, throat, sinuses, and inner and middle ears. In Elrod's case, it involved the sinuses and ear canals, which are connected and play an important role in regulating pressure in the head. There were no antibiotics available for the treatment of such infections in 1938. Andrew Fleming had discovered penicillin ten years earlier at Oxford University, but the first public uses of it did not begin until the early 1940s. Elrod was thus forced to rely on saltwater gargles, nasal irrigations with a saline solution, and steam treatments to relieve the buildup of mucus.

He showed some improvement and was released on December 22. Four days later, though, the infection had taken a drastic turn for the worse. No cause was given for the setback, but he probably attempted to fly and aggravated the left ear all over again. This time he was admitted for nearly two weeks with a diagnosis that modern doctors would recognize: "otitis media, acute." Rather than the generalized fever observed during his first visit, it was clear that he now had a bacterial infection in the middle portion of his left ear. This type of infection typically results from a ruptured eardrum, which allows bacteria to pass through the tear into the middle ear. The same regimen of treatments was begun anew. After making slow progress for the first week, he was at last discharged on January 9, 1939.[13]

At least one of Elrod's commanding officers took note of his behavior and criticized him for being "impetuous" during this period. Major Vernon Megee did not specifically mention the failed dual takeoff attempt or the *Saratoga* incident or the predictable health consequences of flying while infected, but he reported that Captain Elrod "requires considerable supervision." The major general commandant of the Marine Corps, having read this, felt he should send a letter with the full quote from Major Megee to Elrod as a warning. The captain must have been taken aback by the attention, but it was not all bad news. The assessment affirmed that Elrod was "energetic and willing" and, most importantly, perhaps, "improving." Elrod seems to have taken the criticism to heart. In his next report, six months later, Megee confirmed that Elrod was "improving with experience in grade," meaning experience as a captain. He still considered him to be at best an "average unit leader," but he could not deny that Elrod was a "very good pilot."[14]

Although he sometimes required more supervision than other officers, Elrod demonstrated his usefulness. He took part in the sixth fleet landing exercise in early 1940, which was staged again on the Caribbean islands of Culebra and Vieques, just off the coast of Puerto Rico. For the first time, marine landing operations there used the final version of what became known as the Higgins boat, with a hinged front ramp just as the marines had requested during FLEX 4. Whatever doubts the marines had harbored about his leadership qualities in 1939 were largely resolved in the aftermath of FLEX 6. Even Major Megee agreed that Elrod had "contributed materially to the efficiency of the squadron during [the] 1940 exercises."[15]

If he was maturing as a unit leader, however, Elrod was still not taking adequate care of his own health. Once back in California, he insisted on flying with a "severe cold" for several weeks, until it settled with a vengeance into his left ear. He was admitted again on June 3 to the Naval Hospital with the same symptoms as previously and underwent treatments again for two weeks. Doctors judged him fit for duty on June 17, but permanent damage had been done to his ear this time. His right ear was fine. It was still able to hear the ticking of a pocket watch at a distance of forty inches, just like always, but the doctor had to move it more than a foot closer to his left ear before Elrod raised his hand. The "defective hearing" was not considered severe enough to disqualify him from active duty.[16]

That was fortunate, because the marines needed him in 1940 more than ever before. Even with a compromised left ear, his unique set of skills—aerial reconnaissance, aerial combat, island-based amphibious operations, and the ability to do it all from an aircraft carrier—matched the challenges that were expected to present themselves if a conflict with Japan materialized in the Pacific Theater. Such a threat had seemed unlikely just ten years earlier. Even after Japan invaded Manchuria in 1931 and set up the puppet state of Manchukuo, it looked as if the Empire's expansionist goals were aimed mostly to the north. American interests, by contrast, lay safely to the south, in the Philippines. The same was true of the United States' closest allies, Great Britain and France. Their holdings in Hong Kong, Malaya, Singapore, and Indonesia (comprising Vietnam, Laos, and Cambodia) were seen as being too far south and west of the Chinese mainland to be a point of serious Japanese interest.

American foreign policy experts became increasingly concerned with the outbreak of the Sino-Japanese War in 1937. Yet here, too, there was no sense of urgency at first. They believed the war with China would serve to embroil Japan in a damaging conflict that required its full attention, thus preventing further moves to the south. Ironically, that same logic worked to Japan's advantage when Hitler's invasion of Poland in September 1939 forced France and the United Kingdom to declare war on Germany. Defending against the Wehrmacht inevitably forced the Allies to draw forces away from their South Asian colonies, and Japan could not help noticing. There was no official commitment to southward expansion in 1939, but Japanese officials agreed that they should strive to identify and seize opportunities to expand at Europe's expense wherever they presented themselves in South Asia.

Both American and British foreign policy experts recognized this southern shift of Japanese attention, and they began a prolonged series of conversations throughout 1940 about how best to counter it. As a result of those talks, the United States agreed to move more forces into the Pacific. It was hoped that they would serve mainly as a deterrent, forcing Japan to think twice about becoming too aggressive. Yet it was understood by late 1940 that the failure of deterrence could possibly mean war. In order to place its best-prepared assets in a position to be of assistance, the marines ordered Squadron VMF-2 to relocate from Naval Air Station, San Diego, to Hawaii in January 1941.

The move presented the Elrod household with a number of dilemmas. The captain's horse had already been repossessed by the lender, so that was taken care of, but the car still needed to be sold. Elrod was a voracious reader and collector of books, with which he could not bear to part. They were boxed up and labeled and carried aboard a naval vessel. Betty's uncle, meanwhile, old Admiral Jackson, then seventy-six, had settled in very comfortably in their spare bedroom. He had come to prize their company and the myriad teas and dinners with old friends and modern-day movers and shakers. It would be hard to say good-bye to all of that and return to a solitary life in Alabama. Pearl Harbor was also a center of naval activity, was it not? And, after all, it had been many years since he'd seen the Sandwich Islands. Perhaps the admiral asked them; perhaps they asked him. One way or another, it was decided that he would go along and continue to live with them in Oahu.

CHAPTER 10

Westward to Wake Island

MARINE FIGHTING SQUADRON VMF-2 WAS NOT ALONE IN BEING transferred to Oahu. Two other squadrons accompanied them in order to round out the marines' full complement of fighting, scouting, and bombing capabilities. This was essentially all the airpower the marines possessed in San Diego. VMS-2, the scouting squadron, was equipped with Vought SB2U-3 "Vindicators," a two-cockpit monoplane. VMB-2, the dive-bombing squadron, had just received twenty-one Douglass SBD-1 "Dauntless" airplanes. All three squadrons parked their aircraft on the deck of the USS *Enterprise* in mid-January and arrived, after a little more than a week at sea, at their new base.[1]

As it turned out, there was not much of a "base" waiting for them. This was the first permanent deployment of marine aviation units beyond the US mainland, and very little had been done to prepare for their accommodations. The navy had established a base at Pearl Harbor on the southern coast of the island of Oahu in 1899, but marine pilots were a new development in 1941. They were assigned to an abandoned dirigible field at Ewa (pronounced *Eva*), about five to six miles to the west of the main harbor, where a mooring mast had been constructed in the 1920s for lighter-than-air ships. All three airships that had once been scheduled to fly to the field were destroyed before arriving, and the navy discontinued the program in the mid-1930s. So it had never been used at all; the leathernecks could have it.

Because the mooring mast was still standing when they showed up, many of them continued to refer to the airfield as "The Mooring Mast at Ewa," even after it was officially commissioned as "Marine Corps Air Station–Ewa." Aside from the old mooring mast, there was no runway suitable for military airplanes, no hangars for the airplanes, no refueling stations, and no housing for any of the enlisted men, officers, or civilian workers stationed there. To make matters worse, much of the area that had been assigned to them was infested with a formidable growth of bamboo. From this humble beginning, MCAS-Ewa developed in the course of one year into the most important staging point for Marine Corps aviation operations in the Pacific Theater during World War II.

Since it was not operational upon arrival, the pilots flew their airplanes first to the Naval Air Station at Ford Island and were driven by truck to Ewa. The first order of business was to clear bamboo and cane thickets. Pilots and ground crews swept the area together, armed with machetes. With that done, a new runway was graded and paved so the planes could be flown over and parked. By the end of 1941, the marines had constructed a second runway that intersected the first to form a cross. Yellow lines were painted on it to show the size of an aircraft carrier deck, so the pilots could practice deck landings while on land. The pitted coral landscape around the runways was leveled off to allow airplanes and ground vehicles to maneuver and be stored. Meanwhile, the crow's nest at the top of the old mooring mast, which stood about fifty feet high when the marines arrived, was closed in and converted to a radio-equipped control tower. The enlisted men were put to work constructing wooden platforms for framed tents. This "tent city" served as the enlisted quarters for most of 1941. By November, a traditional barracks for enlisted marines and a barracks for the officers had been completed.

The Elrods rented an apartment in Pearl City, a small suburban community about five miles away, on the northern shore of Pearl Harbor. This gave the admiral a grand view of Ford Island, which occupied the center of the harbor and served as the main hub of US naval operations. The entire shore of Ford Island was ringed with docks to service the major warships of the US Navy, including the *Lexington*, the *Enterprise*, the *Saratoga*, and the *Oklahoma*. It meant that Captain Elrod had to commute each morning to work at the Mooring Mast, but this was not much farther than he had once walked to Thomasville High School. And there were always bicycles, cars, and motorcycles for sale by soldiers and sailors in the process of transferring out.[2]

The Territory of Hawaii in 1941 had changed in many ways from the independent republic that had once been ruled by Queen Liliuokalani in the nineteenth century. The most obvious of those changes was the US military presence. Annexed at the start of the Spanish-American War in 1898 because of their strategic significance, the Hawaiian Islands came to be regarded as the centerpiece of American naval power in the Pacific. Pearl Harbor was one of nearly a dozen military bases operating throughout the islands.

The American presence, in turn, encouraged economic change. Pineapple and sugarcane plantations became important factors in Hawaiian business and political life, while plantation workers recruited from China, Japan, Portugal, and the Philippines made the territory increasingly diverse. In addition, recreation and tourism had begun to emerge as important players in Hawaiian economic life by the time the Elrods arrived, with much of this activity focused on the bustling city of Honolulu, just seven miles south of Pearl Harbor. It was home to a little over 340,000 people in 1941, and stateside travel literature was already celebrating its most famous beach, Waikiki. Yet getting there was still a major undertaking. A flight aboard Pan American's *China Clipper* took thirteen hours from Oakland, California, a distance of 2,400 miles. Not many Americans could afford the tickets, either, which could run from $200 to $600 for a round-trip flight.

Most tourists deplaning from the *Clipper* in Oahu had no idea that they had just experienced a facet of United States defense policy. Had they propped themselves up on their beach towels and shaded their eyes the following morning, though, they might have watched the airplane lift off from the harbor to continue westward on the next leg of a weeklong transpacific run. From Honolulu the *Clipper* flew 1,380 miles to Midway Island. After an evening's stay there, it lifted off again for a 1,260-mile flight to Wake Island, where it stayed for another one-night layover. Then, it was off to Guam, 1,450 miles further west. The last leg of the journey took it 1,550 miles to Manila in the Philippines. The journey was impossible without those refueling stops along the way, and each of them was an American protectorate, with Wake and Midway Islands under naval jurisdiction.

Pan Am wanted, first and foremost, to make money, but in order to gain access to those properties, it persuaded the navy that a regular air route across the Pacific Ocean would enhance American control and influence in South Asia without violating the terms of the Washington Treaty of 1922, in which the United States had agreed not to fortify territories in the Eastern Hemisphere. Commercial flight facilities on Wake and Guam, it argued, would maintain the spirit of the treaty and be less threatening to the Japanese than a US military presence. The airline even promised to make use of its radio equipment at each station to monitor Japanese transmissions, sharpening the eyes and ears of US intelligence efforts.[3]

For its participation in this symbiotic relationship, the United States benefited in several ways. Beginning in 1935, Pan Am established a permanent civilian presence on Midway and Wake, giving the United States a more compelling case for ownership, and it began work on extensive improvements. On formerly uninhabited Wake Island, for instance, the company built an impressive hotel for its guests, complete with a screened veranda from which to enjoy the sunset, a fully stocked bar, and tennis courts. It brought in oil storage and maintenance equipment and built roads. Because the *Clipper* was a seaplane, there was no need to build a runway, but the lagoon in the middle of the island was initially too shallow for safe landings and pitted with coral outcroppings. A good deal of money and labor were thus expended to blast out a channel with dynamite and remove the rubble and mark it with buoys.[4]

This military/civilian arrangement worked well for both parties during its first five years, but the developments of 1938–1940 forced a reassessment on the military side. The same concerns that had prompted the marines to bring their West Coast squadrons forward to Ewa applied with even greater urgency to these exposed Pacific outposts. Affairs in Europe had weakened the British presence, and Japan was on the hunt. The US military assessed the situation and concluded that, should Japan strike first, not all American protectorates could be held. Guam was considered especially vulnerable. As the southernmost of the Northern

Mariana Islands, the rest of which were occupied by Japanese forces, it would be impossible to defend.

Wake Island, on the other hand, was nearly seven hundred miles away from the nearest Japanese military presence, the island of Kwajalein, far to the south in the Marshall Islands. That isolation would make it a difficult target if properly fortified. A detachment of marines, it was proposed, might be able to hold the island until reinforcements could be sent from Midway or Pearl Harbor. If supplied with marine air units, moreover, Wake could provide vital reconnaissance and advance warning for the defenses of Midway and Hawaii.

Plans were drawn up for Wake Island's new defensive scheme as early as 1939, but Congress could not agree on funding until 1940. Actual work did not begin until January of the following year. It was a clear departure from the treaty system that had guided US relations with Japan for the previous two decades, but American officials saw no point in pretending any longer. "By January 1941 . . . ," US Secretary of State Cordell Hull remembered, "we considered Japan's expansionist ambitions an eventual danger to our own safety."[5]

At just about the same time that Captain Elrod and the rest of Squadron VMF-2 were extending the runway and preparing the grounds around the Mooring Mast at Ewa, civilian workers were launching an even more ambitious project on Wake Island. Theirs was almost tantamount to the challenge of terraforming a foreign world, since the island produced virtually nothing, aside from fresh air, necessary for human life. There were no sources of freshwater whatsoever, and the volcanic rock and coral that lifted the place just barely above sea level were sufficient only to support the most stubborn of weeds and scrub brush. There was no indigenous wildlife to speak of, except for rats and migratory seabirds. The marines who were later deployed there, to be fair, also reported seeing a strange brown flightless bird, about seven inches long, known as a "rail." None of it could be expected to support long-term civilization.

In the spring and early summer of 1941, workers installed desalinization machinery and catch basins to collect and store rainwater. The navy brought in a half dozen shipments of supplies, provisions, and equipment. The improvements made by Pan Am were of some value, but not as much as hoped. Naval aviators needed more than a narrow seaplane channel in the lagoon and a fully stocked hotel bar. To make matters worse, a typhoon had battered the island toward the end of 1940 and lessened the value of the Pan Am facilities even more. According to a supply ship captain who arrived on January 9, 1941:

> All of Panair's equipment had been swept away and the beach was a tangled rat's nest of steel rails, wire cable, timbers, coral boulders, driftwood and debris of all sorts. High up on the shore line lay the wreck of a fine, new Panair boat, the battered remnants of their float and the wooden lighter which they had used in handling supplies. Throughout the scrub trees, which had been swept bare of leaves by the gale, lay several hundred drums of aviation gasoline plentifully interspersed with sticks of "mushy" dynamite from what had been the Panair powder house. One of our first tasks was to break up this unholy alliance by collecting all of the visible sticks and carrying them gently down the beach where they were exploded.[6]

That first supply run managed to set a crane and two bulldozers ashore. They cleared a more extensive supply road, whimsically named "Wilshire Boulevard," and a camp for the workers of the Civilian Engineer Corps. Before the end of January a lighting plant and radio station were completed. Summer saw the construction of two paved runways, able to accommodate the largest military aircraft of the day.[7]

It was a breakneck pace, to be sure, but the navy feared that time was running out. The United States had placed a broad set of economic sanctions on the Japanese Empire that spring, restricting the sale of iron, steel, and high-octane gasoline. The pro-military faction of the Japanese government, as a consequence, had become increasingly strident in its rhetoric. President Roosevelt and Secretary of State Hull recognized there were other factions within the Japanese government that were more amenable to dialogue and compromise, but they feared that the militants had captured the ear of the public. These expansionists considered access to raw materials a matter of national security, since Japan possessed within its own shores none of the resources required to maintain itself as an industrial power. They framed their agenda to the public, with increasing success, as a matter of urgent national survival.

For the United States, any doubts about who was in control of imperial politics disappeared when American cryptographers deciphered the Japanese code. By means of a covert operation known as "Magic," the Roosevelt administration was in a position by the late spring of 1941 to read secret diplomatic communications from Tokyo while engaging with Japan's ambassador in Washington, DC, Admiral Kichisaburo Nomura. As the summer progressed, these intercepted messages made it abundantly clear to Secretary Hull "that the Japanese government was going ahead with its plans of conquest even while talking of peace with us."[8]

Hull may have been taken aback by the swiftness with which the Japanese put those plans into action, but he could not have been terribly surprised when its forces invaded French Indochina on July 21. With Paris occupied by Nazi soldiers, there was not much France could do about it. Ambassador Nomura continued to promise that no further advances would be made into Southeast Asia, but the Roosevelt administration knew better.

Frustrated, Hull discontinued talks with the Japanese ambassador for the time being and counseled Roosevelt to take a harder line. The United States, it was felt, must use every form of leverage it possessed to force Japan to reconsider its program of expansion. All Japanese financial assets and investments within the United States were thus ordered frozen by means of an executive order on July 26, and further restrictions were placed on trade with Japan. One result of those restrictions was that oil shipments were effectively embargoed. Ironically, this latter move served mostly to add urgency to the Japanese quest to control the oil deposits in the Dutch East Indies. With these actions, the United States had exhausted every form of peaceful influence it still possessed, leaving at its disposal only military deterrence and the threat of war. "From now on," Cordell Hull recalled, "our major objective with regard to Japan was to give ourselves more time to prepare our defenses."[9]

American military bases in the Philippines and Hawaii were placed on high alert, and the pace of work on Wake and Midway Islands was accelerated. The Marine Corps was authorized to increase its numbers, both on the land and in the air. Since this entailed the creation of additional squadrons, the marines created at the same time a new system of numbers for units. Captain Elrod's squadron, for instance, VMF-2, became VMF-211 in July. At the same time, the two other marine squadrons at Ewa, scouting and bombing, were reclassified as "scout/bomber squadrons," VMSB. They remained distinct squadrons, but they were each now expected to pursue comprehensive scouting and bombing training and operations.

VMF-211 was also informed in July that they would be receiving new Grumman F4F-3 "Wildcat" fighter planes to replace their old F3Fs. This was welcome news indeed. It was a direct design evolution from the plane they had been flying for the last two years and looked very similar. Yet the new Wildcat incorporated many significant improvements. It was, first of all, a monoplane, so the F4F was able to dispense with the elaborate strut system required to support and stabilize two wings, thus reducing wind drag. Along with this aerodynamic improvement, the F4F boasted a more powerful air-cooled Pratt & Whitney fourteen-cylinder engine. As a result, its top speed was increased to about 290 miles per hour. That was better than their old biplanes, but as the pilots of VMF-211 would soon learn, it was not nearly as fast as a Japanese Zero.

There were some new features, nevertheless, that gave it a fighting chance. The new Wildcats were made entirely of metal, with additional armoring around the cockpit to protect the pilot. The Zeros, by contrast, were built of canvas stretched over wooden frames with no cockpit armor. A well-directed burst of machine-gun fire could inflict fatal damage on a Zero, while the Wildcat was able to absorb an enemy's barrage, much like the heavyweight boxing champion that year, Joe Louis, and return it shot for shot.

In terms of firepower, too, the new F4F was head and shoulders above its predecessor. The F3F that Elrod was flying when he first landed at Ewa was equipped with a single machine gun mounted in front of the cockpit. Its firing mechanism, like that of the Vought O3U-6 Corsairs that Elrod had flown at Quantico, was linked to the engine with a timing belt so that bullets fired in between the rotating propeller blades. The designers of the new F4F had taken that load off the engine and increased the firepower by mounting two .50 caliber Browning machine guns on each wing, firing around the propeller rather than through it.

The Wildcat's landing gear, unfortunately, was unchanged. Pilots still had to manually lower the wheels prior to landing, about thirty rotations of the crank wheel with the right hand, while guiding the plane down to the carrier deck or runway with the left hand. The wheels were still configured directly beneath the fuselage as well, giving the F4F-3 Wildcat, like its predecessor, a very narrow footprint when landing.

The pilots of VMF-211 had to wait until October to try the new planes out, but Elrod and the rest of them were passionate about flying and spent long hours to make up for the late start. Their first order of business was to obtain carrier qualification. This was easily done, since the USS *Enterprise* and *Yorktown* were both stationed near Hawaii. The squadron spent at least a week practicing carrier takeoffs and landings alternately on each carrier, and they found the F4F-3 a little harder to handle than their old biplanes. With only one wing to provide lift, they had to come in for landings a little faster and, for the same reason, gun the engines more fiercely on takeoff. One pilot complained that the rudders on the rear edge of the wings were just too small, making it noticeably less responsive on final approach to the carrier deck. Because the Wildcat's landing gear was so narrow, the pilot was obliged to stomp on the pedals more aggressively to level the plane and bring both wheels down on the deck at the same instant.[10]

Once the pilots had passed their carrier tests, they collaborated with the new radar installations on the coasts of Oahu for scramble drills in November. A decoy plane would fly toward the airspace around the island unannounced to test the radar operators. Once they had established its position and rate of approach, they radioed those coordinates to MCAS-Ewa. The entire base then launched into action. The ground crew prepped and started the Wildcats, while the pilots suited up and ran to be strapped into their cockpits. The squadron took off and attempted to intercept the decoy over open water. The results were analyzed afterward. These tests were ongoing through early and mid-November, requiring Elrod to stay on the base many nights in the newly built officers' barracks.[11]

On one such evening in late November, the squadron commander for VMF-211, Major Paul A. Putnam, asked Captain Elrod to join him for a private talk. Putnam had no office at Ewa, so perhaps they walked out beside the runway and leaned up against one of the Wildcats. Because Elrod was the squadron's executive officer, Putnam said, he wanted to share some confidential information with him that must not be divulged to anyone. Naval intelligence experts had decoded several Japanese messages that indicated a major military strike against a United States base, or bases, was to take place sometime within the next few weeks. The squadrons at Ewa were therefore being mobilized for deployment to forward bases at Midway and Wake Islands. The scout/bombers were headed to Midway, while the fighters of VMF-211 were being sent to Wake. They were to select twelve pilots out of the squadron's total of eighteen to go. The other six would remain at Ewa. There was, moreover, to be no delay. They were ordered to get under way by November 28. Lastly, Putnam said, he and Elrod were not to reveal the true nature of the mission. They would tell the pilots instead that they were going on a brief "night exercise" to Maui and would be back in a day or two.

This was a heavy secret to carry for both of them. For Elrod, especially, it must have been hard to maintain composure as he said good-bye to Betty. Some historians suggest he was informed by Putnam only the night before the departure, yet Elrod had gone over to Hickam Field on November 21 to sign a power of attorney document, allowing a representative of his bank to pick up his paychecks and deposit them. So he knew at least a week in advance that he was headed out somewhere for an extended period, even if he wasn't yet sure exactly where.[12]

At any rate, he and Putnam (who shoved a fishing rod and some tackle under his seat before departure) were the only members of VMF-211 who took more than a toothbrush and a shaving razor. Most of the pilots had no doubt they would be home the next day, just as Putnam and Elrod promised, and saw no need to pack a change of clothing.

They flew out November 28 to Ford Island Naval Air Station to await further orders. A few hours later they were told to proceed to the USS *Enterprise*, which lay about a half-hour flight away off the southern coast of Oahu. Only eleven pilots, however, made it into the air.

Lieutenant Holden's airplane would not crank. He was shuttled out to the *Enterprise* by a naval plane, leaving his Wildcat behind on the tarmac. Once they touched down on the *Enterprise*, the illusion of a brief training exercise began to dissolve. Some members of the navy ground crew may have spilled the beans about Maui not being the real destination by joking around with the marines as they climbed down to the deck. Those who were spared this ribbing soon heard the PA system announce that the *Enterprise* was headed to Wake Island, and that "Battle Order No. 1" was in effect for the duration of the journey.

What was Battle Order No. 1? The pilots found out as soon as they walked into a briefing room belowdecks, where members of Admiral William F. Halsey's staff were waiting to greet them. They were each given a mimeograph copy explaining the order:

1. The ENTERPRISE is now operating under war conditions.

2. At any time, day or night, we must be ready for instant action.

3. Hostile submarines may be encountered.

4. The importance of every officer and man being specially alert and vigilant while on watch at his battle station must be fully realized by all hands.

5. The failure of one man to carry out his assigned task promptly, particularly the lookouts, those manning the batteries, and all those on watch on the deck, might result in great loss of life and even loss of the ship.

6. The Captain is confident all hands will prove equal to any emergency that may develop.

7. It is part of the tradition of our Navy that, when put to the test, all hands keep cool, keep their heads, and FIGHT.

8. Steady nerves and stout hearts are needed now.

That was sobering enough, but the marines were dismayed to learn officially that they would not be returning to Oahu anytime soon. They were being deployed for at least six weeks, maybe longer, to Wake Island. A few of them must surely have cast an angry look or two at Elrod and Putnam as they took it all in.[13]

Halsey, they learned, was taking no chances. "Since it was vital for delivery of these planes to be concealed from the enemy," the admiral explained in his memoirs, "I was prepared to destroy his snoopers, preferably before they could make a radio report of our presence." The task force accompanying the *Enterprise*, nine destroyers and three cruisers, was thus given orders to "sink any shipping sighted and shoot down any plane encountered." When one of his officers expressed concern that this would be taken as an act of war, the admiral acknowledged as much. The officer lost patience at that point and exclaimed, "Goddammit, Admiral, you can't start a private war of your own! Who's going to take the responsibility?" Halsey turned to him and said "I'll take it! If anything gets in my way, we'll shoot first and argue afterwards."

While Halsey did not divulge the contents of the decoded Japanese messages he had been shown a few days earlier, he knew an attack was imminent. He did not know where, but he was convinced that it "was a matter of days, possibly hours." The admiral was done playing games with the Japanese Empire. The task force maintained complete radio silence all the way to Wake, communicating ship to ship only by means of semaphore, or signal flags.[14]

It was a five-day cruise. It began with a waxing gibbous moon that grew bigger and brighter with each night of the journey. The weather was good for most of it, and the marines spent a fair amount of time relaxing on deck, watching the navy planes take off and land to maintain continuous air surveillance of the waters ahead. At the same time, though, the navy had generously organized a brisk schedule of daily informational seminars to get the pilots of VMF-211 up to speed on their new home base. They unrolled maps and aerial photographs and discussed every aspect of the mission, as far as it was known.

Wake Island, it turned out, was actually three islands lying in close proximity to one another. The largest one, shaped like a V, was Wake, and at the tip of each leg of the V lay two smaller islands: Wilkes and Peale. Together, they offered less than three square miles of solid ground in the midst of a seemingly endless Pacific Ocean, providing cover for a shallow enclosed lagoon. They formed a coral atoll, ringed by a forbidding reef that prohibited naval vessels from approaching too close.

For Elrod, peering at the maps, this presented a unique challenge of reverse engineering. All of his experience in the fleet landing exercises had involved islands very similar to the Wake atoll in size and, to a lesser extent, topography: San Clemente off the coast of California and, especially, Culebra in the Caribbean. His job back then had been offensive in nature—how to identify enemy assets and configure a combined air and amphibious assault to neutralize them. In short, his goal was to capture the island. Now the roles were reversed. He began thinking about how American assets (airplanes, fuel storage, shore batteries, antiaircraft guns) could be disguised against Japanese reconnaissance flights. No one knew better than Elrod what those pilots would be looking for and what they expected it to look like from the air. He began thinking, as well, about how he would attack the island and what types of defenses could be presented to counter the most likely attempts.[15]

It was an assignment that invited questions and creative thinking, in part, because there were no clear answers provided at the outset. Putnam and Elrod asked about mission objectives but received no response. In a secure communication to Ewa, Putnam complained that "my orders . . . are not so direct. In fact, I have no orders." This was an awkward position for a squadron commander to occupy, having just fed their pilots a bill of goods about the mission. Failing any formal guidance, Putnam tried to connect the dots as best he could. "I have been told informally by lower members of staff," he said, "that I will be given orders only to fly off the ship and go to the island." When he wondered whether there might be more guidance once he reached his destination, he was told "that there will be nothing in the way of instructions other than to do what seems appropriate at the moment."[16]

One thing seemed abundantly appropriate to all of them. If they were to hold the position, or even put up a meaningful fight for it, they would need to become masters of their new airplanes. Despite their hard work over the last month, they were still finding their way. Major Putnam asked Admiral Halsey if the pilots of the navy fighter squadron then on board the *Enterprise*, VF-6, would be willing to offer some training to his men. VF-6 had been flying the Grumman F4F-3 for a few months longer. Its pilots had even practiced firing the machine guns, whereas half the Wildcats of VMF-211 were still waiting for their wing armaments to be installed.

Naval Fighter Squadron Six agreed to help the marines become a little more comfortable with issues of targeting, maneuvering, and handling. When Halsey learned about the missing wing-mounted machine guns, he immediately ordered the mechanics of the *Enterprise* to get to work installing them. Truth be told, Major Putnam added, most of VMF-211's airplanes were still without homing equipment and targeting sights. In fact, Lieutenant Kinney and several other pilots had given up on the government and resorted to screwing a bolt into the front of their engine cowlings and painting small yellow ovals inside their windshields. Without official gun sights, they felt, it was the only way they would have a ghost of a chance of leading their targets accurately. Halsey put the *Enterprise* mechanics to work on these problems as well.

Added to it all, there was the issue of the airplane that would not start at Ford Island. VMF-211 had twelve pilots but only eleven airplanes. Halsey ordered the *Enterprise* to sell one of its Wildcats to VMF-211 for a token fee to be settled at some future date. All twelve Wildcats were ultimately painted in what Putnam called "the standard blue & gray." This was the navy's combat scheme: dark blue on top so they would blend in with the color of the sea for enemy planes looking down from above, and light gray underneath so they would be harder to spot against the background of the sky. Major Putnam was grateful, but he confided to a friend that all the special treatment made him a little nervous as well. "I feel a bit like the fatted calf," he said, "being groomed for whatever it is that happens to fatted calves."[17]

About nine hundred miles west of Wake Island, they crossed the International Date Line, separating the Eastern and Western Hemispheres. Nothing much changed outwardly, except that December 2 instantly became December 3. The following day, December 4, when the *Enterprise* had approached to within two hundred miles of Wake Island, the marines of VMF-211 were given the order to launch. This allowed the task force vessels to turn and begin the return trip to Pearl Harbor. This time all twelve engines started, and all twelve pilots took to the air: Major Putnam; captains Hank Elrod, Frank C. Tharin, and Herbert Freuler; first lieutenants John F. Kinney, George A. Graves, and David D. Kliewer; second lieutenants Frank J. Holden, Henry G. Webb, and Carl R. Davidson; and sergeants William J. Hamilton and Robert O. Arthur.

They soon rendezvoused with a navy patrol plane assigned to fly along with them as an escort, rose up above the cloud ceiling, and headed west. Once again they maintained radio silence en route, requiring the squadron to fly in tight formation in order to see hand signals from Putnam. Two hours later they picked up the radio homing beacon from Wake Island's brand-new airstrip and began their descent. Observers on the ground reported that VMF-211 was flying in four V formations, with three planes in each V, when they first emerged from the dense clouds. A sizable crowd of civilian workers and marines had gathered along the runway to cheer their arrival. Putnam landed first, followed in quick succession by Elrod, Tharin, and Freuler.[18]

As soon as they turned the engines off and climbed down to the crushed coral "paving" of the runway, the pilots were greeted by a sea of faces. Some they knew already. About forty enlisted members of the MCAS-Ewa ground crew, for instance, had sailed out several weeks earlier on what they were told was a six-week training exercise, only to find themselves dropped off at Wake instead. It was a story, no doubt, that they spent some time comparing over the next few days with the "overnight" exercise to Maui that had been sold to the pilots. They brought the total marine presence on the atoll to 449 men, not counting the new squadron members. There were many new faces as well. Nearly half of the 1,200 civilian workers on the island came out to watch the landing, eager to see if the runway they had built really worked.

There were formal greetings as well. The officer in charge of the base, Commander Winfield Cunningham, came forward first to shake hands with Putnam and Elrod and the rest of the squadron. They spent a few minutes exchanging pleasantries.

Cunningham had much in common with VMF-211. He was a naval aviator himself and was able to speak knowledgeably about ground support and aerial tactics. Yet he was not a marine. Because the navy claimed jurisdiction over Wake, a navy officer was sent to command it. Like the pilots, moreover, he was a newcomer, having arrived only ten days earlier. This turned out to be a handicap. He was still learning about the base and its defenses and personnel. He was so new, in fact, that many of the marines on the island later testified they were unaware that Cunningham was the officer in charge. They were under the impression that Major J. P. S. Devereux, USMC, was still the commanding officer. Devereux had been on the island since August, supervising the disbursement of supplies, the placement of shore batteries, and other works. He too stepped forward to shake hands with the pilots. They would likely be taking orders directly from him in case of combat, while he in turn took orders from Cunningham. Yet it was Cunningham who gave the first orders of the day, instructing the pilots of VMF-211 to begin regular patrol flights the following morning.[19]

After lunch, Elrod got to work chopping out post holes in the coral for a tent. The squadron had been assigned an area next to the runway for their camp, but nothing much had been done to build it prior to their arrival. In fact, there was quite a bit still to be done on many levels. It was not quite as bad as day one at Ewa, but the runway needed to be widened so that more than one Wildcat at a time could be scrambled into the air. There were no "revetments"—that is, concrete shelters and hangars to protect the planes in case of attack—and there were not enough parts and tools for maintenance. Even if there had been, none of the mechanics on the island, they soon discovered, had ever worked on a Grumman F4F-3 Wildcat before. The plane was just too new. The pilots searched through the meager supplies that had been left for them to see if maybe the quartermaster had thought to include a Grumman repair manual. No such luck.

They bedded down that night with a great deal on their minds, not least of which was the constant pounding of the surf about eighty yards away. It was one of the distinctive features of the island. The coral reef created a near constant crashing of waves all around the shoreline. Older hands generally learned to tune it out, but newcomers could sometimes find it irksome.

The island now had a formidable complement of defenders, as formidable as it would ever get. A full moon shone down on the endless ocean around them.[20]

CHAPTER 11

Three Days to Prepare for Two Days of Infamy

FRIDAY, DECEMBER 5

As the sun rose on December 5, Captain Elrod woke to the roar of the surf. He and the rest of VMF-211 set about a more thorough assessment of their surroundings. They did not know it yet, but they had only three days left to get ready for the day that would "live in infamy," which fell on December 8 on their side of the International Date Line.

Two radio installations had been set up close to the runway by marine communications specialist Major Walter Bayler, who had arrived on the island just a few days earlier to begin that work. The one closest to the runway was intended solely for ground-to-air coordination and received its first real test when the morning patrol of four planes took off. Elrod was likely part of it. Major Putnam would have wanted his most experienced pilots to make that first patrol circuit in order to work out problems and provide guidance for later patrols. The same went for Frank Tharin, Elrod's usual wingman. The two had been inseparable since their first squadron assignments at Quantico, and Major Bayler made note of it again on Wake Island. The dawn patrol was initially to be followed by one at noon and another in late afternoon, but Putnam managed to convince Cunningham to start the squadron off with just two patrols per day. They were to fly on a fifty-mile radius from the island. That computes to a total flight path of about 314 miles, which probably took between two and three hours for the Wildcats to complete.[1]

The patrol was far from routine. None of the planes had been provided with radio homing equipment, so the pilots were forced to practice dead reckoning on note paper in the cockpit in order to find their way back. The calculations had to be spot on, too, because the island was so small. Even a slight error could leave them miles away, wandering over open water in search of visual cues. It was a daunting prospect, since "scattered clouds cast shadows on the ocean that, from the air, looked just like so many islands."[2]

Major Devereux complained that the Grumman F4Fs were "fast short-range fighters, of little value for scouting," but he acknowledged that they were better than nothing. And nothing was about what they had had in terms of reconnaissance prior to the arrival of VMF-211. Naval authorities at Pearl Harbor had promised to send a radar unit, but Devereux was disappointed again and again in November to learn that it had not been loaded onto the latest supply ship. After the war, there was some speculation that the navy had harbored concerns about placing

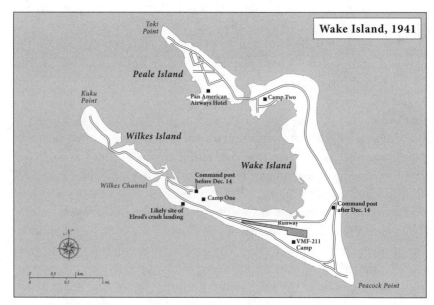

Map of Wake Island. Adapted from Robert Debs Heinl Jr., *The Defense of Wake* (Washington, DC: Historical Section, Division of Public Information, US Marine Corps, 1947).

top-secret technology in such a vulnerable position, fearing the consequences if Japanese scientists were given a chance to reverse-engineer the
captured equipment. No documentation has come to light to confirm or
refute this; whether the lack of radar was a matter of tactical caution or
mere disorganization or incompetence, it meant that "our own eyes and
ears," as Devereux put it, "were the only detection devices we had."

Ears, in fact, were of limited value due to the constant background
noise of the breakers and surf. A Japanese reconnaissance plane, for
instance, had made several high-altitude passes over the island on
December 4 without anyone hearing its engines. Devereux stationed
marines atop two fifty-foot water towers, provided them with binoculars,
and hoped for the best. In this context, the Wildcats at least extended
vision another fifty miles beyond the shore.[3]

The pilots had pointed out the narrowness of the runway and the lack
of revetments on landing, so Major Putnam began pressing for bulldozers
to be brought down from the civilian camp as soon as possible. There
was a general sense that time was running out for such improvements.
For this reason, perhaps, the normally calm and collected squadron
commander lost his temper when the work crews failed to show up in a
timely manner. His fury apparently rose to such heights that the pilots
remembered him uttering several choice words never heard from him
before. It was not his preferred approach, but it worked. The bulldozers
eventually showed up.

Even with all this activity, Putnam ordered four airplanes to be
parked at the southern end of the runway, ready to scramble in case the
patrols spotted trouble. The remaining four Wildcats were moved to the
tie-down area for maintenance.[4]

Problems seemed to multiply as December 5 wore on. The patrol
flights offered the squadron a valuable chance to fly for the first time
with a full complement of bombs and ammunition. They knew that
the weight of two 100-pound bombs and 1,800 rounds of .50 caliber
machine-gun ammunition would change the feel and performance of the
Wildcats in ways that only flight time could reveal. Yet when the ground
crew attempted to load the bombs onto the wing racks, they discovered
that the latching mechanisms were not in alignment. They were not even

close. The dilemma was of paramount concern to the pilots, and several ideas were tossed about as they crouched under the shade of a wing.

It was ultimately the squadron's gunnery and ordnance officer, Captain Herbert C. Freuler, who solved it. He inspected the latching gear on the water-filled dummy bombs that had been sent for the squadron to use for target practice. Seeing that they fit the bomb racks on the planes, he devised a way to remove them from the practice water bombs and attach them to the live ones. Freuler was so confident in his idea that he volunteered to try it out himself in a test flight. Sure enough, the bombs remained secure for both takeoff and landing. The ground crew thus began the work of refitting all 291 bombs possessed by the squadron. Without that innovation, the history of the island's defense would be far different.[5]

SATURDAY, DECEMBER 6

Not a day went by without many such dilemmas cropping up, but the men of VMF-211 kept solving them. Loose coral fragments beside the runway threatened to clog the engine intakes while the planes were idling or warming up, so they built special platforms to control the debris. Water contaminated some of the gasoline. Oil leaks soiled the points of the spark plugs. The tie-down stakes were loosened and pulled free from the hard coral due to the vibration of the engines. In case after case, they met the challenge with ingenious stopgaps. Freuler was not alone in solving them, either; every man in the squadron had his moment sooner or later.[6]

By the end of December 6, the squadron had established itself nicely on and around a smoothed rectangular parking area that ran along the southern edge of the runway. We have a moderately good idea of how the marines arranged themselves because Major Bayler, who was flown off the island just prior to the Japanese invasion, drew a map of it from memory once he was back on Oahu.

The most conspicuous features, positioned right in the middle of the parking area, were two enormous 25,000-gallon gasoline storage tanks. Close by, six hundred drums of aviation fuel stood ready for use. All the airplanes were tied down here when not in use, with a command tent just behind the storage tanks. Close beside the command tent, others were erected to house radio operations, engineering work, and supplies. Finally, along the rear edge, where the smoothed surface of the parking area gave way to the rough debris and scrub of the natural landscape, the marines chopped away at the coral in several spots to create an underground storage area for ordnance, a radio operations bunker, and the most important feature of the entire operation, a latrine.

Farther out in the scrub, they placed two gasoline-powered generators with lines running in to all the lightbulbs, so they could work at night. As living quarters, they initially set up tents among the stunted trees and cover to the west of the parking area, close enough to scramble their planes if need be. By the time Bayler was evacuated, however, the tents had been taken down, and the marines had begun to burrow down in personal bunkers as best they could. Bayler therefore penciled in the word "Bivouac" on his map.[7]

For the gregarious Captain Elrod, the most important facility on the island was likely the officers' club. A short fifteen-minute walk up the coral road toward Camp Number One, where most of the marine infantry were housed, it consisted of a tent erected over a wooden floor. A board positioned across two supports—barrels, perhaps—had been set up at one end of the tent to serve as the bar, with a stack of voucher cards waiting if there was no attendant on duty. Not much to look at as architecture, the club nevertheless boasted a cooler that was stocked at all hours with ice and beer. It also offered hard liquor and several felt-covered card tables, replete with poker chips and cards, for those eager to test their luck.

Hank Elrod had a keen interest in all of these offerings. Marines who recalled his presence there had likely seen him in such surroundings many times before, but he apparently wasted little time in amassing additional lore at Wake Island. John McAlister, for instance, remembered Elrod accepting a challenge late one night to a formal wrestling match with "big McKinstry." This was Clarence McKinstry, who had just been put in command of Battery E on Wilkes Island. He had once been featured in an advertisement for shaving cream, which described him as six-foot-three and 220 pounds. Elrod apparently felt that his grappling skills could overcome McKinstry's height and weight advantage.

The two stripped down to their skivvies, "half naked," and "went to it . . . on the bare wooden floor [of the officers' club], which was plenty rough itself and splintery." The card tables had probably been moved out of the way. McAlister did not say who won the contest, but he remembered both men standing up "with scratches and colorful abrasions from stem to stern." Major Walter Bayler, the radio specialist, remembered a more cerebral version of the same thing: verbal contests with no holds barred. Elrod's approach, he recalled, was to "toss some provocative statement into the conversation, then defend it tooth-and-nail against criticism and attack." Although some of these "debates," he said, never really managed to rise above the level of "noisy arguments," Captain Elrod "always shone." The Yale education that once put him at odds with his father likely found its way into many such encounters.[8]

The most notable event of December 6, however, was an unannounced drill. Major Devereux gave orders for a "dummy run on general quarters" for the entire marine detachment, "sending all units to their positions as though we were being attacked." Artillery crews rushed to the five-inch gun emplacements. Antiaircraft crews manned the three-inch guns, and machine-gun crews fed ammunition belts into their weapons and swiveled them to face the beaches. The men of VMF-211 revved all eight of the remaining Wildcats (four were already out on patrol) and stood at the ready for takeoff. Although everyone had been too busy with basic construction to devote much time to training, the major was pleasantly surprised by the efficiency with which his marines performed the drill. As a reward, he gave them the rest of that day and all day Sunday off.[9]

SUNDAY, DECEMBER 7

There was only so much downtime the men of VMF-211 could allow themselves, of course, having arrived so late. They were still solving a host of problems, such as how to prevent air bubbles from forming (and thus allowing condensation of water) at the tops of the gasoline drums during hand-pumping operations. And patrol flights still needed to be done twice a day. Yet the free day gave them enough time to do a few things unrelated to aviation. Lieutenant Kinney managed to solve the air bubble issue and still take a leisurely stroll for the full length of the seven-mile access road, running along the beachfront of the main island. Marines inclined to take in a film could even catch a showing of *The Beloved Brat*, starring Bonita Granville and Donald Crisp. To date, no records have come to light revealing how Hank Elrod spent his last precious hours of downtime, but there were two baseball games organized that Sunday, one pitting marines against civilians and one close by the airfield involving VMF-211. As a former coach and player for the Quantico marine team, Elrod could hardly have resisted the opportunity to dust off his skills at second base. Playing by the odds, though, we should probably stack a few chips on drinking and gambling at the officers' club as well.[10]

If that bet is correct, we may lay equal odds that Frank Tharin was there with him. Major Bayler described them as the "Damon and Pythias of Aviation," a reference to the famous disciples of Pythagoras who ran into trouble with the ruler of Syracuse, Dionysius I, in the fifth century BC. When Damon was sentenced to death by the local tyrant, his friend Pythias volunteered to take his place and occupy his jail cell so that Damon could return home to settle his affairs and say good-bye to his loved ones. The cynical Dionysius was convinced that Damon, once freed, would never be seen again. So Pythias went a step further and agreed to be executed in place of Damon if his friend failed to return. When Damon eventually returned as promised to be executed, Dionysius was overwhelmed, flummoxed, changed. Their powerful demonstration of brotherly love and devotion brought the tyrant briefly to his senses, and he set them both free. Bayler did not explain the reference in his 1943 memoir, but his intended message was simply that Elrod and Tharin stood ready to give their lives for each other.[11]

That final day of leisure, Sunday, December 7, 1941, was anything but a day of infamy on Wake Island. The weather was temperate and lovely, and the island's military and civilian population made the most of it.

On the eastern side of the International Date Line, it was still December 6 for Betty Elrod in Hawaii. The weather was moderately good there, too, with only scattered clouds. She had learned officially by then that her husband would not be returning from an overnight exercise.

Old Admiral Jackson had seen such things many times. He likely did his best to reassure her that it was all just part of military life. It was a good day for hanging out clothes to dry.

Ironically, the weather between Hawaii and Wake Island was horrific. The *Enterprise* aircraft carrier, having delivered VMF-211 to Wake, was having a slow go of it. The carrier was originally scheduled to arrive back at Pearl Harbor by the morning of December 7, but rough seas delayed it.

MONDAY, DECEMBER 8

By the time the sun rose on December 7 in Hawaii, the day that President Roosevelt later declared "a day that will live in infamy," it was already December 8 on Wake Island. The USS *Enterprise* was still far out at sea, but the vast majority of America's naval strength in the Pacific was docked at Ford Island.

The first wave of the Japanese attack on Pearl Harbor began at 7:48 a.m. That was the most memorable action, yet there were other targets close by that have received less attention from historians. The other half of VMF-211, for instance, still stationed at Ewa, came under attack a few minutes later. One of the lines of approach for attacking aircraft led in from the coast directly over the marine air station, and Japanese pilots made a point of strafing and bombing the Wildcats on the tarmac. Some of the marines initially thought it was an Army Air Corps drill gone horribly wrong until they saw the "meatballs" painted on the sides of the planes. A mix of Zero fighter planes and light bombers, between twenty and thirty in all, flew low over the airfield, picking their targets with care. "They were so low and so slow," recalled one of the handful of marines on duty, "that you could see the gunners in particular . . . you could see their teeth! They were having a great time just spraying the whole area." Not a single Wildcat managed to get into the air, and none were fit for duty afterward. The runway, meanwhile, was badly cratered.[12]

From there, the Japanese planes continued on, following the only paved land road to Pearl Harbor, where they joined the primary attack on the US fleet. As such, they flew almost directly over the Elrod and Jackson households on the harbor's northern shore. Betty and the admiral watched from their doorstep for a minute or two, but when the old man heard an explosion that he could not see, he decided to walk to the end of the street to a wharf. It was directly "opposite," he said, from "the *Lexington*'s berth on Ford Island."

Concerned for his safety, Betty went with him. The two were standing there on the wharf when the planes that had just attacked the marine air station flew overhead. Some of them opened fire with machine guns just before they got over open water, targeting one ship or another on the far side of the channel. Betty and Admiral Jackson were unharmed, but spent shell casings rained down all around them, some falling softly in the grass, some plopping into the water, a few pinging onto the wooden planks of the wharf. Betty felt compelled to walk about and pick them up for no good reason. Then she went back and stood beside the admiral, holding a dozen or so brass casings. She knew the same bullets would soon be seeking her Talmage in the skies above Wake Island, if they had not found him already.[13]

At seventy-six years old, the admiral had lost none of the mental acuity and eye for detail that had once made him such an effective fleet commander. From 7:55 a.m. until 8:30 a.m., when he marked the termination of the first attack, he made notes of every development. He observed, for instance, that

> practically all planes had leveled off as they came down the Northwest shore of the peninsula, passing over three nests of destroyers and apparently heading directly for the *Lexington* and the *Curtiss* berths. Several of these planes flew quite low and not much higher than the *Curtiss*'s masts, and banked to the right as they left the harbor.

His report was considered so thorough and detailed, in fact, that the navy sent it forward as part of the official account laid before President Roosevelt. The first sentence of the document explained that "the attack was observed from the wharf in front of my house at 649 Coral Avenue, Pearl City Peninsula and from the door step of the house." Captain Elrod had other things to worry about on Wake at that moment, but he would have been shocked to know that the president of the United States would soon know where he lived![14]

According to a story that circulated among the men of VMF-211, Betty drove out to Ewa to check on the marines after the first wave of attacks had ended. She was "parked in front of the officer of the day's tent" at 9:00 a.m. when the second wave of Japanese airplanes appeared. Rather than ducking for cover, she ran to the car, rummaged about for a few seconds in the glove compartment, then walked out into the middle of the street with a .45 automatic and began firing up at the Zeros as they bore down on her. "Now that could not have done any good even if she hit them," one of the squadron mechanics mused many years later, "but . . . by God, she was out there with that .45 doing everything she could do."[15]

There can be little doubt, once those airplanes blew past her, that if Mrs. Elrod had believed there was even the slightest chance a .45 caliber bullet could travel one thousand miles across the Pacific Ocean, across the International Date Line to December 8, she would have turned and continued firing westward to try and help her husband, too.

In their shock, radio operators at Hickam Field did not think to pass on the news until about ten minutes after the end of the first wave, at 8:40 a.m., Sunday. That was 6:40 a.m., Monday morning, on Wake Island. The radio set beside the Wake runway picked up a repeating SOS, followed by an uncoded message that read "Island of Oahu attacked by Japanese dive bombers. This is the real thing." It was rushed immediately to Major Devereux's office, but he was not present. A messenger ran to his private tent, where the major was reportedly about half done shaving, and rushed in unannounced with the news.

According to Devereux, he finished his shave and then hurried to the command tent to verify its authenticity. He knew he could not issue orders on an uncoded message, so he contacted the radio crews to ask if the message had come in coded or not. They confirmed that it was not coded, but added that a new message had just come in, and this one *was* coded. They were still working to decode it. Based on this information, Devereux ordered the marines to battle stations and passed the information up the chain of command to the island's naval commander, W. S. Cunningham. Unfortunately, he, too, could not be found for a distressingly long interval.[16]

Elrod had been awake since the regular sounding of "Reveille" at 6:00 a.m., but now he paused his morning routine to listen to a baffling medley of unexpected bugle calls that included in rapid succession a call to church, a fire alarm, and a number of efforts to clear spit. The panicked bugler eventually remembered the correct melody for "General Quarters," and everyone began hustling.

Well, almost everyone. A few skeptics initially thought it was another dummy run like the one on Saturday morning. Elrod knew better when a messenger ran up to him with orders from squadron commander Paul Putnam. He was ordered to scatter the airplanes as much as possible to prevent a single lucky strike from taking them all out, and to do the same with personnel.

Elrod knew there wasn't much room for separating the planes, since the parking area was so small. Rolling them over the rough coral outside the parking area was out of the question. It risked lacerating the tires, and the landing gear of the Wildcats was so narrowly set that even a moderate dip of one wheel into a crevice could slam a wing down on the coral, damaging the ailerons or machine guns or bomb racks or gas tanks. "To move the airplanes out of the regular parking area entailed grave risk of damage," Putnam remembered many years later, "and any damage meant the complete loss of the airplane, because of the complete absence of spare parts." Nevertheless, Elrod gathered a detail as quickly as he could and began putting space between the planes, careful to keep them all on the leveled parking area. Putnam later endorsed the decision to keep them on the parking area. He had hopes that fortified revetments to protect the planes would be functional by that afternoon.[17]

Half a world away, Captain Elrod's little sister, Farrar, launched herself into action even faster than some of the marines when she heard the news. The first NBC radio broadcasts began to break into regularly scheduled programming back in the States at about 3:15 p.m., Eastern Standard Time. Given the time difference, this was about when he was dispersing the airplanes on Wake. Farrar ran out onto the front porch at 942 North Avenue in Atlanta, Georgia, and began shouting over and over, "The Japanese have attacked Pearl Harbor!" My father, then eight years old, was playing marbles in the front yard just beneath the porch railing. He remembered his mom standing there, distraught, screaming the news to no one in particular, "just shouting it out to the neighborhood." Both of them believed "Uncle Talmage" was still posted at Ewa in Oahu. The truth would not have been reassuring.

When the morning patrol flight returned to Wake at 8:00 a.m., Putnam called all his pilots into the office tent and shared the news about Pearl Harbor. Patrols at dawn and dusk were no longer sufficient, he explained, given the circumstances. He wanted four Wildcats up there all day long. These, moreover, would be combat patrols, with orders not to venture out beyond sight of the island. There is some disagreement about who flew that first combat mission. Some remembered Putnam going up himself.

The flight schedule for the day, however, suggests otherwise. Written by the squadron flight officer, Frank Tharin, the first patrol operating under combat status went up at 8:30 a.m., with Graves, Holden, Conderman, and Arthur at the controls. The schedule shows the complete day's rotations, with airplanes destroyed later that day still scheduled to fly. It is thus a portrait of how Putnam expected things to go. As of 8:00 a.m., December 8, at any rate, Putnam had scheduled himself to take to the air at 12:20 p.m. as part of the day's third sortie. That flight never took place.

It is possible that Major Putnam, unable to resist the lure of action, amended his original flight schedule in the heat of the moment, without bothering to write down the changes. Yet, several years later, Captain Tharin, who had originally signed the schedule in the early-morning hours of December 8, confirmed again that the document was accurate and authentic without noting any changes. It simply makes good military sense for the squadron commander to remain on the ground in the early stages of combat to oversee preparations and provide encouragement. In this context, it is frankly hard to imagine a commanding officer of sound mind putting himself at the forefront of battle while his unit is left to figure things out as best they can in a moment of extreme duress.[18]

All sources agree that Elrod went up in the second sortie sometime after 10:20 a.m., along with second lieutenants Carl R. Davidson and John F. Kinney, and Technical Sergeant William J. Hamilton. Captain Elrod was patrol commander. They ascended together as a group, headed west, and were observed from behind by Japanese bombers who were just then descending into the clouds to begin their bombing run. According to one of the Japanese pilots, Norio Tsuji, "suddenly at this time 3 or 4 enemy Grumman F4-F3 fighter planes climbed steeply, far in the distance. A worthy foe! As I watched, they did not even notice our large formation and climbed higher and higher into the skies and disappeared."

It was a narrow miss, but Elrod never knew how close. He took his patrol up to 12,000 or 13,000 feet, then divided into two patrols of two planes each. Elrod took Davidson with him on a sweeping arc of the northern shore of the island, while Kinney and Hamilton looped back to fly along the southern shore.

It was not a good day for flying. The island was shrouded for the most part in dense cumulus clouds with poor visibility. At about the same time, the bombers began their descent through the clouds until they had reached an altitude of "less than 2,000 feet." While descending, the Japanese raid was all but invisible from both above and below. By the time they dropped out of the cumulus formations and were spotted by observers on the ground, the planes were almost over land. According to Major Putnam, "within less than fifteen seconds of their first being sighted their bombs and machine gun fire were on the ground."[19]

In the heat of the moment, Putnam remembered seeing "18 Japanese twin-engined land-based bombers, flying wing to wing in line formation." Walter Bayler, on the other hand, saw "two V's of twelve planes each" as he ran from the mess tent to seek shelter in the nearby scrub. The discrepancy may be due in part to differing perceptions of the two waves of the attack, separated by about a minute. Either way, they were looking at the bombers of the Chitose Air Group, based on the island of Roi-Namur in the Kwajalein atolls of the Marshall Islands.

There was no fighter escort available for the Japanese bombers, on this occasion, because the Zeros on Roi could not fly the 1,400-mile round-trip to Wake Island and back. So Putnam and Bayler were looking at between thirty-four and thirty-six Mitsubishi G3M2 Type 26 bombers, later referred to by US servicemen as "Nells." They came in two waves separated by at least a minute. Their primary objective was the airfield—revealing that previous reconnaissance flights had done a good job of identifying targets.

Bayler left his lunch behind and scrambled to safety, but others still in the mess tent took a direct hit a few seconds later. At least one of the two enormous 25,000-gallon fuel tanks was hit by a bomb, and shrapnel from that explosion likely took out the other at the same time. Both erupted into towers of flame and smoke, spraying the entire area with flaming gasoline.

First Lieutenant George A. Graves had no thoughts of self-preservation. He instantly began running toward Wildcat 211-F-7 to try and get it in the air and give the Japanese a little more to think about than merely an attack on sitting ducks. As soon as he lowered himself into the cockpit, however, the plane was struck directly by a 200-pound bomb. His body was flung under the right wing. As flames reached the Wildcat's 100-pound bomb, hanging just above him, it too detonated, "further mutilating his already dead body."

"Strawberry" Conderman, so nicknamed because of his red hair, had the same thought, but strafing fire passed through his legs and neck before he could reach his plane. As he lay dying on the runway, Conderman directed his fellow marines to help others who had a better chance of survival.[20]

The morning patrol was scheduled to return shortly after noon, but the field and crew were in no condition to receive it. Once again, sources suggest several interpretations about what really happened. According to Bayler, three of the planes touched down without mishap, but the "fourth just failed to clear a mess of heavy debris which was cluttering up the coral strip and finally came to rest with a bent propeller." His account suggests a sequenced landing, with the "fourth" plane bringing up the rear, although he did not explicitly state this. He did not identify the pilot of the plane that hit the debris, but was grateful that he was not hurt. John F. Kinney, meanwhile, one of the patrol members, confirmed that one of the planes did indeed hit some debris, resulting in damage to the propeller, and went a step further by identifying the pilot of the damaged Wildcat as Henry Talmage Elrod. Thus far, the accounts are reconcilable. Yet Kinney added some information that complicates the portrait. He claimed that he stayed in the air another thirty minutes "to make sure that the ground crews had time to remove any debris from the landing strip." This suggests that Elrod and Davidson may have landed first and encountered debris on the runway, at which point Kinney and Hamilton were either waved off visually or ordered by radio to remain aloft awhile longer.[21]

As further evidence that Kinney's half of the patrol came in later than Elrod's, Kinney remembered that the "decision to remain aloft as long as I did after the raiders departed saved me from actually witnessing all the human carnage." Elrod was not so lucky. He and Frank Tharin, who was injured himself but still ambulatory, joined the rest of the survivors in a desperate search for the wounded and the dead. At a reunion of Wake Island defenders in the mid-1980s, my father spoke with a member of the ground crew who had been found by Hank Elrod. He was badly hurt, he said, and buried under debris. He believed he was going to die, but then Elrod lifted a tin panel up off of him. He remembered gazing up at Elrod's face for a few seconds, framed by the sudden brightness of the sky. Then Elrod turned his head and yelled "Frank! Here's one shot up pretty bad!" My father was not a historian and did not record the man's name or the date of the conversation, yet he never forgot the man's tears as he told the story, nor his enduring gratitude to Hank Elrod for having saved him.[22]

Casualties were light across the island generally, but the Pan American facilities on Peale Island and VMF-211 were the exceptions to that rule. At least ten Pan Am employees were killed, and the radio station there was destroyed. The bulk of the day's damage, by any standard of judgment, was directed at the marine airfield. Major Putnam recorded a casualty rate for VMF-211 of 62 percent. Total squadron strength was fifty-nine men, of whom four were flying patrol at the time of the attack. According to Putnam, "of the fifty-five (55) officers and men present, twenty-three (23) were killed outright or died before the following morning." Eleven more were wounded.

The casualty rate for the eight parked airplanes was even greater, at 100 percent. The Japanese bombers had managed to score direct hits on several of them, and came close enough to several others to set them afire or disable them with shrapnel. Only one of the Wildcats on the ground managed to escape bomb damage. It was nonetheless crippled by machine-gun fire as the bombers strafed the area. Once the casualties had been tended to, Putnam stepped off the distance between bomb craters to try and understand whether the Japanese had just gotten lucky or knew what they were doing. Finding the distance between each crater to be identical, he described it as "pattern bombing," perhaps coining for the first time a term that became common parlance later in the war.[23]

That tactic managed to inflict tremendous damage on the squadron, but it also missed a few things. Fortunately, the electrical generator, which had been placed in the scrub beyond the cleared parking area, emerged with no damage. Perhaps for the same reason, some of the radio equipment survived the attack. Here again, there is some disagreement. Kinney claimed that "Major Bayler's ground-to-air radio gear was reduced to so much scrap metal," whereas Putnam reported that the "radio station" had been spared. Major Devereux, too, identified the "radio shack" as one of the few things to escape damage at the airfield, while Bayler himself, the radio specialist, wrote that his "radio tent" had been hit by a fragmentation bomb. As a result, he claimed it was "practically obliterated." Bayler is surely the most reliable voice on this score, since he was responsible for the radio. He judged that there was enough left to rebuild the system with a great many borrowed parts from the navy. He did not give a precise date or time for the completion of repairs, but confirmed that "later . . . I was able to re-establish ground-to-plane communications."[24]

Any way one cut it, the attack left the airstrip, as Devereux put it, a virtual "slab of hell." Most of the tents had been shredded or burned. Many members of the squadron, sadly, would not be needing such accommodations ever again. Yet the survivors were left with little more than the cold ground to sleep on.

It hardly mattered for the moment, for none of them went to sleep. Elrod and every other man not actively losing blood worked through the night to finish building revetments to protect the four precious Wildcats still able to fly. A few civilians showed up to help, but the command of the civilian contractors was badly shaken during and immediately after the attack. The work that night was done mostly by the squadron itself. They began chopping away at the coral to make foxholes where they could shelter from the next bombing raid. There was little doubt, of course, that there would be more bombing, and that the airfield and the men of VMF-211 would be high on the list of targets.

Putnam and his surviving pilots, only nine of them now, gathered together to discuss where the bombers had come from and when they would likely return. They all agreed the planes were too large to have taken off from an aircraft carrier. The Marshall Islands, they concluded, must be their point of origin. Reasoning that Japanese pilots would seek to avoid flying by night over such a vast expanse of open water, a 1,200- to 1,400-mile round-trip, they calculated that the next raid would likely occur between the hours of 11:00 a.m. and 1:00 p.m.[25]

Once they had time to think things through a bit more thoroughly, they realized that the bombing was probably intended as preparation for a landing attempt. With that in mind, as if they did not have enough to do already, Elrod and Tharin devoted much of the night to burying explosive charges up and down the runway. Each one was wired through a single switch, and that, in turn, was connected to the generator. If the Japanese managed to take the island, the men of VMF-211 would at least deny them the use of the runway. They completed the night's projects under the darkness of an island-wide blackout, aided only by the light of a waning gibbous moon.[26]

As the sun finally rose over Wake Island on December 9, the days of infamy were done. Now it was time for war. And marines know what to do with war.

CHAPTER 12

Defending Wake Island in the Air

FEW MEMBERS OF VMF-211, OFFICERS OR ENLISTED, NEEDED TO HEAR
"Reveille" on Tuesday, December 9. Most were awake. Most were working. But there it was anyway, riffing down from Camp Number One. The
mess tent had been blown to shreds. There was no breakfast to be had.
Yet someone had brought a pot of coffee to a boil, and that was enough
under the circumstances. A motley assortment of exhausted marines
staggered toward the aroma from all sides of the airfield. Farther north
on the island, Major Devereux, also awake most of the night, had come
to regard coffee as a sort of "plasma for the soul" for marines. When
hunger became too much for even coffee to assuage, squadron members
kicked through the debris of the mess tent, searching for cans of stewed
tomatoes or green beans or condensed milk. They cracked the claw side
of a hammer through the lids and swallowed the contents cold.[1]

With only three Wildcats ready for flight, Major Putnam ordered
two patrols in the air at dawn and dusk, each consisting of two airplanes.
These were intended mainly to scout for the approach of Japanese naval
vessels and provide an early alarm for the expected landing attempt,
yet each plane was loaded with two 100-pound bombs and full belts of
ammunition for the wing-mounted machine guns should they happen
to encounter enemy aircraft. The real witching hours for air attacks
had already been narrowed down to the hours between 11:00 a.m. and
1:00 p.m., so Putnam ordered all available fighters in the air at midday.
Elrod may have flown one or both of the patrols, for his flight certificate
indicated that he logged about three hours and fifty minutes that day.

Yet only three pilots went up to do battle with the incoming bombers at noon, and he does not appear to have been among them. Wildcat number nine had proven a bit more difficult to fix than first hoped. When Elrod struck debris the previous day, it did more than merely bend the propeller. The suddenness with which it stopped spinning created a series of cascading failures within the system, most notably a burned-out prop motor and a network of blown relays.[2]

In his absence, Hamilton, Kliewer, and perhaps Freuler engaged a formation of twenty-seven Japanese bombers at an elevation of about eleven thousand feet. Their task was aided substantially by the lack of a fighter escort, but even so, the Wildcats faced a withering barrage of machine-gun fire as they closed on their targets. They scored at least one kill, possibly two, and forced the bombers in the process to descend a few thousand feet closer to the ground-based three-inch antiaircraft guns. As a result, several more were seen to be trailing smoke as they departed, with one of those exploding while still within sight of the island.[3]

Major Putnam described the tactics of day two as being a significant departure from day one, when the bombers had inflicted severe losses on the airfield with a low-altitude attack. "Their original raid was tactically well conceived and skillfully executed," he recalled many years later, "but thereafter their tactics were stupid." As much of a surprise as the first attack had been, the daily attacks that followed became routinely predictable, coming in at very high altitudes to avoid the island's "triple A," or antiaircraft fire. According to Putnam:

> The hour and altitude of their arrival over the island was almost constant and the method of their attack invariable, so that it was a simple matter to meet them, and they never, after that first day, got through unopposed, even though the squadron never had more than four airplanes in operation and usually could muster only two or three.[4]

VMF-211 emerged from the December 9 raid with considerably less damage than it had sustained on the day of infamy. Yet other parts of the atoll suffered. On the northeastern wing of the island, the civilian camp took several direct hits, including the hospital tent. Civilian casualties may have numbered as many as fifty, and many patients in the hospital, too wounded to evacuate, were now killed outright. "That," remembered Walter Bayler, "was the crowning infamy." The navy radio station also sustained damage, making the army radio truck at the southern end of the airfield the only way of picking up communications from the outside world. From those transmissions the scope of the Japanese offensive slowly came into focus during the day. Pearl Harbor and Wake, it became clear, represented only part of a vast initiative that saw Japanese forces mobilized against American bases in the Philippines and Guam and British bases in Malaya. Wake and Hawaii were not alone, moreover, in the magnitude of damage inflicted. The Japanese had done their homework well and delivered a thorough drubbing against all of their chosen targets.[5]

Whether the Wildcats managed to bring down one or two bombers, Devereux declared it "first blood" in retribution for the previous day's losses. It did much to lift morale across the entire island. The Marines manning the three-inch guns felt good about their performance as well. It was easier to hit a slow-moving target at 8,000 to 11,000 feet than one zooming just overhead at only 1,300 feet, and they knew they had scored some hits. Like everyone else in the squadron, Elrod and Tharin had chiseled out foxholes for themselves as best as they could the previous night, but several civilian volunteers brought in heavy equipment to dig proper dugouts once the bombing ended on December 9. The two moved their belongings into one of them and began stocking it with needful supplies that came to hand. Over the course of the siege, in fact, the Elrod/Tharin bunker gained a reputation as having an especially abundant supply of canned and dry goods. According to Walter Bayler, "Duke Tharin and Baron Elrod lived in luxury becoming to the nobility; their hole-from-home had a sandbag revetment and it was common knowledge that they had stocked the larder with twelve cases of canned food and five five-gallon containers of water."[6]

I happened to be present at a conversation in which my father asked then general Frank Tharin about it years later. As a floundering college student interested mostly in a good time, I found the general's response noteworthy, and it stuck with me long after I had forgotten much else.

He acknowledged that they had squirreled away a lot of "good stuff" down there. Then, he paused a moment, as if trying to think of something he could tell us that he had never told anyone else. With a big smile, he said, "But we also had *the* good stuff." After some prodding, he explained that he and Elrod had managed to lay hold of an entire case of whiskey. He did not say where they had acquired it, but it could only have come from one place: the demolished officers' club. Bayler, too, had visited the ruined club that Tuesday and had seen "bottles of liquor . . . strewn all over the place, many of them unbroken." He "salvaged a bottle of bourbon to take to [his] dugout." Elrod and Tharin were far more ambitious![7]

The next day, Wednesday, December 10, saw all four surviving Wildcats restored to action. Having just returned from the morning patrol, Elrod had only a few moments to stretch his legs before being strapped back into the cockpit at 10:00 a.m. for the midday rendezvous with incoming bombers. The fighters by this time had come to be regarded by many as emblematic of the entire garrison's prospects, and Elrod held a place of special esteem even within that elite band. According to the prize-winning historian Gregory J. W. Urwin, "Without a doubt, the garrison's favorite pilot was Capt. Henry Elrod." He had always enjoyed good relations with enlisted men, having begun his career as a private, but on Wake he used it to foster an esprit de corps in a variety of ways. Urwin interviewed one marine gunner, for instance, who remembered that Elrod always made a point of flying low over their battery before zooming up to do battle. "I can remember Elrod taking off over our position," Guy Kelnhofer recalled, "and all of us standing up and applauding him as he went off, you know . . . All of us, you know, just cheering him, because he was such a tremendous pilot, and he was so, so fearless . . . and he would wave [to] us and he would go over our heads . . . and we were all shouting, cheering him. Because we were a team, working together."[8]

On this day, having completed his traditional salute to the gun crew, Hank Elrod climbed toward the rising sun and put on one hell of a show for his artillery friends. The bombers appeared a little early this time, about 10:45 a.m., and a good deal higher than the day before, at 18,000 feet. They had suffered at the hands of the island's three-inch antiaircraft guns the previous day and hoped to rise above them now. For the Japanese bombardiers, this meant that the ground-based fire would be less deadly, but it also ensured that their own bombs would be less accurate in return. For the pilots of VMF-211, it meant climbing up to a height that required the use of supplemental oxygen.

This was a bit more of a challenge than it should have been, since most of the squadron's supply had been destroyed on the first day's surprise attack. Once again, Herbert Freuler, who had already delivered one engineering miracle by finding a way to attach bombs, applied his expertise to the problem. He devised a method by which the oxygen from welder' tanks could be transferred into the handful of flight bottles still left. There were no masks on the island, so the pilots flew with a tube in their mouth when operating above 13,000 feet. Thus equipped, they faced between eighteen and twenty-six twin-engine bombers a few miles out from shore. Elrod appears to have closed with the enemy first and engaged the formation "single-handedly" for some time. Observers on the ground could hear the fight in the distance before they saw it, but soon enough it came within view. Elrod had plunged his Wildcat into the thick of the Japanese formation and was weaving in and out among the planes, delivering machine-gun fire with each pass and taking a good deal of punishment himself. One of the bombers began tumbling from the sky. Now the gunners really had something to cheer about. Someone on the ground was heard to exclaim "Hammering Hank is sure giving 'em hell!"[9]

As the planes came within range of the island's guns, they too opened up. Most pilots would have veered off at this point to avoid the island's antiaircraft fire, yet even as shells burst all around him, Elrod continued pounding his Wildcat down through the formation, trying to disrupt their discipline, shove them a little off their line of attack. Then he climbed back through it, gunning all the while at engines and gasoline tanks, to repeat the procedure. Two more bombers went down. Officially, Elrod was credited with two kills and ground-based gunners with one, but there was no reliable way to determine who had done the more telling damage with everyone throwing everything at the same enemy all at once. That, after all, was exactly what Guy Kelnhofer meant when he said "We were a team, working together." Many of the Japanese bombs missed their targets that day. Some fell harmlessly in the lagoon while others blew craters in useless coral. No casualties were reported. The Japanese did manage to hit one of their primary targets, a gun emplacement on the southern shore of the island. But the marines, suspecting that the position had been spotted, had worked the previous night to move those eight-ton guns several hundred yards to the west, so the bombers succeeded only in destroying some decoys made to look like artillery. Whoever it was who called him "Hammering Hank" must have had a lot of friends standing close by, for once Elrod touched down that day, he was always "Hammering (or Hammerin') Hank" wherever he went for the last thirteen days left to him.[10]

If there was ever an afternoon or evening for opening one of those bottles of whiskey back at the Elrod/Tharin pleasure dome, this was one of them. Yet the looming threat of a landing enforced moderation. They could not let their guard down. An amphibious assault might rouse them to action at any moment during the night. Major Putnam and the squadron leaders had made every effort to anticipate how this might happen and prepare for all eventualities. In order to defend, for instance, against enemy gliders coming down quietly while they slept, they drove all the heavy equipment out onto the runway at the end of each day.[11]

Major Devereux was thinking the same way. He moved his command post into an empty powder magazine at the southern tip of the island that night, a complex operation that required all telephone lines to be linked through his new location. He had just managed to lie down and close his eyes when one of those lines called him back to wakefulness a little before 3:00 a.m. One of the lookouts had seen some type of "movement" off the southern shore of the island. The lookout could not provide any details, "just something seemed to be moving. Then we couldn't see it anymore." Devereux did not want to wake his tired marines for a false alarm, so he called every lookout. Two of them reported seeing something similar but couldn't be sure. He walked out to the beach himself with binoculars. A half-moon still threw enough light on the water to provide some sparkling relief to the surf and the distant surface of the sea, but for several minutes he saw nothing. Then, sweeping a little to northward, Devereux muttered to himself "Well . . . there they are."[12]

He immediately phoned Commander Cunningham with the information. The two men had some disagreements after the war about whose idea it was, but the consensus that morning was to withhold artillery fire and keep the searchlights dark to lure the ships in as close to the island as possible. The marines had been using their three-inch guns to spar with the bombers for the last few days, so they were no secret, but they also had some long-range five-inch guns, six of them, that could come close to matching the firepower of the guns aboard the Japanese ships. Had the fleet commander, Rear Admiral Sadamichi Kajioka, known this, he would simply have kept his ships at a distance and pounded the island in safety.

Devereux reported that a cruiser was leading the flotilla forward. This was the *Yubari*, a fast, shallow-draft light cruiser with six-inch-gun turrets at each end of the ship. It approached within 8,000 feet of the southern tip of the island, Peacock Point, just below the airfield, then turned northward, parallel to the shore, and began firing at between 5:00 and 5:20 a.m. It sailed the entire length of the island, blasting away. In Devereux's judgment, it was "trying to find out what we had, firing to make us open up if we had anything left." The marines had been ordered to hold their fire until the order was given, "It was a calculated risk," Devereux remembered, "that the enemy would think the bombings had knocked out our guns."

Encouraged by the lack of resistance, the Japanese fleet continued to close on the island. Now three destroyers moved forward and began firing. The marines crouched by their guns, hoping they would live long enough to return the favor.

In his memoir, Devereux reported that the four Wildcats of VMF-211 took off when he finally gave the order to fire, but his memory failed him on this particular. The historian Robert J. Cressman was the first to compare Devereux's timeline with the firsthand accounts of the surviving pilots who took part in the action. Cressman concluded that the Wildcats took off a few minutes before the *Yubari* started shelling the island, perhaps around 5:15 a.m. It made good military sense to send them up out of harm's way rather than holding them on the ground at the risk of incurring damage. In Cressman's interpretation, they did not go on the attack, since the defenders were still trying to bait the Japanese to come closer at that point. The pilots, Major Putnam and captains Elrod, Freuler, and Tharin, were ordered simply to rendezvous at about twelve thousand feet over Toki Point (the northernmost beach of Peale Island) and observe. Elrod was flying Wildcat #11. This was prior to sunrise, but enough refracted light spilled over the horizon to give them an early glimpse of the enemy's true numbers.

Keeping tabs on a notepad, Freuler counted a total of fourteen vessels: two cruisers, six destroyers, and the rest either transports or some other type of vessel. It was not a good day for flying or observing, with significant and shifting cloud cover, but he was almost spot on with his count. His only mistake lay in thinking he saw two cruisers. There was, in fact, only one light cruiser: the *Yubari* itself. To their astonishment, the pilots could see no aircraft carriers anywhere on the seas beneath them. Every available Japanese carrier in the region, as it turned out, had been mobilized for the attack on Pearl Harbor. There were simply none to spare for little Wake Island. In practical terms, this meant the Wildcats would have no opposition in the air.[13]

The island's batteries were at last given the order to fire around 6:10 a.m. The first salvos missed their marks in many cases, though not by much. The battery at Peacock Point overshot the *Yubari* by about five hundred yards, but within a minute or two the gunners had made their adjustments and began to find their marks with deadly precision.[14]

Elrod and Tharin dutifully observed and reported the results: "They got her! The gunboat! Every shot hit her close to the waterline . . . She jumped ten feet in the air, an' now she's listing like nobody's business." According to Major Putnam, the Wildcats delayed their own aerial attack by as much as an hour, "not joining in the surface fight until just about the time the attacking force had begun its withdrawal."[15]

Based on radio chatter, Elrod and Tharin appear to have been especially impatient during this period. "So we're to observe results, eh, Baron?" Tharin was heard to ask over the radio. "Now what would you say's the best way to do that?" To which Elrod responded, "Why, Duke, I'd say the best way to observe anything is to get as close to it as possible. Mebbe we oughta do that, huh?" "I reckon we ought," said Tharin.

"If we're going to be observers, we wouldn't want to miss anything, would we?"[16]

When Putnam gave the order to attack, his pilots went into a steep dive in pursuit of their targets. "The first air attack on the surface ships was coordinated," he later recalled, "but thereafter each plane renewed the attack individually as fast as it could be re-armed and refueled." Walter Bayler, who was manning the radio in the command post bunker, reported that he "could hear the wind screaming past and the roar of the engines as they went into a power dive. A few moments of breathless suspense, then the sharp rattle of machine guns as they opened fire on the enemy deck."[17]

Once the planes had cleared the target and begun climbing again, the radio picked up "a joyous shout from Elrod."

"Duke! You hit him!" shouted Elrod. "You hit him with your second!"

"Yeah?" replied Tharin. "I was traveling too fast to notice . . . You didn't do so bad yourself, Baron. Your first rattled his rivets."

With only two bombs apiece, there was only so much they could do in a single sortie.

"C'mon," called Elrod, "let's go back for nourishment. My gas is low and so's my ammunition."[18] By "nourishment," he meant another bomb hooked up under each wing and fresh belts of Browning .50 caliber shells for each machine gun. Much of this ordnance work was done by civilian volunteers, who stepped forward to help the squadron after the loss of essential personnel on December 8.

Eager to get back upstairs and into the thick of it, the pilots usually jumped down from the cockpit just long enough to pace back and forth beside the plane until it was ready to go. One member of the ground crew remembered that Elrod had blood streaming out of both of his ears during one of these refueling stops. This was likely the result of the sudden change in air pressure as he dove from twelve thousand feet to sea level at approximately 350 miles per hour, but it may also have been a consequence of his previous ear infections and hearing loss in Hawaii.[19]

On occasion, the armorers had more trouble than expected or needed to take extra time to solve a problem. During one strafing run, for instance, Elrod's guns had threatened to jam, so the ground crew inspected them to try and identify the cause of the glitch. Such delays allowed Elrod and Tharin just enough time to run over to the command post, only a short jog to the southward, to get some water or coffee or smoke a cigarette. It also gave them a chance to get updates on the battle. The Japanese ships were now in full retreat, attempting to get beyond range of the shore batteries, but one destroyer-class vessel, the *Hayate*, had been sunk outright.[20]

A shout from the re-arming pits let them know their planes were ready, but Elrod delayed a moment. He had a question for squadron commander Putnam, who happened to be on the ground at that moment too.

"Sir," he began, "there's a Japanese cruiser out there. We think she must be the flagship of the outfit, because she's been hanging back and keeping out of range while shelling the island. . . . Duke and I have been thinking of attacking her if—if it's okay."

Based on their description of the ship, Putnam seemed hesitant. Two fighter planes against a cruiser was not a fair contest, and to make matters worse, the island's batteries had begun to fall silent as the fleet drew farther and farther out of range.

"All right, Captain Elrod, you may attack," Putnam answered at length. "Bear in mind, though, we're rather shy of planes. Keep reasonably high, and make a point of dodging the antiaircraft."

Even the dauntless Frank Tharin appeared to have some doubts about the project. As he and Elrod headed for their Wildcats, he was overheard to say "Y'know, Baron, I've heard it said it's impossible to sink a capital ship with small bombs."

"Well, if it's impossible," Elrod replied, "it'll take a little longer, so let's get started."[21]

At this point, the battle shifted from a general exchange between ship and shore batteries to one involving only the fighters of VMF-211 and the fleeing Japanese fleet. Loaded for game once again, Elrod and Tharin rose up and pursued them to southward.

The "fog of war," as the Napoleonic-era military strategist Carl von Clausewitz once termed it, had clouded their eyes to some extent. This was the tendency of combat to warp perception, to provide too much information about some things and not enough about others. Whatever ship they had originally sighted was certainly not the flagship, as they believed it to be, and the ship they caught up with was not a cruiser. It was a destroyer named the *Kisaragi*, the Japanese word for "February."[22]

They did not let their confusion interfere with their fighting, however. As they closed on what they presumed to be the flagship cruiser of the Japanese fleet, Elrod radioed Tharin: "See that big fat sonofabitch straight ahead?"

"I see him," said Tharin, "let's get him!"

"Sashay off to the right and come down on him from your side," Elrod continued. "I'll do the same from mine. That way we'll divide his fire. . . . All set?"

As they prepared to dive, Elrod called it in: "Come in, Command Post. Pilot Elrod calling CP . . . Pilots Elrod and Tharin, only two-man squadron of the skies, about to attack enemy for umpty-umph time. Hope some of you are keeping count. I lost track long ago."[23]

The pilots were not the only ones peering through the fog of war. Few accounts at the time were in total agreement about how many times Elrod and Tharin attacked the *Kisaragi* and returned for nourishment to renew the campaign. Bayler recorded four round-trips, which amounted to sixteen 100-pound bombs delivered and many thousands of rounds of machine-gun fire.[24]

On one of the runs, Tharin's machine guns jammed and would not fire. He filled the airwaves for a few seconds with some angry shouts and swore about malfunctioning machine guns and civilian armorers. "I'm going down, anyway," he called to Elrod. "I'll feint a frontal assault and draw their fire while you come in from the side." As they finished the dive and turned back toward home, Tharin continued pumping the triggers in frustration. Suddenly the guns came back to life and fired off a round. "If it's Wake you're shooting at," laughed Elrod, "try to pot an armorer." It may be worth noting here that when Betty Elrod read this version of the Elrod/Tharin dialogue two years later, some of Tharin's lines "strained [her] credulity." As she explained in a letter to Tharin's wife, "I have never seen Frank mad enough to do much swearing." On the other hand, she had to admit, her own husband's dialogue sounded all too true to form: "I bet Elrod had the air blue most of the time."[25]

In addition to the questionable language, Elrod and Tharin were also disobeying orders. They had been counseled to "keep reasonably high," but they were clearly diving in through flak to deliver punishment at close quarters. Back in San Diego, Elrod had once been cautioned during target practice about holding his bombs until the very last moment, releasing them with only an inch or two to spare between his plane and the top of the target. There is no clear evidence that he took unusual risks of that nature against the *Kisaragi*, but it would have been out of character for him to play it safe with so much on the line. On the last sortie, whatever number it was, Elrod held his bombs long enough to put them right where he wanted them.[26]

It turned out to be a kill shot. According to Putnam, "a bomb dropped by Captain H. T. Elrod apparently got below decks on the light cruiser and set her afire." Thereafter, he observed that the ship "hove to," or slowed to a stop as if disabled. It began moving again, "slowly," but "at a point thirty miles south of the island the Squadron Commander personally witnessed an explosion from within her which caused her to sink within a matter of seconds."

After the war, Japanese sources confirmed that the *Kisaragi* was carrying a large supply of depth charges for use against American submarines. One of those sources claimed that Elrod's bombs "exploded amidst depth charges stored on deck, causing a greater explosion which tore the ship apart." Either way, the rapidity with which the destroyer went down gave other Japanese vessels little time to rescue survivors. All hands were lost, about 160 men. This apparently was the final straw for Rear Admiral Kajioka. If he had been thinking of standing beyond range of the island's five-inch guns and lobbing in artillery to degrade the shore batteries, the Wildcats made him reconsider. He now decided to call off the invasion completely and sail seven hundred miles back to the Marshall Islands.[27]

Having delivered his coup de grâce, Elrod had a much shorter journey home, but it must have seemed like seven hundred miles. Antiaircraft fire from the *Kisaragi* had ripped through his engine. Some remembered a shell having cut the fuel line, others, the oil line. Either one could have meant ruin for plane and pilot. Elrod's harrowing flight back to the island was observed in its final stages by several marines, including Majors

Devereux, Putnam, and Bayler, and Captain Frank Tharin. "We could see the plane was in serious trouble," remembered Devereux, "wobbling badly, losing altitude all the time, as if it were being dragged down." By the time Major Bayler saw it, the engine had stopped. The propeller was not turning.[28]

"Obviously it couldn't make the airfield," he recalled thinking at the time, "and for a few minutes it didn't seem as if it would make the island at all." Bayler held his breath, "expecting it to plunge into the sea." As the plane was about to make its last wobbling drop into the ocean, however, Elrod "somehow lifted her the few extra feet which enabled him to make a 'dead stick' landing on the beach, just above the creaming surf."[29]

It was not a gentle landing. There was a "flurry of spray and sand" as the Wildcat crashed among the coral boulders. There was no chance it could ever be repaired, and the pilot's chances were initially assumed to be about as dismal. Bayler began running toward it, "dreading what I would find in the wreckage." While still some distance away, he "saw a figure rise from the ruins, jump to the ground, and turn to look dejectedly at the crashed plane. It was like seeing a newly buried corpse pop up from the grave." As he got closer, he saw that it was Elrod.[30]

Not much was said at first. Hammerin' Hank "stood a moment in silence, looking at his plane, then reached out and touched it gently." He had a gash in his right cheek, caused perhaps by his head being thrown against the side of the canopy on impact, and probably blood from both ears again. As Devereux and Putnam arrived, he became a little more talkative. "His first words to us," Devereux recalled, "were an apology for failing to bring his plane safely home, and he kept on apologizing for it, over and over, as though it had been his fault." Duke Tharin remembered that Elrod still had his oxygen tube in his mouth as he made those first apologies, slurring and gurgling some of the words. Devereux wanted to hear about "the death blow he'd dealt an enemy cruiser," but Elrod had only one thing on his mind. As they walked back to the airfield, he turned to the major again and said, "Honest, I'm sorry as hell about the plane."[31]

Together, air and land forces on Wake had sunk two Japanese battleships, inflicted significant damage on several others, and killed as many as five hundred to seven hundred sailors. They had turned back a major invasion attempt. It was the only victory notched by United States forces anywhere in the Pacific Theater during the first few weeks of World War II. Aside from Elrod's face and ears, there were no serious injuries reported on the island. While Elrod continued apologizing to anyone who would listen, Putnam, Freuler, Hamilton, and Kinney were still rotating into the air to harass the fleeing ships.

It was not yet 10:00 a.m., but the day had additional challenges in store. The regular bombing raid would be showing up at any moment, so Putnam eventually stopped pursuing the ships and ordered his least exhausted pilots, John F. Kinney and Carl R. Davidson, to patrol. Within about fifteen minutes of reaching twenty thousand feet, seventeen bombers appeared. Kinney maneuvered so that he could dive down out of the sun, tearing through the formation and sending one of the bombers down in flames. Davidson managed to take out two more.

Later, while flying the afternoon patrol at 4:30 p.m., David Kliewer spotted a Japanese submarine about twenty-five miles to the southwest of the island. It had surfaced to recharge its batteries. He too maneuvered his plane so that he could approach the vessel with the sun behind him and strafed it with machine-gun fire. Then, before it could submerge, he lined up for a perpendicular bombing run against the hull. Kliewer released his bombs at such close range that the shrapnel punctured his own tailfins as he passed. When Putnam flew over the location to finish it off a little while later, he observed only an oil slick. The general assumption was that it had sunk.[32]

While Putnam was still in the air surveying Kliewer's handiwork, Elrod received an unusual message from the command post. A mysterious signal had been spotted off the northeastern shore of the island, consisting of what appeared to be three inflated red balls and a column of smoke. The smoke was apparently not the result of a wrecked Japanese airplane or ship, as some initially speculated, for it was repeated again about fifteen minutes later with the appearance of three more inflatable red balls.[33]

Major Devereux requested that a Wildcat take a closer look. As acting squadron commander in Putnam's absence, Elrod assigned himself the job. He hopped in the lone operational fighter plane and charted a course for the unidentified floating object. Once he had crossed the full length of the island, he began cruising at low altitude to survey the ocean surface. Soon enough, he spotted the red balls, only about three thousand yards off the shore of Peale Island, Wake's northernmost point. A short distance beyond them, moreover, he caught sight of a surfaced submarine.[34]

With Kliewer's story still fresh in his mind, Elrod must have had visions of yet another kill, but he held his fire until he had done a close flyover. There was not much difference between the profile of a Japanese sub and an American one, and both tended to have an Arabic numeral on the conning tower. Kliewer claimed to have seen a Japanese character on the one he sank, but Elrod saw only the number "198" in white paint on this one. The reports do not provide enough detail to say for sure how Elrod made the identification. Perhaps they had raised a US flag. At any rate, he relaxed his finger from the machine-gun trigger and radioed back that a United States submarine was hailing the island. It turned out to be the USS *Tambor*, which had observed that morning's battle through its periscope and was now curious about the outcome.[35]

The rest of the day was uneventful by comparison. John F. Kinney and William Hamilton immersed themselves for the next twenty-four hours in the mechanical complexities of trying to restore the last three Wildcats to flying condition. Freuler's engine had been shot up almost as badly as Elrod's, but he managed to glide to the runway.

That evening, some of the men managed to tune in to a Japanese radio broadcast hosted by an English-speaking woman, one of many such broadcasters later nicknamed "Tokyo Rose." In her news report, she claimed that Japanese forces had attacked Wake Island successfully that day and had now taken control of it. The marines got a good chuckle out of that. Although at the same time, their own estimate of the day's outcome may also have been influenced by some partisan exaggeration. In his official report, Major Devereux overstated the island's success by a significant margin. He was under the impression that his gunners had sunk nine enemy ships during the day's fighting.[36]

Nevertheless, his pride was justified. A legend quickly began to circulate that he or island commander Cunningham had concluded a radio message to Hawaii that evening with a defiant request to "send more Japs," but both men denied it. According to Devereux, he first became aware of the quote from an American radio broadcaster that many of the marines on the island liked to listen to on their private radios whenever they could get the signal. After the war, Devereux speculated that perhaps one of his radio operators, energized by what the island's defenders had accomplished, added it unofficially. More recently, historian Gregory Urwin solved the mystery of the quote by locating the famous language in the "padding," or preliminary coding, of a radio message sent by Commander Cunningham. As such, it was never meant to be an official message, but rather a bit of test language to give radio operators in Hawaii time to tune in properly.[37]

CHAPTER 13

Defending Wake Island on the Ground

THE VICTORY DID WONDERS FOR THE GARRISON'S MORALE AND BOOSTED the spirits of Americans back home. A small band of marines numbering less than five hundred had turned back an overwhelming Japanese landing force, inflicting significant losses of life and equipment while incurring virtually none in return. Granted, Elrod's airplane could no longer fly, but there had been no deaths on the island. His name was not mentioned in early reports about the sinking of a Japanese destroyer, but the news of its sinking was heard in every American household that cared to listen the next day. Most such reports attributed it broadly to "naval planes." One especially inaccurate broadcast claimed the ship had been sunk by an "Army pilot." Marines who gathered around the handful of personal radio sets with access to electrical power knew they were a hot topic of conversation and pride in the States. They were pleased to hear the word "gallant" used frequently in almost every description of their performance.

Yet they also knew they were in a bad situation, and many of the news reports they managed to pick up only reinforced that reality. One big-name radio personality began referring to them in every installment as the "Alamo of the Pacific." With the exception of one young man from Texas, who got a kick out of it, most marines on Wake recoiled from the reference. They remembered from their school days what had happened at the end of that story. Even the *New York Times* gave them front-page treatment with headlines like "Marines Keep Wake" and "Small Force Fights Off Foe Despite Loss of Some Planes." The paper rejoiced that

Japanese forces had at last been forced "to pay the red price of war." Yet there too the shadow of the Alamo crept into the stories. "Wake may be captured," one article conceded, "but if its 'leathernecks' add another glorious chapter to their history and inflict further losses on the enemy, they will not have died in vain." It was that last phrase that gave them pause. Whether the fight was ultimately judged to be in vain or worthwhile, they preferred to believe there might be an outcome other than death on the table.[1]

Some on the island also worried that stateside reports were giving too much information to the enemy by constantly emphasizing the contrast between the smallness of the defending force and the power of the Japanese fleet. Even President Roosevelt played into this trend in his very first press conference. Speaking from the White House on December 12, he confirmed to reporters that Wake Island was still holding firm against Japanese attacks. "We are all very proud," he said, "of that very small group of Marines who are holding the island." The statement about the defensive force being "very small" likely seemed a point too obvious to conceal at the time, but Japanese military officials had come away from their December 11 defeat with a very different impression of the island's capabilities. They may have been trying to justify their failure to superiors, but Rear Admiral Kajioka and others represented Wake Island in their official reports as being well armed and formidable, "the most strongly fortified island in the Pacific." There was no good reason, some marines thought, to correct them.[2]

Regardless of whether the secret of their weakness could be kept, the defenders knew they could not hold out indefinitely without reinforcements. There was no question in anyone's mind that the Japanese would return as soon as they were able to augment their forces. The island's fate therefore depended on the ability of officials at Pearl Harbor to organize a relief expedition faster than the Japanese navy could organize a second landing attempt. It was a tall order, given the level of destruction meted out on the Pacific Fleet a few days earlier. Based on anecdotal evidence, however, the marines on Wake appear to have been almost unanimously optimistic about the prospect, especially in the heady days just after their victory.

As of December 12, they believed, rightly, that they had earned it. More importantly, they felt their success had bought them a little extra time. It would take the Japanese at least a few days to sail back to the Marshall Islands, a few more days to refit, and a few more on top of that to return. Very few doubted that the US Navy should, and would, show up first. Naval officials understood that timetable, too, and high-level discussions about reinforcing the island were indeed under way as early as December 10. They moved forward with added urgency after news of the December 11 miracle. The basic plan was to ship in the Fourth Defense Battalion of marines, along with ammunition, supplies, and additional armaments, and take off the one thousand civilian workers trapped on the island.[3]

December 12 presented VMF-211 with a few new wrinkles that had not been seen before, but overall it was a subdued day by comparison to its predecessor. Just prior to dawn a lone Japanese seaplane appeared over the island and began dropping bombs indiscriminately. Wake's defenders had implemented a complete blackout every night, so there were no visual cues to guide the bombardier to his targets. As a result, the "raid" was entirely ineffective in terms of damage inflicted. This, however, was not its primary objective. The seaplane intended merely to harass the enemy, to interrupt a good night's sleep, to irritate.

In this it succeeded admirably. Elrod and Tharin staggered from their dugout along with the rest of the squadron, but it was Tharin on this occasion who strapped into a Wildcat and gave chase. The slow-moving seaplane tried to disappear into the clouds, but, unfortunately for its crew, the harassment tactics had achieved their desired effect. Tharin was now appropriately irritated. He followed it in and cut loose with enough machine-gun fire to shoot down an entire weather front. The plane went down in flames. According to Japanese records, several other seaplanes initially took off as part of this particular mission but were unable to locate the island in the darkness. They returned to Kwajalein in the Marshall Islands without dropping their bombs.[4]

Mysteriously, the same fate befell the regular bombing raid a little later that day. Angered perhaps by the defeat the day before, the bombers took off shortly after midnight, intending to hit the island by surprise just after daybreak. But as the sun rose on December 12, they could see nothing beneath them. They too returned to the Marshall Islands with a full complement of bombs and ammunition. VMF-211's noon patrol, now reduced to only two functional airplanes, had gone up to do battle as usual, but no victims ever presented themselves. Some marines began to speculate that perhaps the submarine attacked by David Kliewer had been broadcasting a radio beacon each day for the bombers to follow. For whatever reason, the bombers could not find the island on this day. The Wildcats stayed in the air waiting a little longer than usual, but no one complained when they finally landed without incident.

December 13 brought the same eerie calm. No Japanese bombs fell on the island at all. As a fitting symbol of that deceptive peace, Captain Elrod's wrecked Wildcat #11 still lay sprawled on the rocky beach where he'd crashed it. It would fight no more. Yet it offered a wealth of spare parts for Second Lieutenant John Kinney and his mechanics as they sought to keep the two other Wildcats in the fight.

A detail was formed to go down and drag the plane back to the runway. This was probably done by attaching chains to the Wildcat and then dragging it behind a bulldozer. Marines may have walked alongside it, holding each wingtip level so they wouldn't catch on the jagged coral. The job couldn't have taken very long, since Elrod was in line with the runway when his engine had frozen. Gregory Urwin claimed that the shell of Wildcat #11 was placed on the lagoon side of the runway to serve as a decoy once it had been gutted for parts, but John Kinney remembered the decoy plane as being Wildcat #12. In all likelihood, they were both out there. Both planes, at any rate, were later dragged to the eastern end of the runway and placed in a scrapyard by Japanese occupying forces. Wildcat #11 was photographed there by Americans when they returned to the island in 1945.[5]

At about the same time that Elrod's Wildcat was being dragged off the beach, Rear Admiral Kajioka's battered invasion fleet limped back into port at Kwajalein in the Marshall Islands. Japanese naval officials arranged to have an additional destroyer assigned to the fleet to replace the *Kisaragi*, which had been sunk by Elrod and Tharin. In addition, a

The Wildcat Elrod flew on December 11 to sink Japanese destroyer *Kisaragi*. Naval History and Heritage Command, Photo Section, Photo 80-G-179006.

light cruiser was assigned to replace the *Hayate*, which had been sunk by the Wake Island shore batteries.

By far the most significant upgrades to the Japanese invasion fleet were two aircraft carriers that had participated in the Pearl Harbor attack. They were ordered to divert from the main task force as it traveled home and proceed to the Marshall Islands to join the Wake Island invasion fleet. These new additions were surely the result of Kajioka's report about the effectiveness of the US fighter planes, which were judged to have "stalemated" the initial invasion attempt. The two aircraft carriers would allow Kajioka to bring dozens of high-speed "Zero" fighters into the contest when he next approached the beaches of Wake Island. Although more lightly armored than the Marine Wildcats, they were faster and more agile. None of the surviving pilots of VMF-211, Elrod included, had ever laid eyes on one. It hardly bears noting that several dozen versus two, whether we are discussing medieval knights or Civil War regiments or World War II aircraft, presents an overwhelming numerical advantage for one side that can seldom be overcome by pure skill and courage on the part of the other.[6]

Meanwhile, in Hawaii, the United States Navy was moving forward with sending reinforcements to defend the island. One important difference in the two efforts, of course, was that the US Navy had just suffered staggering losses of equipment and personnel at Pearl Harbor, while the Japanese navy was undiminished and heavily concentrated in the waters between Hawaii and Wake Island. Despite this handicap, the United States managed to assemble three different task forces for the operation. Two were to act as diversionary forces, while the third one, Task Force 14, would go directly to Wake.

Task Force 14 consisted of one aircraft carrier, the *Saratoga*, and one destroyer, the *Tangier*, supported by a fleet of smaller supply ships and cruisers. Fourteen hundred marines boarded the USS *Tangier* on December 13 and 14, along with substantial cargoes of ammunition for the three- and five-inch shore artillery and machine-gun ammo for the remaining Wildcats. Several Buffalo Brewster fighter planes were stored on the *Saratoga*. The Buffalos looked very much like the Wildcats, but they were bigger and slower in the air, and less reliable. Nevertheless, they would have brought VMF-211 back up to full strength. Lastly, three new radar sets were also loaded onto the ship. It was a serious and well-planned expedition.[7]

The bottom line, however, was that the US relief fleet was working toward a projected D-Day at Wake Island of December 24, Christmas Eve, whereas the Japanese invasion fleet had established a deployment date of December 23. When American intelligence officers picked up radio messages indicating that a Japanese invasion of Wake was imminent, Task Force 14 increased its speed to make up time.

Yet Japanese officials also picked up US radio transmissions and suspected that relief efforts might be under way. They promptly moved their deployment date up to December 22. So while there were many complicating factors along the way, such as bad weather and the removal of Admiral Kimmel from active command of Pacific naval forces in the midst of the expedition, the United States simply had too much water to cross in too little time. When Kimmel's temporary replacement, Vice

Admiral William S. Pye, was briefed on the situation, he too was determined to get to Wake at all costs. When it became clear that Japanese ships would likely be in control of the waters around the island, Admiral Pye still did not waver. He gave orders to prepare for combat and proceed. Unfortunately, preparing for combat meant "topping off" the fuel tanks of all the ships in the task force so they would be able to maneuver at full speed for prolonged fighting if need be. That's where the bad weather played a part. With every wave around them cresting high with white-caps, that simple operation took a full day to complete. It was a day they did not have.[8]

Henry Talmage Elrod knew nothing of these things. He took it as a matter of blind faith that his country would come to his aid if it possibly could, and he kept on fighting. The commanding naval officer of the island, Captain Winfield Scott, received radio confirmation of the expedition, but he did not make it common knowledge to the garrison. Perhaps he feared that dashed hopes in the end might be more damaging to morale than mere uncertainty in the interim.

As the days wore on, however, doubts and misgivings began to creep into everyone's thoughts. From the heights of euphoria following the December 11 victory, the Wake defenders increasingly worried that reinforcements might not reach them in time, or, worse, might not be coming at all. These worries were compounded by the grinding hardships of life on the island after December 8. For Elrod and the men of VMF-211, they were too numerous to list. The squadron had been the primary target of the first attacks and had suffered proportionally greater deaths and injuries than any other unit. In the days following, the daily bombing raids continued to target the airfield for special treatment. Daily meals, moreover, did not always reach them from the civilian commissary. Civilian delivery trucks delivered lunch as quickly as they could to the nearest encampments and batteries before the midday bombing raids, but they usually hunkered down for the raids before reaching the airfield (which they knew would be a target). Located on the southeastern point of the atoll, the airfield personnel were the last on the delivery route and frequently received smaller portions, or none at all. As a result of poor nutrition, dysentery became a chronic problem for VMF-211. Squadron commander Putnam made sure that the pilots took a vitamin pill from his personal supply every morning, but that provided only limited protection against fatigue, demoralization, malnutrition, sleep deprivation, and a host of untreated injuries.

As if that were not enough, the brief respite from bombing the marines had enjoyed after December 11 came to a jarring end on December 14. Japanese bombers began finding their way to the island again. They had probably succeeded in posting another submarine near the atoll to guide them in by radio beacon. Bombs fell almost every day thereafter, with only December 18 free of daytime raids. At this point, the squadron was still able to send up only one or two Wildcats to battle them on most days. In addition to the high-altitude bombing that the garrison had become accustomed to, the Japanese now began sending seaplane bombers at all hours of the night. Since the island continued to observe a total blackout between sunset and sunrise, the bombardiers could see nothing beneath them and had little chance of making precise hits on these runs. But that was not their objective. They sought mainly to interrupt the sleep of the defenders and wear them down psychologically.

After one such sleepless night, the bleary-eyed men of VMF-211 were watching and listening for the incoming bombers when someone caught sight of a single Japanese airplane. It was slightly before noon, about when the bombers typically made their appearance. Yet today there was just this one plane. One observer described it as flying at high altitude in a straight line down the middle of the island, neither dropping bombs nor strafing. Others saw it circle back over certain areas for a second look. No bombs. Too high to even hear the engines.

Having begun his aviation career with an observation squadron, Hammerin' Hank Elrod recognized its movements instantly: This was a reconnaissance flight. He petitioned Major Putnam for permission to go up and kill it before it could carry its photographs back to base. Putnam agreed, and Elrod strapped into the only functional plane that day, Wildcat #8. He gave his traditional wave to the shore battery as he rose up into the sky, then turned in the direction of the Japanese plane. At thirteen thousand feet, he switched on his oxygen canister and continued climbing. The Japanese crew must have seen him coming, however, for the reconnaissance plane turned away from the island and began heading out to sea. Elrod gave chase but could not catch it.[9]

The next two days brought new developments. On December 19, Elrod received confirmation by radio that his wife Betty was okay. Uncertainty about her safety must have occupied his thoughts incessantly from December 7 onward, especially since their apartment lay just across the water from Ford Island, the main focus of the Japanese attacks. He was never informed, thank goodness, about her harrowing duel with a Japanese Zero that fateful morning, wielding only a .45 caliber pistol.

Then, on December 20, a US Navy patrol plane glided in for a landing on the island's lagoon. It had flown from Pearl Harbor via Midway with a few essential supplies and written confirmation for Captain Cunningham that reinforcements were on the way by means of Task Force 14. The plane was not intended to support the island long-term. Instead, its orders were to return as quickly as possible to Midway Island. The crew, however, offered to take some brief messages back to loved ones, provided they were brief enough to be sent by telegram. The offer was extended only to officers, and only if they could write them quickly enough.

Captain Elrod waited for a turn at the squadron typewriter, fearing that his message might end up missing the flight. He wrote the following:

Saturday, 20 December, 1941

My Darling Elizabeth,

I have little hope that this will get out today but I am hoping that it will. There is little news that you don't have or can't imagine. We are still clinging grimly on to what little that we can still call our own. Everything is very secret to everyone except the Japs who seem to know it all before the rest of us. Hoping again that this gets off today and that you are well and safe. Have a Merry Christmas and a Happy New Year and I love you more and more—

Always and Always.

He signed off as "Talmage" and dropped the letter on the stack with everyone else's so they could be driven up to the command post.[10]

What happened next is purely conjecture, based on the context of his following letter.

Although no flight schedule survives for December 20, Elrod appears to have been scheduled for the dusk patrol that day. There were two Wildcats able to fly, so perhaps he had a wingman with him as he circled the island. If so, it was surely Tharin, who had also typed a message to his wife. Each pilot must have cast a nervous glance back at the lagoon now and then, expecting to see the patrol plane lift up at any moment and turn slowly east toward Hawaii. When they landed again after sunset, however, the plane was still moored in the lagoon. It had been held over until dawn.

In the interim, island commander Cunningham had decided to send Walter Bayler, the radio specialist for VMF-211, on to Midway Island. That much is not conjecture. His initial orders were only to set up the radio equipment on Wake and then depart, but he had been stranded on the island since the outbreak of war.

The change of plans gave Elrod the chance to write a more extended letter. He and Bayler were old friends, having spent many nights together playing poker and debating the issues of the day at Ewa field in Oahu. Bayler promised to carry a letter personally to Betty Elrod, and deliver it by hand once he got back, so there was no need to shorten it to telegram length. Elrod thus sat down at the typewriter again to compose a more thoughtful statement, this time on official navy airmail stationary. Although portions of the letter have been quoted extensively in other works, the full text is printed here for the first time:

My Dearest Darling Sweetheart,

I never suspected this afternoon when I wrote my other short note that I would be sitting down writing another tonight. But here we are. I just got in a few minutes ago and have just learned that Walt Bayler is returning and he has kindly consented to deliver this personally, so I am very thankful for the moment.

Of course there isn't a lot of news that I can write about. And you probably know more real news than I do anyhow. I am missing you terribly and am undergoing a few *new* experiences, but also is everyone else. We have had considerable rain today and it is still cloudy. The wind has been very low, however. The weather on the whole is nothing to complain about but I would like to see a good old-fashioned typhoon swamp this entire area.

I imagine there is an awful lot of whitewashing going on now in high places. It certainly will be a criminal shame if they succeed in covering over everything.

I am writing this in something of a hurry and under somewhat difficult circumstances. I'll think of a million things that I should have said after I have gone to bed tonight. But now I am going to say that I love you and you alone always and always and repeat it a million times or so.

Give my love to Mary also. Between the two of you, you have it all—there isn't any for anyone else. I know that you are praying for me and I have nothing more to ask than that your prayers be answered.

Yours devotedly and loving,

Talmage

PS: Betty, please mail the enclosed message to the address written thereon. If you think of anything and wish to do so, Gruber says that you may add a postscript to it.

Love again.[11]

The letter provides a number of important clues. Elrod's preoccupation with the weather reflected more than idle banter here. As a pilot, he knew how hard the rain and cloud cover made it to take off and land and navigate. Yet he was not complaining, for the Japanese bombers had failed to locate the island on that particular Saturday due to cloud cover. In that context, too, his desire to "see a good old-fashioned typhoon swamp this entire area" was more than simple grumbling. He knew that such weather would make a Japanese amphibious landing impossible. Most importantly, his suspicion that there was "an awful lot of whitewashing going on now in high places" tells us about his state of mind at that moment. As executive officer of the squadron, he may have felt some measure of guilt or anger for leading his men into the desperate state of affairs that now threatened their lives. He and Putnam, after all, had initially told the pilots they were merely flying out for an "overnight" maneuver to Maui. Now, many nights later, several of those men were dead or gravely injured, and the survivors faced the prospect of death every day. For Elrod, at least, it must have seemed abundantly clear that someone at a very high level had made a grave strategic miscalculation. He wished to see them held accountable. If they were not, he felt it would be a "criminal shame."

The arrival of the patrol plane spurred a flurry of speculation on the island. Some viewed it as a sign that the United States had not forgotten them and that reinforcements would soon follow. Others took the opposing view. The plane's crew, of course, had delivered sealed orders to Commander Cunningham confirming the approach of the relief force, but he continued to keep that information to himself.

For Elrod and the men of VMF-211, the matter was settled in an unexpected way the next day, December 21. It was a Sunday, and it started off predictably enough. Walter Bayler rowed out to the patrol plane where it lay rocking on the calm waters of the lagoon. He had folded Elrod's letter neatly in his duffel bag. Shortly after sunrise, the patrol plane took off for Midway. So far, so good. For the men of VMF-211, the next order of business on a typical day would have been breakfast and prepping the Wildcats, as many as were still airworthy, for the midday battle with long-range Japanese bombers from the Marshall Islands.

This, however, was no ordinary day. At about 9:00 a.m., eighteen Type 99 Japanese bombers hit the island. They did not release their bombs at high altitude like the usual raids. They dove instead toward their targets and released their bombs with deadly accuracy at close range. These were, in fact, the same dive-bombers that had just devastated Pearl Harbor two weeks earlier. They were accompanied, moreover, by eighteen Mitsubishi A6M2 fighter planes. Zeros! The regular high-altitude bombing raids that the squadron had become accustomed to had never had fighter escorts, because their range was too limited. The sudden appearance of these Zeros could mean only one thing: They were operating from Japanese aircraft carriers.[12]

This realization changed things in several ways. First, the defenders of Wake surmised at once that the Japanese invasion force must have beaten the American relief effort to the island. They were partly right. The Second Carrier Division of the Japanese navy, composed of two aircraft carriers and four destroyers, had taken up a position about two hundred miles northwest of the island. It was these carriers that had launched the Zeros and dive-bombers. The main invasion force was still a day away but closing rapidly. If American reinforcements were to reach the island now, they would have to fight their way through Japanese naval forces.

Second, the Wildcats of VMF-211 were facing impossible odds. None of them managed to get airborne in time to do battle on December 21, but two of them went up the following day and it did not go well. Against eighteen bombers and eighteen fighters, Carl Davidson and Herbert Freuler managed to shoot down two bombers and three Zeros. Yet they paid a heavy price for their courage. Davidson was last seen over open water engaged in a heated dogfight with six enemy fighter planes. His body was never recovered. Freuler, meanwhile, managed to bring his Wildcat back to the runway, but it was too badly damaged to ever fly again. Freuler himself had to be lifted down from the cockpit with multiple bullet wounds.[13]

The loss of those last two planes brought the defense of Wake Island into its final phase. Major Putnam arranged for the men of VMF-211 to be placed under the command of Major Devereux in order to assist with the ground defense. They were assigned to protect the shore batteries close to the runway, so there was no need to relocate. The historical record offers only a few clues as to Elrod's state of mind during this period. Frank Tharin remembered Elrod telling him "I'm not gonna make it." It was not a complaint or confession of fear, Tharin said, but a simple statement of fact. John Kinney, meanwhile, recalled a conversation with both Tharin and Elrod in which the latter expressed the opinion that "the Japs don't take prisoners." It seems, therefore, that Elrod had given up hope that American reinforcements might still reach the island in time to provide assistance, and, facing the prospect of an imminent Japanese landing, he had no intention of surrendering, come what may. That mind-set was communicated to the enlisted men of the squadron in some unorthodox ways. When Elrod encountered four members of the ground crew around sunset on December 22, he upbraided them for their unkempt appearance. "I want you to all clean up," he said. "This may be your last night on this Earth." Seeing that one of them, Corporal Robert Page of Missouri, looked especially rough, Elrod added shaving to the order. "I want you to shave and clean up," he emphasized, looking directly at Corporal Page.[14]

It seems clear that Captain Elrod was heavily influenced in all of this by the lore of the Last Stand. Historically, such hopeless spectacles, in which a small number of heroic defenders stand defiantly against overwhelming odds, have been fought for the same reasons in age after age: honor, survival, brotherly love, tactical advantage, and so on. The most famous last stand, of course, saw three hundred Spartans under the command of King Leonidas sacrifice themselves at the Battle of Thermopylae in 90 BC. Honor, brotherly love, and tactical advantage were in play on that occasion, but not survival. The Spartans fought to delay the invasion of the Persian king, Xerxes, into Greece. They did not expect to live, and none of them did. As every student of military history knows, the messenger who saw them last reported that they were bathing and brushing their hair in preparation for death. If I am correct, it stands to reason that Elrod himself had "cleaned up" in preparation for his "last night on this Earth." He probably made use of the same tidal pools on the beach that Corporal Page and his friends used. When the high tide receded, it left several tub-sized basins in the coral reef full of water. These were often warmed by the sun during the day, offering the closest thing to a heated bath the marines could hope for after the showers had been bombed.[15]

With some time to think about it, however, Elrod may have begun to regret his apocalyptic language about last nights on Earth. Perhaps he sensed that it would be better for morale if the enlisted men under his command retained some hope of success, whatever his private thoughts about the matter. When he next caught sight of the clean-shaven Corporal Page, he called out "Page . . . do you like to fish?"

The corporal responded enthusiastically, "Yes, sir! You're talking my language."

"If we get out of this alive," said Elrod, "I'll take you on the damnedest fishing trip you was ever on in your life."[16]

As Putnam and Elrod considered how best to defend their ground, they confronted some harsh realities. Not much of the squadron was left standing: four officers and perhaps thirteen enlisted men. Second Lieutenant David Kliewer was placed in command of a machine-gun position at the western end of the runway. Three enlisted marines stayed with him. They were in charge not only of the .50 caliber machine gun but also of the gasoline-powered generator connected to all the mines that Elrod and Tharin had buried along the full length of the runway. The other three officers, Putnam, Elrod, and Tharin, prepared to lead the eleven remaining enlisted marines wherever Major Devereux might order them. The general expectation was that the Japanese would target the beaches south of the runway, since the distance between the coral reef and the sandy shore was only about fifty feet there. Yet no one knew for sure. The moon had been reduced from the slender crescent of the day before to nothing at all, a new moon. It was thus a pitch-black night. Lookouts all over the island had difficulty seeing anything, and their imaginations ran wild in some cases. There were at least three false reports of movements at sea before midnight. Several of the enlisted men stretched out on the ground beside Putnam's command dugout and tried to sleep. "To die, to sleep. To sleep, perchance to dream. Aye, there's the rub . . ."

At about 3:00 a.m., Captain Elrod nudged them all awake. There had been a confirmed landing on Wilkes Island, the westernmost tip of the atoll, and fighting was under way.

Devereux had ordered all marines to general quarters. Once everyone was on their feet again, events on the main island of Wake unfolded rapidly. A beach detail just south of the airfield commanded by Second Lieutenant Robert Hanna spotted a Japanese transport vessel headed directly toward the reef at full speed. To counter the bad weather and choppy waves, the Japanese had devised a plan to run their big ships straight ahead onto the coral and let their "Special Landing Forces," the Japanese Imperial version of marines, splash the rest of the way to the beach. As chance would have it, there was a three-inch artillery installation close to the spot where the transport was headed, but it was unmanned. Hanna called in the sighting to Devereux with his field phone and requested permission to operate the abandoned artillery piece. He was looking right at it, he said, and there was no one posted to it. Devereux gave permission, and Hanna began running up the beach. In the heat of the moment, he forgot to leave orders for the rest of the detachment or tell them what he was doing. Two or three civilians ran after him to try and help.

Although he had never operated a three-inch artillery piece, Hanna managed to load a shell into the breech. He quickly realized why no crew had been posted to the gun: Its sighting equipment had been cannibalized for another position.

He screwed the barrel down to what appeared to be the right elevation, but his first shot whistled over the deck and splashed harmlessly in the ocean. With his second salvo, he began eyeballing the ship's hull by looking through the barrel before inserting the shell. It was, after all, only a few hundred yards away. Almost every shot thereafter rang a bell. The ship's hull was punctured. Its deck caught fire, and as Hanna and his two civilian helpers continued blasting away, the magazine exploded, sending out a blazing display of tracer bullets, depth charges, and grenades. Darkness was no longer as much of a handicap for the defenders. The spectacle of the burning transport lit up the scene all too well. They suddenly saw that hundreds of Japanese soldiers were wading in, holding their weapons above their heads to keep them dry. There was nothing to stop them once they reached the shore, except the three-man gun crew.

As the situation became clear, Major Devereux ordered VMF-211 to rush down and set up a skirmish line in front of Hanna's gun. Putnam, Elrod, and Tharin grabbed their weapons and began leading the enlisted men down to the beach. A small contingent of civilians followed along of their own accord, eager to help, but Putnam warned them to stay put. Most of them were unarmed, he pointed out, and the Japanese would likely treat civilian combatants more harshly if captured. They should seek cover and stay out of the way. The civilians would not hear of it, however, and Putnam at length relented.

They did not have far to go, about sixty yards. The path from the airstrip down to Hanna's three-inch gun was virtually the same one that Elrod, Page, and others had likely taken earlier that night to get "cleaned up." This time they stopped short of the water and deployed in a line running from the scrub brush just above the sand back up toward the airfield. The civilians were ordered to the rear and assigned to carry ammunition from the dugout to the artillery piece so that Hanna and his helpers could focus entirely on loading and firing. The area had already been infiltrated to some extent by Japanese landing forces. In fact, Hanna had been forced to suspend firing the gun at one point in order to defend himself with a pistol. So VMF-211 laid down a steady barrage of fire to clear the brush in front of them and establish control of the area. Kiyoshi Ibushi, a member of the Japanese Special Landing Forces that night, described it as "a terrific net of fire from their concentration of rifles and artillery." According to some reports, Elrod moved to secure and hold the "right flank." From Hanna's perspective, this would have been the end of the line closest to the airfield, but there is no way to establish his exact location. His best friend Frank "Duke" Tharin commanded the opposite flank. By process of elimination, the squadron commander Major Putnam must have held the center.[17]

The battle took shape around three basic realities: terrain, darkness, and tactical differences between Japanese invaders and American defenders. In terms of terrain, the ground held by VMF-211 was covered with scattered scrub growth of between one and three feet in height as the position rose away from the sandy beach, on the one hand, and interspersed scrub and stunted trees of five to six feet in height, on the other, as the position approached the runway. This represented a total increase above sea level from the beach to the runway of about five to six feet. None of this vegetation provided much cover for either side during the engagement, so both sought to keep as low as possible. "We hugged so close to the ground," Ibushi remembered, "the edge of our helmets dug into the earth." The darkness aided in this effort for most of the engagement. Even with the light thrown out by the burning ship, US marines aimed more often than not at muzzle flashes rather than clear targets. The Japanese occasionally fired flares into the air to illuminate the scene for a few seconds. For most of the engagement, moreover, a light rain fell intermittently.

In terms of tactics, the marines held their ground by means of small-arms and light-machine-gun fire, anchored to the position of the three-inch gun. Elrod, for instance, was armed with a Thompson machine gun and a pistol. The Japanese, by contrast, sought to crawl forward little by little to put themselves in better position for a bayonet charge. They made many such attempts prior to daybreak, with the marines beating each one back. During one of these onslaughts, Elrod was seen to stand and sweep the field back and forth with his tommy gun. While thus hotly engaged, he nevertheless maintained sufficient coolness and presence of mind to provide helpful advice and guidance to his fellow marines by shouting "Kill the sons of bitches!" over and over. Soon after, he wrestled a light machine gun away from a Japanese soldier and began using that. He handed his tommy gun and pistol to nearby marines who were in need of arms.[18]

As Japanese numbers increased and attrition took its toll on VMF-211, the situation became increasingly dire. A second Japanese transport had run itself aground a few hundred yards west of the first one, and fresh soldiers began moving up to support the frontal bayonet charges. They also sought to encircle the marine position by crawling along the edge of the runway to their north. By happenstance, while Japanese landing forces felt their way forward among the dust and coral of the airfield, they discovered the wire connecting the gas generator to the explosive charges that Elrod and Tharin had buried. Close by they found the telephone lines that connected the rest of the island to the command bunkers of Major Devereux and Captain Cunningham, both located at the southern end of the runway. They cut all the wires.

Cunningham had managed to send out a radio message earlier: "Enemy on Island. The issue is in doubt." Now, with no information at all coming in, the issue became even more doubtful.

As dawn approached, the darkness gradually gave way to subtle shades of gray. Silhouettes and movement could be discerned. The sun's disk first inched over the horizon at 7:23 a.m. on December 23, 1941, but Elrod's earlier warning about "your last night on this Earth" proved to be prophetic in his case. He did not survive to see the new day. In the ambient predawn glow, the marines discovered the ground to be littered with bodies on all sides. One of those Japanese casualties, however, was not quite dead. He lay still among the corpses of his comrades until Elrod rose to throw another grenade, then he lifted his pistol and shot.

Conclusion

American naval officials back in Oahu suspected that Wake Island had fallen by the evening of December 23. Japanese radio reports of victory could not be taken at face value, since they had also claimed victory on December 11 while in full retreat, with Elrod and Tharin in pursuit. American radio silence, on the other hand, spoke volumes. By Christmas Eve, the US Navy had issued a statement that the island had fallen. Some newspapers and radio broadcasts managed to include this information on December 24, but most published the grim news on Christmas Day. The details of the engagement, however, remained obscure.[1]

For Elrod's immediate family back in the States, the uncertainty was overwhelming. After a week of futile telephone calls, my grandmother wrote the US Marine Corps in early January of 1942, "to get some information as to the welfare and location, if possible, of my brother, Major Henry Talmage Elrod." She was apparently unaware, even then, that he had been deployed to Wake Island. "He was stationed in Hawaii until the last of November," she wrote. "Since then we have heard nothing from him." She directed the letter to no one in particular, simply "The Marine Corps," and addressed the envelope "Washington, DC." By some miracle it reached the proper desk, and the marines sent her a response explaining that "Elrod was stationed on the Island of Wake at the time it was attacked by Japanese forces on December 7, 1941, and, as his name does not appear on any casualty list thus far received, it is probable that he is now a prisoner of war."[2]

His wife Betty spent the early months of 1942 in the dark as well. As Elrod's "next of kin," she received all official correspondence. This included paperwork confirming that he had been approved for promotion to the rank of major. Sadly, the rank was to take effect on January 1, 1942, exactly one week after his death. Betty also received notice in mid-January that President Roosevelt had issued a special citation recognizing the bravery of the First Defense Battalion and VMF-211, but there was no news about whether Elrod had survived. Her hopes soared in February when a navy list of those "presumed" to have been captured on Wake included her husband's name. Shortly afterward, in March, she learned along with the rest of the nation some of the details of his time on the island when the marines released for the first time the names of the two pilots who had been involved in the sinking of the Japanese destroyer, *Kisaragi*: Elrod and Tharin. The story was taken up enthusiastically by virtually every newspaper in the country, with most including a brief biography of both men and an account of the sinking. At last, the American public had faces and names for its Wake Island heroes.[3]

This information had no effect on the Paramount Pictures version of the siege, creatively titled *Wake Island*. Seeking to capitalize on the nation's patriotic anger, the movie was rushed into production only about two weeks after Tharin and Elrod were publicly recognized, and the movie's director John Farrow had no interest in revising the script any further. Thus, the pilot who sinks the Japanese destroyer in the Hollywood treatment was a fictionalized collage of Elrod and Tharin, renamed Lieutenant Bruce Cameron. Like the actual pilots, Cameron has a wife in Hawaii, but to heighten the emotional stakes, she is killed during the attack on Pearl Harbor. Had Farrow known the truth of the matter—that Betty Elrod had stood in the middle of the street firing a .45 up at an oncoming Zero—he might have thought twice about doing a little more revision. In the movie, Cameron dives through withering Japanese antiaircraft fire, just like Elrod, to deliver the killing blow, then manages to get his Wildcat back to the runway before dying of his wounds. Once again, Elrod's survival of a crash landing on the beach might have made even better theater. Nevertheless, the film was advertised as factual and American audiences flocked to theaters. *Wake Island* was ultimately nominated for four Academy Awards that fall.[4]

Betty remained in Oahu for the rest of the winter, hoping for more news. Then, she arranged to move back to San Diego in the spring.

Admiral Jackson moved with her, and they shared an apartment in Coronado. As the Red Cross sent confirmation of POW status to other wives and family members, even addresses in Japan to which letters and care packages could be mailed, she became increasingly frustrated and stepped up her search for information. She even contacted the Columbia Broadcasting System in May to ask if their overseas correspondents had heard anything. "After checking several local sources of information," she was informed, "we were unable to discover anything at all regarding Captain Elrod."[5]

Admiral Jackson, meanwhile, used his considerable connections to continue searching for answers, and on June 12 he received a fateful telegram from the commandant of the Marine Corps, Lieutenant General Thomas Holcomb: "Cable from International Red Cross states medical officer from Wake Island now a prisoner of war reports Major Henry T Elrod died December 23 X Letter en route to Mrs. Elrod X Please convey to her my deepest sympathy." Mercifully, therefore, the news appears to have been delivered personally by her uncle, who must have handed her the telegram at some point. It was among the papers she bequeathed to the Marine Corps Archives at the end of her life. When the official letter arrived in her mailbox a few days later, she already knew what it said.[6]

The rest of 1942 saw efforts at commemoration begin to gain momentum. These focused initially on the garrison at large, with Congress approving a special expeditionary medal for the Wake Island defenders. Most of the survivors would have to wait until they were freed at the end of the war to receive their awards, but Betty received her husband's medal in the mail in September. Strangely, the award letter concluded with a cautionary note that the medal was only to be worn by the actual recipient and not by the "next of kin."[7]

Elrod and Tharin had already emerged as the public faces of Wake Island heroism, but in November Elrod began to be singled out for special recognition. The initial impetus came from his squadron mates in the other half of VMF-211, still stationed on Oahu. Stirred by the stories of his exploits and perhaps increasingly by the recognition that Elrod in particular had made the ultimate sacrifice, they persuaded the commanding officer of the Marine Air Station at Ewa, Major John Young, to submit a formal petition to have the station renamed "Elrod Field."[8]

"It is felt that the daring and successful exploits of the late Major Henry Talmage Elrod, USMC, during the siege of Wake Island," Young argued, "were so outstanding in character and importance and typified such unselfish devotion to duty as to make his name the most appropriate available for this field." The marine commandant disapproved the proposal on the grounds that there were no other Marine Air Stations in the Pacific Theater at that time and, hence, no need to distinguish it from others by a personal name.[9]

Elrod's stature continued to rise in 1943 with the publication of Lieutenant Colonel Walter Bayler's memoir of the Wake Island fight, *Last Man Off Wake Island*. Bayler was the radio specialist working with Squadron VMF-211 during the first two weeks of hostilities. He lived to tell about it only because he was ordered to evacuate to Midway on December 21, two days before the Japanese victory. In addition to his regular duties thereafter, he somehow managed to write and publish a 367-page narrative of the siege. Bayler had been the man listening to the air-to-air radio transmissions of Elrod and Tharin as they dove repeatedly through enemy fire to hammer the *Kisaragi* on December 11, 1941, and he transcribed their dialogue in gripping detail. He had also witnessed Elrod's dramatic crash landing on the beach. Bayler's depiction of the ghostly pilot, presumed dead, rising out of the wreckage, climbing down to the rocks, and laying a mournful hand against the cowling of his ruined plane captured the hearts of American readers everywhere. My grandmother rushed out and bought copies for everyone in the family. In the book she gave to my father, she wrote this inscription on the front endpapers: "I know that you are going to be as fine and brave as your Uncle Talmage. When you read this book, remember that he was once a little boy nine years old, too."

Although she must have been heartened by the efforts of his old squadron and Hollywood and Lieutenant Colonel Baylor to honor her husband, Betty made her own statement in 1943. On May 24, she enlisted in the newly created Marine Corps Women's Reserve. After receiving basic training as a private in San Diego, she transferred later in the year to the Officer Training School at Camp Lejeune in North Carolina. By the end of the war, she had risen to the rank of captain.

In 1944 the marines at Quantico, Virginia, began searching for ways to honor Elrod's memory as well. The librarian on staff there at the time said, "We are planning to name the training camp for aviation Ground Officers School Camp Elrod." This effort appears to have met with more success than the Ewa proposal. While it is not clear whether the training camp was ever renamed, the road leading to it was named "Elrod Avenue" and continues to bear that name today. Most importantly, the memorial effort at Quantico produced a well-researched article-length biography of Elrod, and a high-quality photo suitable for publication was loaned out by the Marine Corps historical center in Washington, DC. These items later became part of the Marine Corps' nomination of Elrod for a Medal of Honor.[10]

By far the most significant influence on Elrod's legacy was the return of the Wake Island POWs in 1945. Their stories added compelling detail to the narrative and served to confirm the public image of his heroism. Squadron commander Paul Putnam's testimony played an especially important role in this process. Putnam made a point of awarding credit for the sinking of the *Kisaragi* to Elrod alone. He did this in official recommendations for awards, but also in numerous public interviews that gained a broad distribution. Although Putnam himself had also strafed and bombed the *Kisaragi*, he graciously deferred credit to Elrod. "It was that first hit by Elrod that did the damage," he maintained again and again, "and to him must go the credit for being the first man in naval history to sink an enemy warship with light bombs from a fighter plane."[11]

Putnam's influence can be discerned in the language of President Truman's Medal of Honor citation in 1946, which repeated many of the same points:

> [by] executing repeated bombing and strafing runs at extremely low altitude and close range, [Elrod] succeeded in inflicting deadly damage upon a large Japanese vessel, thereby sinking the first major warship to be destroyed by small-caliber bombs delivered from a fighter-type aircraft.[12]

This distinction continues to be regarded as one of Elrod's most notable achievements in the defense of Wake Island. The Grumman F4F-3 Wildcat fighter plane was never designed to function as a bomber, and no other pilot flying one succeeded in doing what Elrod did. Perhaps he just got lucky. Yet he was unique even among marine pilots for his willingness to take chances. Above all, he is remembered today for embodying the marine spirit—for his willingness to throw his whole effort into every challenge, whether in the air or on the ground.

On November 9, 1946, the award was presented to Betty in a formal ceremony in Washington, DC, by the commandant of the US Marine Corps, General A. A. Vandegrift. Had he lived to see that day himself, Elrod would certainly have said that others in his squadron deserved it too: Freuler, Kinney, Tharin, Putnam, Davidson. Yet somehow it was Elrod who became the face of their collective heroism.[13]

The original makeshift memorial on Wake Island, ca. 1945, featuring Elrod's wrecked propeller and airplane cowling. Collections of the National Naval Aviation Museum, Pensacola, Florida.

American forces reoccupied Wake Island shortly after the Japanese surrender in September 1945, and a makeshift memorial was erected on the island in honor of those who had fought there. Elrod's wrecked propeller and airplane cowling served as the centerpiece for the monument.

Attention then turned to the grim task of trying to identify the bodies of marines and civilian workers who had been hastily buried without adequate records or markers. In Elrod's case, the job was especially difficult because the Japanese landing forces, still angry perhaps at the stiff resistance they had encountered, coerced survivors to tumble his body into a mass grave without any effort to mark the remains. By some miracle, his body was identified by means of dental records in 1947 and returned to the States for a proper burial. "Proper" in this case turned out to be Arlington National Cemetery in Washington, DC, with President Harry Truman in attendance to make a brief speech about patriotism and sacrifice.

Elrod was not alone. Twenty other coffins lay on either side of him, waiting to be lowered into their graves. The speech was not recorded or transcribed, but a journalist observed that the president stood in silence for a few minutes after he had finished his remarks, gazing at the flag-draped coffins. During that interval, "an unidentified woman," as the newspaper described her, walked forward and knelt beside one of them with her head bowed, as if whispering a final message.[14]

Notes

Introduction

1. "Henry Talmage Elrod Letters from Yale to Emily," excerpted transcripts of letters, n.d., in author's possession. Emily Neal gave these excerpts to my uncle, Henry Elrod Ramsey, sometime in the 1980s, but she tore out sections, including the dates, that she did not want anyone to read. She did so, Henry noted on the transcript, "for reasons which she does not presently seem ready to divulge."

Chapter 1: 1905–1920

1. *Thirteenth Census of the United States Taken in the Year 1910: Volume II, Alabama–Montana* (Washington, DC: Government Printing Office, 1913), 362, 397–98.

2. *Thirteenth Census of the United States, 1910: Georgia: Troup, Turner, Twiggs, and White Counties*, Microfilm T624, roll 217, National Archives and Records Administration, Washington, DC.

3. For my great-grandmother's "reticence" and retiring nature, I rely on my father's stories. When she came to live with my grandparents in Atlanta in her final years (1930s–1950s), he remembered her mostly as being unusually still and silent. She sat all day in a rocking chair on the front porch and rarely said a word to anyone. He called her "Grandbelle." For Primitive Baptist beliefs, see James Leo Garrett, *Baptist Theology: A Four Century Study* (Macon, GA: Mercer University Press, 2009), 209–10; and John G. Rowley, *Primitive Baptists of the Wiregrass South: 1815 to the Present* (Gainesville: University Press of Florida, 1998), 55–64.

4. *Thomasville Daily Times-Enterprise*, December 15, 1915, 4.

5. William Rogers, "Thomasville," *New Georgia Encyclopedia*. Accessed 12/26/2022, https://www.georgiaencyclopedia.org/articles/counties-cities-neighborhoods/thomasville/.

6. Henry E. Ramsey and W. L. Ramsey Jr., *Elrod's Wake* (Manuscript).

7. "Fourteen Reasons Why Boys and Girls Should Attend Norman Institute," *Thomasville Daily Times-Enterprise*, June 26, 1920, 6.

8. The student's name was Iris Payne. She later married and became Iris Payne Boyle. My uncle, Henry Elrod Ramsey, somehow managed to track her down in the 1980s, and she told the anecdote about the bugle. See Ramsey and Ramsey, *Elrod's Wake*, 15. My

grandmother told a similar version of this story in "Notes and Chronology on Henry Talmage Elrod," Henry Elrod World War II Vet Archival Documents folder, Collections of the Thomasville Historical Society, Thomasville, Georgia. For Talmage's return from the Norman Institute at the end of his eighth-grade year, see *Thomasville Daily Times-Enterprise*, June 1, 1920, 4.

9. *Thomasville Daily Times-Enterprise*, April 8, 1920, 8.

10. *Thomasville Daily Times-Enterprise*, October 23, 1922, 5.

CHAPTER 2: A ROARING START TO THE ROARING TWENTIES

1. Talmage Elrod, Transcript from Thomasville High School, 1920–1923, photocopy in the author's possession; *Thomasville Daily Times-Enterprise*, October 16, 1920, 7; Ibid., November 20, 1920, 6.

2. *Thomasville Daily Times-Enterprise* October 8, 1921, 6; Ibid., November 12, 1921, 3.

3. Emily Neal, "Transcripts of Diary Excerpts," in the author's possession.

4. *Thomasville Daily Times-Enterprise*, October 14, 1922, 6.

5. Neal, "Transcripts of Diary Excerpts."

CHAPTER 3: COLLEGE YEARS, MORE OR LESS

1. Alfred J. Henry, "The Weather of 1923," *Monthly Weather Review* (December 1923): 652–53.

2. "The March of Events," *Pandora 1924* (Athens, GA), 410–14.

3. " 'A' Troop Cavalry," *Pandora 1924* (Athens, GA), 385; Ronald Schaffer, "The War Department's Defense of ROTC, 1920–1940," *Wisconsin Magazine of History*, vol. 53, no. 2 (Winter 1969–1970), 108–20.

4. "The Bullpups," *Pandora 1924* (Athens, GA), 280.

5. Percival Wren, *Beau Geste* (Cutchogue, NY: Buccaneer Books, 1978), 74.

6. Transcript of Henry Talmage Elrod, Registrar's Office, University of Georgia.

7. Excerpts of Seven Letters from Henry Talmage Elrod to Emily Neal, in author's possession.

8. Excerpts of Seven Letters, Ibid.

9. "Modernist Son Leaves Fundamentalist Father," *Fairfield Daily Ledger*, November 27, 1926; also see *Victoria Advocate*, November 29, 1926, and *Oelwein Daily Register*, November 29, 1926.

10. "Modernist Son Leaves Fundamentalist Father."

11. Ibid.

12. Ibid. For information on the suicide of R. H. Elrod, see *Thomasville Times-Enterprise*, March 9, 1926, 1; Standard Certificate of Death for Robert Henry Elrod, 1936, Georgia Death Certificates, #33156, Georgia State Archives, Atlanta, Georgia; *Atlanta Constitution*, March 10, 1926, 6.

13. *Atlanta Constitution*, March 10, 1926, 6; *Thomasville Daily Times-Enterprise*, March 9, 1926, 1.

14. *Thomasville Daily Times-Enterprise*, March 10, 1926, 2.

15. Building Permit for Canal Bank and Trust Company, 1926, Permit #29818, City Archives, New Orleans Public Library; "Modernist Son Leaves Fundamentalist Father."

16. Excerpts of Seven Letters. For the full text of the Hooker poem, see Brian Hooker, "The Commemorative Poem," *Yale Alumni Weekly*, vol. 28 (July 3, 1919): 1060–61.

17. *Thomasville Daily Times-Enterprise*, July 5, 1926, 9.

18. For the telegram exchange with Mrs. Elrod, see "Postal Telegrams," November 25, 1927, Doc. 19, Personnel File, National Archives and Records Administration [hereafter, "NARA"]; for Elrod's date of enlistment, see "Enlistment Papers," November 26, 1927, Docs. 20–22, Ibid., NARA.

CHAPTER 4: ENLISTED, 1927–1931

1. "U.S. Marine Corps Service Record Book of Henry Talmage Elrod," Personnel File, Docs. 1–18, Record Group 127, NARA, Washington, DC.

2. Ibid.

3. Elmore Champie, *A Brief History of the Marine Corps Base and Recruit Depot San Diego, California, 1914–1962* (Washington, DC: Historical Branch, G-3 Division Headquarters, US Marine Corps, 1962), 9.

4. E. P. Moses, "Recruit Depot, Marine Corps Base, San Diego, California," *Leatherneck*, vol. 15, no. 6 (June 1932): 11; for Elrod's assignments during basic training, see "Service Record," Personnel File, Doc. 12, Record Groups 127, NARA.

5. Champie, *A Brief History of the Marine Corps Base*, 10; for Elrod's participation in team sports, see Monroe M'Connell, "San Diego Marines Win Title," *Leatherneck*, vol. 11, no. 4 (April 1928).

6. Professional and Conduct Record of Henry Talmage Elrod, in "Service Record," Personnel File, Doc. 7, Record Group 127, NARA.

7. William F. Trimble, *Hero of the Air: Glenn Curtiss and the Birth of Naval Aviation* (Annapolis, MD: Naval Institute Press, 2010), 104–14; Elretta Sudsbury, *Jackrabbits to Jets: The History of Naval Air Station North Island, San Diego, California* (San Diego: San Diego Publishing Co., 1992).

8. Charles A. Lindbergh, *The Spirit of St. Louis* (New York: Charles Scribner's Sons, 1953).

9. Professional and Conduct Record of Henry Talmage Elrod.

10. Sudsbury, *Jackrabbits to Jets*, 120.

11. E. H. Brainard, "Marine Corps Aviation," *Marine Corps Gazette*, vol. 13 (March 1928): 24–26.

12. "Service Record Book," 11, Doc. 012, Doc. 007, Personnel File, NARA; *Marine Corps Manual* (Washington, DC: Government Printing Office, 1926).

13. Sudsbury, *Jackrabbits to Jets*, 125; "Service Record Book," 4–5, Doc. 007, Personnel File, NARA.

14. The Three Sea Hawks pilots in 1928 were D. W. Thomlinson, W. V. Davis, and A. P. Storrs. For a description of their typical performance, see *San Diego Evening Tribune*, July 24, 1928, 9. Also see Sudsbury, *Jackrabbits to Jets*, 125.

15. *San Diego Union*, August 24, 1928, 6; *The Flying Fleet*, MGM, 1929.

16. "Service Record Book," Personnel File, Doc. 007, Doc. 025, Doc. 013, NARA.

17. *The Flying Fleet*; "The Chief of the Bureau of Medicine and Surgery to the Major General Commandant, U.S. Marine Corps," October 19, 1928, Personnel File, Doc. 028, NARA.

18. Sudsbury, *Jackrabbits to Jets*, 126.

19. "Service Record Book," Personnel File, Doc. 005, Doc. 007, Doc. 010, Doc. 012, NARA; "Promotion to Corporal," April 1, 1929, Personnel File, Doc. 037, NARA; "Detail to Duty Involving Flying," May 6, 1929, Personnel File, Doc. 042, NARA.

20. Sudsbury, *Jackrabbits to Jets*, 124; for the revocation of Elrod's aviation duty, see "Revocation of Detail to Duty Involving Flying," May 31, 1929, Personnel File, Doc. 045, NARA.

21. Frank Capra, *The Name Above the Title: An Autobiography* (New York: Macmillan, 1971), 108–10; photo of Henry Talmage Elrod in the author's possession.

22. Capra, *The Name Above the Title*, 108–10; *Flight*, Columbia Pictures, 1929.

23. Capra, *The Name Above the Title*, 108–10; *San Diego Evening Tribune*, June 13, 1929, 8.

24. "Movie 'Battle' Turns Real as Cameras 'Cut': 200 Marines 'Burn Rear' of 1,000 Mexicans Who Forgot Instructions," *San Diego Union*, May 23, 1929, 3.

CHAPTER 5: COMMISSIONED

1. Herbert Hoover, "Republican Nominating Convention Speech," August 11, 1928.

2. Deposition of Belle Rainey Elrod, September 21, 1929, Thomas County Courthouse, Official Military Personnel File, Doc. 051, NARA.

3. Letter of H. R. Mahler, December 30, 1929, Military Personnel File, Doc. 057, NARA.

4. Assignment to Class of Candidates for Commission, June 7, 1930, Military Personnel File, Doc. 074, NARA.

5. Paul J. Vanderwood, *Satan's Playground: Mobsters and Movie Stars at America's Greatest Gaming Resort* (Durham, NC, and London: Duke University Press, 2010), 105–6; for Elrod's trips to Tijuana during 1938–1940, see "Henry E. Ramsey interview with Elizabeth Jackson Carleson," 1985, in Ramsey and Ramsey, *Elrod's Wake*.

6. Vanderwood, *Satan's Playground*, 238–39.

7. Memo for the Assistant to the Commandant, May 26, 1930, Personnel File, Doc. 071 (p. 48), NARA; Record of Proceedings of a Marine Examining Board, January 12, 1931, Personnel File, Doc. 077, NARA.

8. Final Pay Voucher, February 25, 1931, Personnel File, Doc. 082, NARA; Acceptance and Oath of Office, February 26, 1931, Personnel File, Doc. 084, NARA; Assignment to Duty, February 24, 1931, Personnel File, Doc. 088, NARA; Detail to Duty Involving Flying, April 10, 1931, Personnel File, Doc. 096, NARA; "Philadelphia Marines Win Two Rugby Tilts," *Leatherneck*, vol. 14, no. 5 (May 1931).

9. Basic School Record of Second Lieutenant Henry T. Elrod, 1931–1932, Personnel File, Docs. #098–105, NARA.

10. "Baseball," *Leatherneck*, vol. 14, no. 9 (September 1931).

11. "Basic School Graduates," *Leatherneck*, vol. 15, no. 8 (August 1932).

12. "Request for Flight Training," July 26, 1932, Personnel File, Docs. 109–113, NARA; "Medical Examination Report," July 30, 1932, Personnel File, Doc. 113, NARA; "Change of Station Order," September 1, 1932, Personnel File, Doc. 115, NARA.

13. "Change of Station," September 1, 1932, Personnel File, Doc. 115, NARA; "Naval Message," November, 4, 1932, Personnel File, Doc. 116, NARA.

CHAPTER 6: PENSACOLA, 1932–1935

1. Dual Instruction Log, November 29–December 2, 1932, Military Personnel File, Doc. 125, NARA.

2. Dual Instruction Log, December 5–9, 1932, Personnel File, Doc. 126, NARA; Dual Instruction Log, January 9–February 8, 1933, Personnel File, Doc. 130, NARA.

3. Dual Instruction Log, February 9–24, 1933, Personnel File, Doc. 131, NARA.

4. Personal communication with Henry Elrod Ramsey relating to his interview with Elizabeth Jackson Carleson.

5. Dual Instruction Log, March 3–13, 1933, Personnel File, Doc. 132, NARA; Check Flight Log, March 15–April 3, 1933, Personnel File, Doc. 137, NARA.

6. Check Flight Log, March 15–April 4, 1933, Personnel File, Doc. 137, NARA.

7. Ibid.

8. Advisory Board Hearing, p. 1, April 7, 1933, Personnel File, Doc. 140, NARA.

9. Advisory Board Hearing, p. 2, April 7, 1933, Personnel File, Doc. 141, NARA.

10. Check Flight Log, April 10–11, 1933, Personnel File, Doc. 134, NARA; Check Flight Log, April 17, 1933. Personnel File, Doc. 139, NARA; Advisory Board Hearing, p. 3, April 17, 1933, Personnel File, Doc. 143.

11. Advisory Board Hearing, p. 3, April 17, 1933, Personnel File, Doc. 143.

12. Photo of Henry T. Elrod and Admiral Richard H. Jackson, Photos Folder, Henry T. Elrod Papers, Marine Corps Archives, Quantico, Virginia.

13. Change of Station, April 27, 1933, Personnel File, Doc. 149, NARA; *The Evening Star*, May 21, 1933 (Washington, DC), 5.

14. Naval Message (Pensacola to Washington, DC), May 12, 1933, Personnel File, Doc. 150, NARA; Naval Message (Washington, DC, to Pensacola), May 12, 1933, Personnel File, Doc. 151, NARA.

15. Major General Commandant to Commandant, Reassignment of Lieutenant Henry T. Elrod, USMC, as a Student Naval Aviator, May 23, 1933, Personnel File, Doc. 157; Commandant to Major General Commandant, Reassignment of Second Lieutenant Henry T. Elrod, May 27, 1933, Personnel File, Docs. 158–160, Personnel File, NARA.

16. Request for Flight Training, October 18, 1933, Personnel File, Docs. 162–163, NARA; Flight Physical Examination, December 22, 1933, Personnel File, Doc. 165, NARA; Change of Duty, January 11, 1934, Personnel File, Doc. 169, NARA.

17. Dual Instruction Log, August 6, 1934, Flight Training Jacket, Henry Talmage Elrod, National Museum of Naval Aviation, Pensacola, Florida; Dual Instruction Log, January 14, 1935, Flight Training Jacket, NMNA; Dual Instruction Log, November 13, 1934, Flight Training Jacket, NMNA; Dual Instruction Log, January 16, 1935, Flight Training Jacket, NMNA; Acceptance of Appointment and Oath of Office, November

20, 1934, Personnel File, Doc. 181, NARA; Final Report of Training, April 24, 1935, Personnel File, Doc. 199, NARA.

CHAPTER 7: QUANTICO, VIRGINIA, 1935–1938

1. Allan R. Millett, *Semper Fidelis: The History of the United States Marine Corps* (New York: The Free Press, 1981), 335–37.

2. A. J. P. Taylor, *The Origins of the Second World War* (New York: Simon & Schuster, 1996), 86–101.

3. Nicholson Baker, *Human Smoke: The Beginnings of World War II, the End of Civilization* (New York: Simon & Schuster, 2008), 52–58.

4. Leave of Absence Report, May 29, 1935, Personnel File, Doc. 202, NARA; E. R. Johnson, *United States Marine Corps Aircraft Since 1913* (Jefferson, NC: McFarland & Company, Inc., 2018), 70–71; "How Aviators Get Oxygen at High Altitudes," *Popular Science Monthly* (January 1919): 60.

5. Johnson, *United States Marine Corps Aircraft*, 70–71; "Planes Are Landing by Radio When Fog Hides the Field," *Popular Mechanics* (February 1931), 205.

6. Award of Diploma for Completion of Course in the Marine Corps Institute, August 8, 1935, Personnel File, Doc. 206, NARA; Confirmation of Orders, January 3, 1936, Personnel File, Doc. 209, NARA.

7. Report on Fitness of Officers of the United States Marine Corps, May 7, 1938, Personnel File, Docs. 248–249, NARA.

8. "Two Marines Die in Plane Crash," *Harrisonburg Daily News Record*, November 17, 1937, 3.

9. Personal communication with Lieutenant General Frank Tharin, USMC, September 21, 1985. This interview took place at the commissioning of the USS *Elrod* at Brunswick, Georgia. I was present, along with my father and uncle, Henry Ramsey. The quote is from Ramsey and Ramsey, *Elrod's Wake*, 30.

10. "Henry E. Ramsey interview with Elizabeth Jackson Carleson," 30; Squadron Photo, Photos Folder, Henry T. Elrod Papers, Marine Corps Archives, Quantico, Virginia.

11. Albert A. Nofi, *To Train the Fleet for War: The U.S. Navy Fleet Problems* (Newport, RI: Naval War College Press, 2010), 40–42.

12. Williamson Murray and Allen R. Millett, eds., *Military Innovations in the Interwar Period* (New York: Cambridge University Press, 1996), 76–77; Lieutenant Colonel Kenneth J. Clifford, *Progress and Purpose: A Developmental History of the United States Marine Corps, 1900–1970* (Washington, DC: History and Museums Division, USMC, 1973), 48–49.

13. The *Tentative Manual* was formally adopted as *Landing Operations Doctrine, United States Navy, 1938, F.T.P. 167* (Washington, DC: US Government Printing Office, 1938). For pre-landing reconnaissance procedures, see *Landing Operations Doctrine*, 151–54.

14. *Landing Operations Doctrine*, 152, 153–54.

15. "Dinner/Dance," *Coronado Eagle and Journal*, March 4, 1937, 5; "Planes to Land at Fort Bragg," *High Point Enterprise*, March 9, 1937, 1.

CHAPTER 8: FLEX 4 AND AN UNAUTHORIZED FLIGHT, 1938

1. Notice of Qualification for Promotion, June 2, 1937, Personnel File, Doc. 224, NARA.

2. "Aircraft One Departs for 'War Games,'" January 28, 1938, *Quantico Sentry*, 1. This airfield was constructed in 1931 and was named "Turner Field" in Elrod's day. It was renamed "Marine Corps Air Facility" at the start of World War II, but it is the same airfield that is still in use at Quantico today.

3. General Holland M. Smith, *The Development of Amphibious Tactics in the U.S. Navy* (Washington, DC: History and Museums Division Headquarters, US Marine Corps, 1992), 27.

4. Smith, *The Development of Amphibious Tactics*, 27–28; for an example of comments related to Elrod's experience on aircraft carriers, see "Fitness Report," March 31, 1939, Personnel File, Doc. 255, NARA.

5. Smith, *The Development of Amphibious Tactics*, 27–28.

6. "Advance Information," March 14, 1938, Personnel File, Doc. 239, NARA.

7. "Fitness Report," May 7, 1938, Docs. 248–249, Personnel File, NARA.

CHAPTER 9: WESTWARD TO CALIFORNIA, 1938–1940

1. William L. Shirer, *The Rise and Fall of the Third Reich: A History of Nazi Germany* (New York: Simon & Schuster, 2011), 322–56.

2. "About People You Know," *Coronado Eagle and Journal*, July 7, 1938, 4.

3. "For Adm. Jackson," *San Diego Union*, December 17, 1939, 2d.

4. "Henry E. Ramsey interview with Elizabeth Jackson Carleson," 31; "Rockets Take Polo Battle," *San Diego Union*, June 26, 1939, 4b.

5. "Henry E. Ramsey interview with Elizabeth Jackson Carleson," 31; Strimple C. Coyle to Henry E. Ramsey, June 3, 1992, manuscript letter in the author's possession. Coyle confirmed that the nickname "Hank" was in use at Pearl Harbor by 1940. It also appears in the June 26 *San Diego Union* account of a 1939 polo match.

6. Report on Fitness, March 31, 1940, Personnel File, Docs. 263–264, NARA; Report on Fitness, March 31, 1941, Personnel File, Docs. 276–277; Photo at Cleveland Exposition, 1937, Photos Folder, Henry T. Elrod Papers, Marine Corps Archives, Quantico, Virginia; "Henry E. Ramsey interview with Elizabeth Jackson Carleson," 30; Lynn M. Homan and Thomas Reilly, *Wings over Florida* (Charleston, SC: Arcadia Publishing, 1999), 86; Eleventh Annual Miami All American Air Maneuvers, January 6, 7, 8, 1939, Official Program.

7. Interview with Frank Tharin, May 18, 1984, Brunswick, Georgia. I was present for this interview, but I am grateful to my father and uncle for writing down Tharin's exact words in Ramsey and Ramsey, *Elrod's Wake*.

8. Marshall Cavendish, *Great Aircraft of the World: An Illustrated History of the Most Famous Civil and Military Planes* (London: Marshall Cavendish Books, 1992), 155–62.

9. *Landing Operations Doctrine*, 157. Brigadier General John F. Kinney, USMC, with James M. McCaffrey, *Wake Island Pilot: A World War II Memoir* (Washington, DC: Brassey's, Inc., 1995).

10. Kinney and McCaffrey, *Wake Island Pilot*, 33–34.

11. Gerald Astor, *Semper Fi in the Sky: The Marine Air Battles of World War II* (New York: Presidio Press, 2005), 18.

12. "Medical Abstract and Vaccination Record," Personnel File, Doc. 646, NARA.

13. Ibid.

14. Major General Commandant to Captain Henry T. Elrod, October 10, 1939, Personnel File, Doc. 267, NARA; "Report on Fitness," March 31, 1940, Personnel File, Doc. 269, NARA.

15. "Report on Fitness," September 3, 1940, Personnel File, Doc. 271, NARA.

16. "Medical Abstract and Vaccination Record," Personnel File, Doc. 646, NARA.

CHAPTER 10: WESTWARD TO WAKE ISLAND

1. Major William J. Sambito, USMC, *A History of Marine Fighter Attack Squadron 232* (Washington, DC: History and Museums Division, US Marine Corps, 1978), 5.

2. Interview with Strimple C. Coyle, April 22, 1994, University of North Texas Oral History Collection, No. 1025, PDF transcription, University of North Texas Archives and Special Collections, Denton, Texas. Kinney and McCaffrey, *Wake Island Pilot*, 36. The Elrods' address was listed as 949 Coral Avenue, Pearl City, Oahu; see Report on Fitness, April 18, 1941, Personnel File, Doc. No. 283, NARA.

3. Jenifer Van Vleck, *Empire of the Air: Aviation and the American Ascendancy* (Cambridge, MA, and London: Harvard University Press, 2013), 94–95; for the Treaty of Washington, see Robert J. Cressman, *"A Magnificent Fight": The Battle for Wake Island* (Annapolis, MD: Naval Institute Press, 1995), 5.

4. Bill Sloan, *Given Up for Dead: America's Heroic Stand at Wake Island* (New York: Bantam Books, 2003), 23–25.

5. Sloan, *Given Up for Dead*, 30–33; Cressman, *"A Magnificent Fight,"* 6–13; Cordell Hull, *The Memoirs of Cordell Hull* (New York: Macmillan, 1948), 2: 982.

6. Ross A. Dierdorff, "Pioneer Party–Wake Island," US Naval Institute, *Proceedings*, vol. 69 (April 1943), 499–506.

7. Sloan, *Given Up for Dead*, 38–45.

8. Jonathan Marshall, *To Have and Have Not: Southeast Asian Raw Materials and the Origins of the Pacific War* (Berkeley, Los Angeles, London: University of California Press, 1995), 14–28; Michael Barnhart, *Japan Prepares for Total War: The Search for Economic Security, 1919–1941* (Ithaca, NY, and London: Cornell University Press, 1987), 17–21; Hull, *Memoirs*, 2: 998.

9. Marshall, *To Have and Have Not*, 125–28; "U.S. and Britain Freeze Japanese Assets: Oil Shipments and Silk Imports Halted," *New York Times*, July 26, 1941, 1; Hull, *Memoirs*, 2: 1015.

10. Kinney and McCaffrey, *Wake Island Pilot*, 43.

11. Ibid.

12. Cressman, *"A Magnificent Fight,"* 62–63. For Elrod's POA, see "Power of Attorney by Individual for the Collection of Checks Drawn on the Treasury of the United States," November 21, 1941, Personnel File, Doc. 290, NARA.

13. Kinney and McCaffrey, *Wake Island Pilot*, 45–46; Cressman, *"A Magnificent Fight,"* 65; Gregory J. W. Urwin, *Facing Fearful Odds: The Siege of Wake Island* (Lincoln and

London: University of Nebraska Press, 1997), 173–74; William F. Halsey and J. Bryan III, *Admiral Halsey's Story* (New York and London: McGraw Hill, 1947), 75–76.

14. Halsey and Bryan, *Admiral Halsey's Story*, 76–77.

15. Urwin, *Facing Fearful Odds*, 174.

16. Paul A. Putnam to Colonel Larkin, December 3, 1941, Correspondence and Military Records, 1941–1953: 0313-Bl-fc, Paul A. Putnam Papers, East Carolina University Archives, Greenville, North Carolina.

17. Cressman, "A Magnificent Fight," 68–69; Kinney and McCaffrey, *Wake Island Pilot*, 48; Putnam to Larkin, December 3, 1941, Putnam Papers, ECU Archives.

18. Cressman, "A Magnificent Fight," 72–73; Sloan, *Given Up for Dead*, 54–55.

19. Cressman, "A Magnificent Fight," 72–74; Sloan, *Given Up for Dead*, 54–56; Kinney and McCaffrey, *Wake Island Pilot*, 50–51.

20. Kinney and McCaffrey, *Wake Island Pilot*, 50–51.

CHAPTER 11: THREE DAYS TO PREPARE FOR TWO DAYS OF INFAMY

1. James P. S. Devereux, *The Story of Wake Island* (New York: Bantam Books, 1989), 17; Cressman, "A Magnificent Fight," 74; Kinney and McCaffrey, *Wake Island Pilot*, 51.

2. Kinney and McCaffrey, *Wake Island Pilot*, 51.

3. Devereux, *The Story of Wake Island*, 16–17, 24. For the Japanese reconnaissance flight, see Cressman, "A Magnificent Fight," 74.

4. Robert D. Heinl Jr., *The Defense of Wake* (Washington, DC: Historical Section, Division of Public Information, US Marine Corps, 1947), 9; Kinney and McCaffrey, *Wake Island Pilot*, 51.

5. Urwin, *Facing Fearful Odds*, 181–82.

6. Ibid., 178–81.

7. Major W. L. J. Bayler to the Commander of Marine Aircraft Group 21, February 18, 1942, Wake Island File, US Marine Corps Archives, Quantico, Virginia.

8. Walter Bayler and Cecil Carnes, *Last Man Off Wake Island* (Indianapolis and New York: Bobbs-Merrill Company, 1943), 70–71. For McKinstry details, see Urwin, *Facing Fearful Odds*, 144.

9. Devereux, *The Story of Wake Island*, 20.

10. Kinney and McCaffrey, *Wake Island Pilot*, 53; *The Wake Wig Wag*, December 5, 1941, Edwin Borne Personal Papers, Box 1, A-28-A-5-2, Marine Corps Archives, Quantico, Virginia.

11. Bayler and Carnes, *Last Man Off Wake Island*, 71.

12. Interview with Strimple C. Coyle, April 22, 1994, Item #1025, 30–32, University of North Texas Oral History Collection, University of North Texas, Austin.

13. Rear Admiral R. H. Jackson, US Navy (retired), "Report of Pearl Harbor Attack," December 12, 1941, Enclosure (E) to CINCPAC action report, Serial #0479 of 15 February 1942, World War II action reports, Modern Military Branch, National Archives and Records Administration, College Park, Maryland; Elizabeth Elrod to Farrar Elrod Ramsey, 1941.

14. Jackson, "Report of Pearl Harbor Attack," December 12, 1941, Enclosure (E) to CINCPAC action report.

15. Coyle interview, April 22, 1994.

16. Devereux, *Wake Island Story*, 22–23; Urwin, *Facing Fearful Odds*, 231.

17. Urwin, *Facing Fearful Odds*, 231; Cressman, *"A Magnificent Fight,"* 83; Paul A. Putnam, "Report of Lieutenant Colonel Paul A. Putnam, U.S.M.C," p. 8, in Reports and Rosters, #0313–61-fg, Paul A. Putnam Papers, East Carolina University Archives, Greenville, North Carolina.

18. Putnam, "Report," p. 8; Major Devereux claimed that Putnam "led off our first patrol." See Devereux, *The Story of Wake Island*, 26; Urwin, *Facing Fearful Odds*, 231; "Flight Schedule, VMF-211, December 8, 1941," Herbert Freuler Collection, US Marine Corps Archives, Quantico, Virginia.

19. The exception here is John F. Kinney, who imagined himself taking off with Elrod at 8:00 a.m. and remaining aloft for almost five hours, far exceeding the Wildcat's normal range of safe operation; see Kinney and McCaffrey, *Wake Island Pilot*, 55–58. For Elrod as patrol commander, see Devereux, *The Story of Wake Island*, 27. For what it's worth, Kinney agrees with other sources about the division of labor for the northern and southern patrols, even claiming it was his idea; "Flight Schedule," Freuler Collection, USMCA; Cressman, *"A Magnificent Fight,"* 83, 86; Norio Tsuji, "An Account of the Aerial Bombing of Wake Island," in Allied Translation and Interpreter Section, Southwest Pacific Area, *Enemy Publications*, No. 6, 30–31; Putnam, "Report," 9.

20. Putnam, "Report," 9; Bayler and Carnes, *Last Man Off Wake Island*, 38, 46; Ikuhiko Hata and Yasuho Izawa, *Japanese Naval Aces and Fighter Units in World War II* (Annapolis, MD: Naval Institute Press, 1989), 103–5.

21. Bayler and Carnes, *Last Man Off Wake Island*, 47. When he wrote his memoir, John F. Kinney was a brigadier general, so perhaps it had become second nature to take sole responsibility for everything he did, for better or worse. There are, however, numerous moments in *Wake Island Pilot* where this mind-set is flatly contradicted by external evidence. Compare, for instance, his claim that "I decided not to conduct our patrol beyond sixty miles out from Wake" (p. 55) with Major Putnam's explicit orders not to fly beyond sight of the island on the December 8 flight schedule. Kinney and McCaffrey, *Wake Island Pilot*, 55, 58.

22. Kinney and McCaffrey, *Wake Island Pilot*, 55, 58. William L. Ramsey Jr., personal communication with William L. Ramsey III.

23. Putnam, "Report," 9; Bayler and Carnes, *Last Man Off Wake Island*, 48–49.

24. Putnam, "Report," 9; Kinney and McCaffrey, *Wake Island Pilot*, 57; Devereux, *The Story of Wake Island*, 32; Bayler and Carnes, *Last Man Off Wake Island*, 53.

25. Devereux, *The Story of Wake Island*, 28; Putnam, "Report," 9–10; Bayler and Carnes, *Last Man Off Wake Island*, 51–52.

26. Devereux, *The Story of Wake Island*, 28; Putnam, "Report," 9–10; Urwin, *Facing Fearful Odds*, 268.

CHAPTER 12: DEFENDING WAKE ISLAND IN THE AIR

1. Bayler and Carnes, *Last Man Off Wake Island*, 52–53.

2. Kinney and McCaffrey, *Wake Island Pilot*, 61; Devereux remembered only two planes in the air on December 9, piloted by Kliewer and Hamilton, and only one shot down; see Devereux, *The Story of Wake Island*, 40–42.

3. Devereux, *The Story of Wake Island*, 40–42.

4. Putnam, "Report," 11.

5. Bayler and Carnes, *Last Man Off Wake Island*, 55–56; Devereux, *The Story of Wake Island*, 44–45; Cressman, *"A Magnificent Fight,"* 100–101.

6. Devereux, *The Story of Wake Island*, 41–42; Bayler and Carnes, *Last Man Off Wake Island*, 119.

7. Lieutenant General Frank C. Tharin interview with William L. Ramsey Jr., Henry Elrod Ramsey, and William L. Ramsey III, September 21, 1985, Brunswick, Georgia; Bayler and Carnes, *Last Man Off Wake Island*, 70.

8. Urwin, *Facing Fearful Odds*, 393–94.

9. Devereux, *The Story of Wake Island*, 48–50; Putnam, "Report," 17; Urwin, *Facing Fearful Odds*, 269.

10. Urwin, *Facing Fearful Odds*, 269; Robert Cressman questioned whether Elrod had actually shot down two bombers based on a Japanese report of only one plane that failed to return from the raid. He did not, however, cite the document that led him to this conclusion. See Cressman, *"A Magnificent Fight,"* 107. For Elrod's nickname, see Devereux, *The Story of Wake Island*, 50.

11. Kinney and McCaffrey, *Wake Island Pilot*, 60–61.

12. Devereux, *The Story of Wake Island*, 50–51.

13. Herbert C. Freuler, "Report of Activities on Wake Island," October 9, 1945, Herbert C. Freuler Papers, Coll. 5550, Box 1, Folder 1: Service Records, 1929–45, A/31/F/7/3, Marine Corps Archives, Quantico, Virginia; Devereux, *The Story of Wake Island*, 52–57. Robert Cressman did not present this argument in the text of his book, but rather in a lengthy contextual footnote, which deserved more attention than it received. See Cressman, *"A Magnificent Fight,"* 117, fn. 4; for context on Freuler's count, see Urwin, *Facing Fearful Odds*, 320. Walter Bayler also reported that the pilots took off prior to Devereux's order to commence firing. See Bayler and Carnes, *Last Man Off Wake Island*, 80. The radio banter transcribed by Bayler corresponds well contextually with Cressman's revised timeline, but Bayler's memoir sometimes presented material out of chronological order, as if he was remembering things as he talked. My narrative here has rearranged Bayler's account of the radio dialogue to correspond with Cressman's timeline.

14. Major Paul Putnam, "Report of VMF-211 on Wake Island," October 18, 1945, p. 14, Paul A. Putnam Papers, East Carolina University Archives, Greenville, North Carolina; Bayler and Carnes, *Last Man Off Wake Island*, 85.

15. Major Paul Putnam, "Report of VMF-211 on Wake Island," October 18, 1945, p. 14, Paul A. Putnam Papers, East Carolina University Archives, Greenville, North Carolina; Bayler and Carnes, *Last Man Off Wake Island*, 85.

16. Bayler and Carnes, *Last Man Off Wake Island*, 85.

17. Putnam, "Putnam Report," 14; Devereux, *The Story of Wake Island*, 54–55.

18. Bayler and Carnes, *Last Man Off Wake Island*, 81–82.

19. Personal communication from William L. Ramsey Jr. to William L. Ramsey III concerning an interview with an unidentified member of VMF-211.

20. Bayler and Carnes, *Last Man Off Wake Island*, 83, 87.

21. Ibid., 88–89.

22. One of the best assessments of how the fog of war worked to cloud perceptions at Wake Island during this particular engagement may be found in Heinl Jr., *The Defense of Wake*, 27, n. 24.

23. Bayler and Carnes, *Last Man Off Wake Island*, 81. Bayler's dialogue does not specifically identify this sortie as being against the *Kisaragi*. I have placed it in context with that attack because it matches the tactics used against the *Kisaragi* as described to the author by Lieutenant General Frank C. Tharin. Frank C. Tharin interview with Henry E. Ramsey, William L. Ramsey Jr., and William L. Ramsey III, Brunswick, Georgia, 1986.

24. Bayler and Carnes, *Last Man Off Wake Island*, 89–90.

25. Ibid.; Mrs. H. T. Elrod to Mrs. F. C. Tharin, May 23, 1943, p. 2, Frank C. Tharin Papers, Coll. 5089, A/12/J/3/6, Marine Corps Archives, Quantico, Virginia.

26. Bayler and Carnes, *Last Man Off Wake Island*, 89–90.

27. Putnam, "Report," 14–15; Masatake Okumiya, Jiro Horikoshi, and Martin Caidin, *Zero!* (New York: E. P. Dutton & Co., Inc., 1956), 123.

28. Devereux, *The Story of Wake Island*, 58; Bayler and Carnes, *Last Man Off Wake Island*, 95–96.

29. Bayler and Carnes, *Last Man Off Wake Island*, 95–96.

30. Ibid.

31. Ibid.; Devereux, *The Story of Wake Island*, 58. Frank C. Tharin's comments about the oxygen tube occurred informally during an interview with another member of VMF-211 that was being conducted by Gregory J. W. Urwin; personal email communication from Gregory J. W. Urwin to William L. Ramsey III, June 29, 2021.

32. For casualties, see Heinl Jr., *The Defense of Wake*, 27–28; Kinney and McCaffrey, *Wake Island Pilot*, 67; Cressman, *"A Magnificent Fight,"* 127–30. Colonel Richard D. Camp and Suzanne Pool, "Wake's Valiant Aviators," *Naval History*, vol. 34, no. 6 (December 2020): 22–29.

33. Urwin, *Facing Fearful Odds*, 347.

34. Ibid.

35. Ibid.

36. Devereux, *The Story of Wake Island*, 79–80.

37. Ibid.; Urwin, *Facing Fearful Odds*, 358.

CHAPTER 13: DEFENDING WAKE ISLAND ON THE GROUND

1. Devereux, *The Story of Wake Island*, 79; *New York Times*, December 12, 1941, 1, 18.

2. Cressman, *"A Magnificent Fight,"* 138; *Complete Presidential Press Conferences of Franklin D. Roosevelt*, vols. 17–18 (1941): 364.

3. Cressman, *"A Magnificent Fight,"* 131–32.

4. Ibid., 135.

5. Urwin, *Facing Fearful Odds*, 353; Cressman, *"A Magnificent Fight,"* 145; Kinney and McCaffrey, *Wake Island Pilot*, 71.

6. Cressman, *A Magnificent Fight*," 147.
7. Ibid., 147–48.
8. Ibid., 147–69.
9. Herbert C. Freuler, "Report on Activities on Wake Island," October 1945, Herbert C. Freuler Papers, Coll. 5550, Box I, Folder 1: Service Records, 1929–45, A/31/F/7/3, Marine Corps Archives Branch, Quantico, Virginia; Bayler and Carnes, *Last Man Off Wake Island*, 130; Cressman, *A Magnificent Fight*," 167.
10. Cressman, *A Magnificent Fight*," 170; Urwin, *Facing Fearful Odds*, 396–97; Henry Talmage Elrod to Elizabeth Elrod, December 20, 1941, Correspondence, Henry T. Elrod Papers, Marine Corps Archives, Quantico, Virginia.
11. Henry T. Elrod to Elizabeth H. Elrod, December 20, 1941, Correspondence, Henry T. Elrod Papers, Marine Corps Archives, Quantico, Virginia.
12. Okumiya, Horikoshi, and Caiden, *Zero!*, 124; Cressman, *A Magnificent Fight*," 177.
13. Paul A. Putnam to the Secretary of the Navy, "Recommendation for the Silver Star Medal, Case of Second Lieutenant Carl R. Davidson," October 25, 1945, Paul A. Putnam Papers, East Carolina University; Paul A. Putnam to the Secretary of the Navy, "Recommendation for the Navy Cross, Case of Captain Herbert C. Freuler, USMCR, Putnam Papers, East Carolina University; Okumiya, Horikoshi, and Caiden, *Zero!*, 124.
14. Personal communication from Lieutenant General Frank Tharin, September 21, 1985, Brunswick, Georgia; Kinney and McCaffrey, *Wake Island Pilot*, 81; Gregory J. W. Urwin interview with Robert E. L. Page, September 10, 1986, Reunion of Defenders of Wake Island, Houston Texas, cited in Urwin, *Facing Fearful Odds*, 439.
15. For a good summary of Last Stand ideology, see Nathaniel Philbrick, *The Last Stand: Custer, Sitting Bull, and the Battle of the Little Bighorn* (New York: Viking Books, 2010), xvii.
16. Urwin interview with Page, September 10, 1986, cited in Urwin, *Facing Fearful Odds*, 439.
17. Kiyoshi Ibushi, "A Detailed Report on the Capture of Wake Island," in Allied Translator and Interpreter Section, Southwest Pacific Area, *Enemy Publications*, No. 6, 27–30, RG 407, National Archives and Records Administration; Cressman, *A Magnificent Fight*," 210–11.
18. Ibushi, "Detailed Report," 27–30. Urwin interview with Page, September 10, 1986, cited in Urwin, *Facing Fearful Odds*, 439.

Conclusion
1. "Wake Falls After Gallant Fight," *Honolulu Advertiser*, December 25, 1941.
2. Farrar Elrod Ramsey to Marine Corps, January 9, 1942, Doc. 306, Military Personnel File, NARA; Major L. Cronmiller Jr., USMC, to Mrs. William L. Ramsey, January 15, 1942, Doc. 308, Military Personnel File, NARA.
3. Appointment as major, January 26, 1942, Doc. 311, Military Personnel File, NARA; "Full List of Yanks Captured by Japs," *Los Angeles Herald Express*, February 19, 1942, 1; "Flyers Who Sunk Cruiser off Wake Are Identified," *Galveston Daily News*, March 10, 1942, 11; see also *Modesto Bee*, March 10, 1942, 1.

4. "Production Notes on the Picture 'Wake Island,'" *Marine Corps Gazette*, vol. 26, no. 3 (September 1942): 34–35, 48–49.

5. Chester J. Doyle to Mrs. Henry T. Elrod, May 18, 1942, Correspondence, Henry T. Elrod Papers, Marine Corps Archives, Quantico, Virginia.

6. T. Holcomb to Admiral R. H. Jackson, June 13, 1942, Western Union Telegram, Correspondence, Henry T. Elrod Papers, Marine Corps Archives, Quantico, Virginia.

7. John Dixon to Mrs. Henry Talmage Elrod, September 2, 1942, Correspondence, Elrod Papers, Marine Corps Archives, Quantico, Virginia.

8. Major John S. E. Young to Marine Commandant, November 9, 1942, Correspondence, Elrod Papers, Marine Corps Archives, Quantico, Virginia.

9. Major John S. E. Young to Marine Commandant, November 9, 1942, Correspondence, Elrod Papers, Marine Corps Archives, Quantico, Virginia. Marine Corps Commandant to Commanding Officer, Marine Corps Air Station, Ewa, Oahu, T. H., January 15, 1943, Correspondence, Elrod Papers, Marine Corps Archives, Quantico, Virginia.

10. Second Lieutenant Betty Smith to Lieutenant Edna Smith, December 20, 1944, Correspondence, Elrod Papers, Marine Corps Archives, Quantico, Virginia.

11. "Story of Wake Island and Life in Prison Camp Is Told by Col. Putnam," October 6, 1945, *Evening Journal* (Washington, Iowa), 4.

12. Henry T. Elrod, National Medal of Honor Museum, https://mohmuseum.org/elrodmoh/, accessed June 28, 2023.

13. "Wake Hero's Medal Is Given to Capt. Elrod, His Widow," *Washington Evening Star*, November 9, 1946, 6.

14. "She Pays Silent Tribute at Heroes' Graves," *Washington Post*, October 31, 1947, 3.

Bibliography

Manuscript Collections
East Carolina University Archives
Paul A. Putnam Papers

Georgia State Archives
Georgia Death Certificates

Marine Corps Archives, Quantico, Virginia
Henry T. Elrod Papers
Edwin Borne Personal Papers
Herbert Freuler Collection
Frank C. Tharin Papers
Wake Island File

National Archives and Records Administration (NARA)
World War II action reports, Modern Military Branch
Henry T. Elrod Military Personnel File
Allied Translator and Interpreter Section, Southwest Pacific Area, *Enemy Publications*

National Museum of Naval Aviation
Flight Training Jackets, Henry Talmage Elrod

University of North Texas Archives and Special Collections
University of North Texas Oral History Collection

Newspapers
Atlanta Journal and Constitution
Coronado Eagle and Journal

Evening Star (Washington, DC)
Harrisonburg Daily News-Record
High Point Enterprise
New York Times
Quantico Sentry
San Diego Evening Tribune
San Diego Union
Thomasville Daily Times-Enterprise

PRIMARY SOURCES

"Baseball," *Leatherneck*, vol. 14, no. 9 (September 1931).

"Basic School Graduates," *Leatherneck*, vol. 15, no. 8 (August 1932).

Bayler, Walter, and Cecil Carnes. *Last Man Off Wake Island.* Indianapolis and New York: Bobbs-Merrill Company, 1943.

Brainard, E. H. "Marine Corps Aviation," *Marine Corps Gazette*, vol. 13 (March 1928): 24–26.

Coyle, Strimple C., to Henry E. Ramsey, June 3, 1992, manuscript letter in the author's possession.

Devereux, James P. S. *The Story of Wake Island.* New York: Bantam Books, 1989.

Eleventh Annual Miami All-American Air Maneuvers, January 6, 7, 8, 1939, Official Program.

Halsey, William F., and J. Byran, III. *Admiral Halsey's Story.* New York and London: McGraw Hill, 1947.

Henry, Alfred J. "The Weather of 1923," *Monthly Weather Review* (December 1923): 652–53.

Hooker, Brian. "The Commemorative Poem," *Yale Alumni Weekly*, vol. 28 (July 3, 1919): 1060–61.

Hoover, Herbert. *The Speeches of President Herbert Hoover.* N.P.: Filibust Publishing, 2015.

"How Aviators Get Oxygen at High Altitudes," *Popular Science Monthly* (January 1919).

Hull, Cordell. *The Memoirs of Cordell Hull.* New York: Macmillan, 1948.

Kinney, Brigadier General John F., USMC, with James M. McCaffrey. *Wake Island Pilot: A World War II Memoir.* Washington, DC: Brassey's, Inc., 1995.

Landing Operations Doctrine, United States Navy, 1938, F.T.P. 167. Washington, DC: US Government Printing Office, 1938.

Lindbergh, Charles A. *The Spirit of St. Louis.* New York: Charles Scribner's Sons, 1953.

M'Connell, Monroe. "San Diego Marines Win Title," *Leatherneck*, vol. 11, no. 4 (April 1928).

Okumiya, Masatake, Jiro Horikoshi, and Martin Caidin. *Zero!* New York: E. P. Dutton & Co., Inc., 1956.

Pandora 1924. Athens, Georgia, 1924.

"Philadelphia Marines Win Two Rugby Tilts," *Leatherneck*, vol. 14, no. 5 (May 1931).

"Planes Are Landing by Radio When Fog Hides the Field," *Popular Mechanics* (February 1931).

Roosevelt, Franklin D. (Franklin Delano), and Jonathan Daniels. *Complete Presidential Press Conferences of Franklin D. Roosevelt*. New York: Da Capo Press, 1972.

Wren, Percival. *Beau Geste*. Cutchogue, NY: Buccaneer Books, 1978.

SECONDARY SOURCES

Astor, Gerald. *Semper Fi in the Sky: The Marine Air Battles of World War II*. New York: Presidio Press, 2005.

Baker, Nicholson. *Human Smoke: The Beginnings of World War II, the End of Civilization*. New York: Simon & Schuster, 2008.

Barnhart, Michael. *Japan Prepares for Total War: The Search for Economic Security, 1919–1941*. Ithaca, NY, and London: Cornell University Press, 1987.

Camp, Colonel Richard D., and Suzanne Pool. "Wake's Valiant Aviators," *Naval History*, vol. 34, no. 6 (December 2020): 22–29.

Capra, Frank. *The Name Above the Title: An Autobiography*. New York: Macmillan, 1971.

Cavendish, Marshall. *Great Aircraft of the World: An Illustrated History of the Most Famous Civil and Military Planes*. London: Marshall Cavendish Books, 1992.

Champie, Elmore. *A Brief History of the Marine Corps Base and Recruit Depot San Diego, California, 1914–1962*. Washington, DC: Historical Branch, G-3 Division Headquarters, US Marine Corps, 1962.

Clifford, Lieutenant Colonel Kenneth J. *Progress and Purpose: A Developmental History of the United States Marine Corps, 1900–1970*. Washington, DC: History and Museums Division, USMC, 1973.

Cressman, Robert J. *"A Magnificent Fight": The Battle for Wake Island*. Annapolis, MD: Naval Institute Press, 1995.

Dierdorff, Ross A. "Pioneer Party–Wake Island," U.S. Naval Institute, *Proceedings*, vol. 69 (April 1943), 499–506.

Hata, Ikuhiko, and Yasuho Izawa. *Japanese Naval Aces and Fighter Units in World War II*. Annapolis, MD: Naval Institute Press, 1989.

Heinl, Jr., Robert D. *The Defense of Wake*. Washington, DC: Historical Section, Division of Public Information, US Marine Corps, 1947.

Homan, Lynn M., and Thomas Reilly. *Wings over Florida*. Charleston, SC: Arcadia Publishing, 1999.

Johnson, E. R. *United States Marine Corps Aircraft Since 1913*. Jefferson, NC: McFarland & Company, Inc., 2018.

Marshall, Jonathan. *To Have and Have Not: Southeast Asian Raw Materials and the Origins of the Pacific War*. Berkeley, Los Angeles, London: University of California Press, 1995.

Millett, Allan R. *Semper Fidelis: The History of the United States Marine Corps*. New York: The Free Press, 1981.

Moses, E. P. "Recruit Depot, Marine Corps Base, San Diego, California," *Leatherneck*, vol. 15, no. 6 (June 1932).

Murray, Williamson, and Allen R. Millett, eds. *Military Innovations in the Interwar Period*. New York: Cambridge University Press, 1996.

Nofie, Albert A. *To Train the Fleet for War: The U.S. Navy Fleet Problems.* Newport, RI: Naval War College Press, 2010.

Philbrick, Nathaniel. *The Last Stand: Custer, Sitting Bull, and the Battle of the Little Bighorn.* New York: Viking Books, 2010.

Sambito, Major William J., USMC, *A History of Marine Fighter Attack Squadron 232.* Washington, DC: History and Museums Division, US Marine Corps, 1978.

Schaffer, Ronald. "The War Department's Defense of ROTC, 1920–1940," *Wisconsin Magazine of History,* vol. 53, no. 2 (Winter 1969–1970): 108–20.

Shirer, William L. *The Rise and Fall of the Third Reich: A History of Nazi Germany.* New York: Simon & Schuster, 2011.

Sloan, Bill. *Given Up for Dead: America's Heroic Stand at Wake Island.* Bantam Books, 2003.

Smith, General Holland M. *The Development of Amphibious Tactics in the U.S. Navy.* Washington, DC: History and Museums Division Headquarters, US Marine Corps, 1992.

Sudsbury, Elretta. *Jackrabbits to Jets: The History of Naval Air Station North Island, San Diego, California.* San Diego: San Diego Publishing Co., 1992.

Taylor, A. J. P. *The Origins of the Second World War.* New York: Simon & Schuster, 1996.

Trimble, William F. *Hero of the Air: Glenn Curtiss and the Birth of Naval Aviation.* Annapolis, MD: Naval Institute Press, 2010.

Urwin, Gregory J. W. *Facing Fearful Odds: The Siege of Wake Island.* Lincoln and London: University of Nebraska Press, 1997.

Vanderwood, Paul J. *Satan's Playground: Mobsters and Movie Stars at America's Greatest Gaming Resort.* Durham, NC, and London: Duke University Press, 2010.

Van Vleck, Jenifer. *Empire of the Air: Aviation and the American Ascendency.* Cambridge, MA, and London: Harvard University Press, 2013.

MISCELLANEOUS

Building Permit for Canal Bank and Trust Company, 1926, Permit #29818, City Archives, New Orleans Public Library.

Flight (film). Columbia Pictures, 1929.

The Flying Fleet (film). MGM, 1929.

Interview with Frank C. Tharin, May 18–21, 1984, Brunswick, Georgia.

Transcript of Henry Talmage Elrod, 1923–1925, Registrar's Office, University of Georgia.